D0873990

Eighteenth-Century Hermeneutics

Eighteenth-Century Hermeneutics

Philosophy of Interpretation in England from Locke to Burke

Joel C. Weinsheimer

Yale University Press New Haven & London

Designed by Nancy Ovedovitz and set in Bembo type by DEKR
Corp., Woburn, Massachusetts. Printed in the United States of
America by Vail Ballou Press, Binghampton, New York.

Library of Congress Cataloging-in-Publication Data

Weinsheimer, Joel.
    Eighteenth-century hermeneutics : philosophy of interpretation in
    England from Locke to Burke / Joel C. Weinsheimer.
    p. cm.
    Includes bibliographical references and index.
    ISBN 0-300-05280-4 (alk. paper)
      1. Hermeneutics—History—18th century.   2. England—Intellectual
    life—18th century.   I. Title.
    B1302.H47W45   1993
    121'.68'09—dc20   92-26062
                                                       CIP

10   9   8   7   6   5   4   3   2   1

For my teachers

Contents

Preface

Eighteenth-century England has not seemed to many a very promising field for hermeneutic research. Among the best recent work in the field, Gerald Bruns's *Hermeneutics, Ancient and Modern* moves directly from Luther to Wordsworth, and Jean Grondin's *Einführung in die philosophische Hermeneutik*, though devoting chapters to Dannhauer, Chladenius, and Meier, finds no Englishman of the period worthy of attention. Indeed, it is no exaggeration to say that the entire period of British thought from the Restoration to the Regency is never discussed and rarely even mentioned in anthologies and general surveys of hermeneutic philosophy.

Whatever the causes of this oversight by students of hermeneutics, however, students of the British eighteenth century have not failed to notice what is quite evident: that a host of thinkers from Locke to Burke accorded the problems of interpretation intense and fruitful scrutiny. The interpretive schisms which, from the Restoration to the mid-century, violently divided Deists from Dissenters, Anglicans from Catholics, High Churchmen from Low Churchmen, gave the need to understand understanding a special urgency in that period. The turmoil in biblical hermeneutics, however, was merely the most evident manifestation of a much more widespread crisis in understanding, one that plagued and invigorated intellectual, political, and indeed all common life.

To glimpse the full breadth of the issues requires an inquiry of considerable scope and diversity. Eighteenth-century studies, such as Hans Frei's *Eclipse of Biblical Narrative* or Douglas Patey's learned and valuable *Probability and Literary Form*, typically concentrate on hermeneutics as it relates to a particular area. The present study, by contrast, ranges from one area to another in order to look at hermeneutic issues common to many areas—to interpersonal as well as textual understanding, to scriptural, legal, historical, political, and literary hermeneutics alike. Comprehensive though not exhaustive, the present study covers all the primary interpretive disciplines.

To say it is therefore multi- or interdisciplinary would be somewhat anachronistic, however, since the boundaries dividing disciplines were a good deal more amorphous then than they are now. Aesthetic taste, judicial discretion, and political prudence, for example, were commonly considered variant species of one interpretive art or skill, variously called "discernment," "sagacity," or "judgment." In our time Emilio Betti and E. D. Hirsch, Jr., strictly differentiate kinds of interpretation (cognitive, performative, and normative) according to the various objects of interpretation (for example, a historical event, a musical score, and a legal statute). Eighteenth-century hermeneutics, by contrast, was much more integrated, each field overlapping the others.

This study, like everything I have written in the last fifteen years, stems from my continued fascination with Hans-Georg Gadamer's *Truth and Method*, not least with his attempt to formulate a unified, rather than a fragmented, hermeneutics like that of Betti and Hirsch. That Gadamer barely makes an appearance in the pages that follow merely testifies to his omnipresence. Everything bears his imprint. Not so much the very brief but suggestive comments he makes about Reid, Hume, and Burke are my starting point as his general approach, which he calls "philosophical hermeneutics." This I have examined elsewhere, in *Gadamer's Hermeneutics* and *Philosophical Hermeneutics and Literary Theory*. Here I need mention only that by calling my present topic "philosophy of interpretation," in the words of the subtitle, I want to indicate that my approach is more philosophical than historical, and that my philosophy is allied to Gadamer's.

By this I mean several things, negative and positive. I do not mean to label Blackstone and Burke philosophers, of course, though my interest is in their interpretive principles. Moreover, the figures I have chosen to discuss—Bolingbroke, for example, rather than Gibbon—have been selected because of the explicitness of their principles, their philosophy of interpretation. Their practice, and its relation to their principles, is another matter, one that is fully worthy of study although it has not occupied me here.

Further, in being primarily philosophical in orientation, this book does not offer a historical narrative. It opens with Locke's epistemological denigration of hermeneutics and ends with Burke's hermeneutic denigration of epistemology. But between these *termini*, no continuous narrative is to be found. In allying my approach with Gadamer's, I mean to suggest that this study of Swift, Locke, Toland, Bolingbroke, Hume, Reid, Blackstone, and Burke is intended primarily as a contribution to hermeneutics, rather than just to the history of it. Not the various authors or even the period as such, but rather the *Sache*, the understanding of understanding itself, is my primary aim. This aim, it seems to me, is best achieved not by a synoptic overview but by intensive, critical analysis of selected figures. The object of such analysis is not just to discover what Toland said or meant, for instance, and not at all to show how he differs from Hobbes or Newman or whether he was really an atheist or a pantheist or whatever. I have tried instead to examine whether and how what he said about interpretation is revealing, significant, and true. Nineteenth-century formulas like *wie es eigentlich gewesen* fall well short of describing my aim and seem not only anachronistic but substantively inappropriate to the eighteenth century in any case. (Anyone wishing to take Bolingbroke's historiography seriously cannot begin with Ranke's historicist assumptions.)

What the reader will find is discussion of a series of interrelated issues, all pertaining to "philosophy of interpretation." In each chapter I ask such questions as: Is interpreting necessary? If so, when and why? If not, what kind of thing is it that does not need to be interpreted (what is clear or plain)? What occasions, obstacles, or purposes make it necessary for interpret? What is the relation of the interpretation to what is being interpreted? What qualities or characteristics make something understandable? What faculties of mind or previous knowledge are requisite to understanding? What kind of a process is interpreting? What does it mean to interpret something? What is not interpreting (for example, altering or copying)? By what signs can a true interpretation be known, and what is its opposite (for example, twisting or wrenching)? What accounts for multiplicity and variance among interpretations?

I take these to be real questions, not just matters of historical curiosity; and in addressing them to eighteenth-century works, I am looking for real answers—that is, answers which bear on our own thought and practice.

All quotations from eighteenth-century authors have been silently modernized following British style.

Special thanks are due to Lisa Woolley, Chip Burkitt, amd Michael Gareffa for their many hours of help on various stages of this project and to the University of Minnesota Graduate School for making this help possible. A grant from the Bush Foundation is likewise sincerely appreciated. Thanks go as well to John Bender, Stephen Daniels, James Farr, Claude Rawson, and Robert Rodes, Jr., for their careful and critical comments on earlier drafts.

Introduction: The Hermeneutics of Knaves and Fools

Seen from the perspective of Jonathan Swift's *Tale of a Tub*, the fundamental problem of eighteenth-century hermeneutics, and of our century as well, might well be called the dichotomy of knaves and fools.[1] Two inalienable though incommensurate interpretations of interpretation divide the field: not nostalgia and affirmation, as in Derrida's formulation, but credulity and curiosity. Defined as the "wisdom which converses about the surface of things," the credulity of the hermeneutic fool consists in being passively open to the obvious, taking things to be what they seem and words to mean what they say. Correlatively, defined as the "reason [which brings] tools for cutting and opening and mangling and piercing [things] and offering to demonstrate that they are not of the same consistency quite through" (173),[2] interpretive curiosity consists in ferreting out the real beyond the apparent, the meaning behind the word. The dichotomy of fools and knaves in Swift's *Tale of a Tub* presents the reader with an impossible choice between two opposed and inadequate hermeneutic factions.[3] Both visions of interpretation seem correct as far as they go, but each is incomplete precisely to the extent that it excludes the other. From the perspective of *Tale of a Tub*, the fundamental problem of hermeneutics consists in formulating a notion of interpretation as whole and undivided, both foolish and knavish, or neither.

"Fixing tropes and allegories to the letter" is what makes credulity foolish, just as "refining what is literal into figure and mystery" (190) makes for hermeneutic knavery. The fool understands everything as plain, the knave as dark and deep.[4] One continually underreads; the other overreads. These corollary deficiencies result from the "converting imagination" (190) which the two share and exercise in common, though in opposite directions, "converting" toward either the literal or the figural. It would seem that adequate, valid, true interpretation could be defined easily enough as that which did not convert at all, which read the letter literally and the allegorical figuratively. This is a fool's solution, however, for it assumes that the distinction between plain and mysterious is itself plain and does not involve interpretation.

It cannot be said, moveover, that the dichotomy between fool and knave is exhausted by the distinction between surface and depth. The distinction is itself knavish, since the operations of curiosity assume it, whereas the defining characteristic of credulity is precisely not to distinguish them. Because credulity perceives "how near the frontiers of height and depth border upon each other" (157–58), it knows nothing of superficial or profound, but only one smooth level without relief. Foolish hermeneutics is therefore monistic; knavish is dualistic or pluralistic, in that it posits two or more levels of understanding,[5] and its very activity consists in discriminating between them. To interpret, knavishly understood, means to "lay open by untwisting or unwinding and either to draw up by exantlation or display by incision" (67); thus knavish interpretation depends on the dualisms of implication and explication, higher and lower, containing and contained, outside and inside, which make possible the operations of interpretive penetration and exposé.[6] "Wisdom is a fox," the knave informs us, "who after long hunting will at last cost you the pains to dig out" (66).

For knavish curiosity, the real is hidden. This means that the object of interpretation is conceived as situated below a covering surface, behind some opaque but enticing hieroglyph, waiting to be deciphered.[7] Sometimes the object is a hidden treasure, as in the decoding of divine mystery. When mystery loses its credibility, however, when Hermes Trismegistus is shrunken into Tristram Shandy and mystery can be understood only as mystification, hermeneutics no longer subserves the hermetic, but demystifies and debunks it.[8] Now what the opaque shell conceals is merely "a nut which, unless you choose with judgment, may cost you a tooth, and pay you with nothing but a worm" (66). Or, at a further extreme, the hidden object comes to be conceived as something hideous, which is concealed because shameful or repulsive. In *Tale of a Tub,* as in psychoanalysis, the hidden secret is typically the body; and not just clothes, but soul, mind, and reason are its concealments. The "mysteries not to be named, giving occasion for those happy epithets of turgidus and inflatus" (151), are "covers" for bodily facts, "for lewdness as well as nastiness" (78).

In the case of false mysteries, interpretive disclosure takes the form not of revelation but disillusioning exposé—like the notable discovery that, for all her loveliness, "Celia shits."[9] The interpreter's very repulsion comes to confirm the veracity of the interpretation. "Freud says the dream is bawdy," Wittgenstein muses. "*Is* is bawdy? . . . There is a strong tendency to say: 'We can't get round the fact that this dream is really such and such.' It may be the fact that the explanation is extremely repellant that drives you to adopt it."[10] Knavish interpretation of the repulsive consists in stripping away its false but "beautiful externals" (67), its surface or skin; hence the predominant figure of exposé in the *Tale* is anatomy. "Yesterday I ordered the carcass of a beau to be stripped in my presence, when we were all amazed to find so many unsuspected faults under one suit of clothes: then I laid open his brain, his heart, and his spleen; but I plainly perceived at every operation that the farther we proceeded, we found the defects increase upon us in number and bulk" (174). Conceived as the outcome of hermeneutic anatomy, *aletheia,* the unconcealed, the true, is the ugly.

For fools, by contrast, truth is beauty. This does not mean simply that they delude themselves with "beautiful externals" while remaining meticulously oblivious to what is "darkly and deeply couched under them" (67). That is a knave's explanation. For credulity, beauty symbolizes the true because beauty exemplifies the nondistinction between internal and external, real and apparent, noumenal and phenomenal. Pure fools take things as they find them and "will by no means be persuaded to inspect beyond the surface and the rind of things" (66). Credulity acknowledges nothing beyond the surface, and so refuses all knavish talk of levels—of distinctions between form and content, vehicle and tenor, outside and in. "*Omnia vanitas:* all is mere outside" (79n.), the *Tale's* commentator explains—though even this states the fool's position too knavishly. For the hermeneutic fool there is nothing "mere" about the outside, since there is no inside with which to contrast it—which is merely to say that things are what they seem. "If this were seriously considered by the world, as I have a certain reason to suspect it hardly will," Swift writes, "men would no longer reckon among their high points of wisdom the art of exposing weak sides and publishing infirmities, an employment in my opinion neither better nor worse than that of unmasking, which I think, has never been allowed fair usage, either in the world or the playhouse" (172–73).[11]

Swift's fool undoubtedly represents the materialist, who "can with Epicurus content his ideas with the films and images that fly off upon his senses from the superficies of things" (174).[12] What constitutes the hermeneutic folly, however, is not the materialism per se but its monism. "Matter has no *inward*," Coleridge writes. "We remove one surface but to meet with another."[13] Matter typifies whatever is impenetrable not because it is too deep, but rather because it is too shallow: it is "of the same consistency"—all surface— "quite through" (173). The same point could be made of Berkeley's idealism: under any monism, exposé becomes impossible, since there is nothing superficial about the monistic surface that would arouse suspicion or invite unmasking. The fool's one-dimensional world, without height or depth, offers no hiddenness to be exposed, no meaning, nothing to interpret. Everything is plain.

Not the surface, then, but the very attempt to penetrate and interpret it constitutes the deception: in a monistic world, it is the knave who is the fool. "If certain ermines and furs be placed in a certain position, we style them a judge, and so an apt conjunction of lawn and black satin, we entitle a bishop" (79). Whatever looks like a judge and acts like a judge *is* a judge; what to *all* appearances is a bishop cannot be other than a bishop.[14] Temporary deceptions are possible, and these are subject to knavish demystifications, of course; but the "*perpetual* possession of being well deceived" (171, my emphasis) is possession of the unfalsifiable truth, and there is no deception in it. People can be mistaken about things for a long time, the fool admits, but there can be no ultimate distinction between appearance and reality. The fool says in his heart, there is no mystery, only ignorance, because it is of the nature of reality to be unmysterious, to appear. If reality manifests *itself,* then that manifestation or appearance cannot be equated with falsehood that needs to be exposed; nor can reality be equated with truth that needs to be revealed by the act of an interpreter. Rather, the real manifests itself. It presents its own evidence, and interpretation is merely complicity with the self-manifestation—the self-evidence—of the real.

For the fool, truth is open to "common understanding, as well as common sense" (171), because what is most certainly true is that which is patent, obvious to everyone.[15] Following Shaftesbury, who took laughter as a test of truth, Thomas Reid, founder of the Scottish commonsense philosophy that we will consider in chapter five, held that whatever contradicts the obvious is not merely erroneous but absurd. Correcting absurdity requires not argument but ridicule, and Reid numbers Swift and other satirists among the champions of common sense.[16] Interpreting the obvious and commonsensical is pointless because it interprets itself. One need only look, without obstruction or mediation, at the self-evident to see what it truly is. Any attempt to go beyond, beneath, or behind it in the misguided desire to get at a deeper truth, Reid showed, actually constitutes falsification, for there is no truth more true than the evident, no depth deeper than a plain surface.

Beauty is the symbol of truth, understood as the nondifferentiability of the apparent and the real. It makes no sense to say of the self-evident, "It seems true, but is it really?" It makes no more sense to say of something beautiful, "It looks beautiful, but is it truly?" What looks beautiful is so: there is no criterion other than appearance because beauty is entirely phenomenal, a matter of seeming, a surface without depth. Beauty evidences itself, is its own evidence. Since it is nothing but what it appears to be, beauty is invulnerable to attempts at falsification, and is therefore an apt symbol of truth. Because it is merely skin deep, the beautiful precludes any distinction between what appears and what is, and the fool's strength consists in not trying to draw any. "Last week I saw a woman flayed," the knave exclaims, "and you will hardly believe how much it altered her person for the worse" (173). But the fools asks, where is all the wonderment? Since beauty is nothing other than what it seems to be, it is not subject to exposé. Strip off the "beautiful externals" and you find not real beauty or true beauty but no beauty, and only a knave would think otherwise.

The wisdom of the fool is his knowledge that in a world without mystery or mystification, without "secret wheels" and "hidden springs" (164), hermeneutic exposé actually covers the truth it pretends to dis-cover. For this ill, there is one sure remedy. If interpretation obscures or falsifies what it would reveal, the easiest solution is to stop interpreting.

There are two reasons to stop: either genuine mysteries exist but, being forever hidden from profane eyes, the attempt to pry into them is pointless; or, more simply, there are no genuine mysteries, in which case trying to interpret things that purport to be mysteries is just plain silly. Just as Swift's *Tale* was for several centuries read as a satire not of the abuses of religion but of religion itself,[17] so the same issue arises with respect to mystery. Swift's targets are all those who dupe themselves into mistaking an empty well for a deep one, who con others into taking their superficiality for profundity, or who cry "Mystery" to conceal self-interest. Swift clearly has lots of fun with false mystery, mystification of self and others; the question is whether he recognizes any other kind.

William Wotton thought not, and so he allies Swift's *Tale of a Tub* with John Toland's *Christianity Not Mysterious,* which is examined in detail in chapter two. Commenting on Peter's use of mystery to veil what he does not wish to be "over-curiously pried into" (88), Wotton writes: "The author, one would think, copies from Mr. Toland, who always raises a laugh at the word mystery, the word and thing, whereof he is known to believe to be no more than a tale of a tub" (319). For several reasons, we ought to be suspicious of Wotton's identification. Swift ridicules Toland in the *Argument against Abolishing Christianity* (4:29, 36); he laughs at Collins for saying that "there is no such thing as mystery" (4:27); and in the process of affirming his faith in the most textually controversial verse in the New Testament (1 John 5:7), Swift calls the Trinity "something dark and mystical" which "it pleased God to conceal from me and from all mankind" (9:161). It was just this kind of talk that Toland wanted to silence. In defense of Wotton's allying Swift with Toland, however, it must be conceded that while the *Tale* exposes plenty of false (that is, Catholic and Dissenting) mysteries, such as transubstantiation and private inspiration, no true (that is, Anglican) mysteries such as the Trinity seem to be mentioned.

"Mystery," we recall, is the knave's term for the object of interpretation; and just as Wotton considers all mystery to be the target of the *Tale,* so the question with regard to interpretation, likewise, is whether Swift's satire goes beyond ridiculing inane or wild misinterpretation to comprehend all interpretation. In *Gulliver's Travels* and elsewhere, Swift stigmatizes political witch-hunts and the consequent hermeneutic paranoia that finds deep meaning everywhere: that is "sure to be mistaken by searching too deep" (8:80), that can "decipher a close-stool to signify a privy council" (11:191) or read "G. R. II" as Jacobite innuendo that George is the second king—that is, the second after the Pretender (12:232). But more than these adepts at discovering "arcana imperii" (8:80), Swift despised lawyers. In England, he complained, laws are "explained, interpreted, and applied by those whose interest and abilities lie in perverting, confounding, and eluding them" (11:132), and so Gulliver refuses to emerge from seclusion until Smithfield is "blazing with Pyramids of lawbooks" (11:6). Swift despised lawyers as venal misinterpreters ready to prove that "white is black and black is white, according as they are paid" (11:248). Did he also despise them just as interpreters? In Brobdingnag, "to write a comment upon any law is a capital crime" (11:136)—not a false commentary, any commentary.

> We found, or we thought we found, an inconvenience in having every man the judge of his own cause. Therefore judges were set up, at first with discretionary powers. But it was soon found a miserable slavery to have our lives and properties precarious and hanging upon the arbitrary determinations of any one man or set of men. We fled to laws as a remedy for this evil. By these we persuaded ourselves we might know with some certainty upon what ground we stood. But lo! differences arose upon the sense and interpretation of these laws. Thus we were brought back to our old incertitude. New laws were made to expound the old; and new difficulties arose upon the new laws; as words multiplied, opportunities of cavilling upon them multiplied also. Then recourse was had to notes, comments, glosses, reports, *responsa prudentum,* learned readings: eagle stood against eagle; authority was set up against authority. Some were allured by the modern; others reverenced the ancient. The new were more enlightened, the old were more venerable. The confusion increased, the mist thickened, until it could be discovered no longer what was allowed or forbidden. . . . Our inheritances are become a prize for disputation; and disputes and litigations are become an inheritance.[18]

The words are Burke's, but the sentiments were Swift's as well.

"Laws penned with the utmost care and exactness and in the vulgar language are often perverted to wrong meanings," Swift observes;

"then why should we wonder that the Bible is so?" (4:248). Among the religious mystifiers and mystery-mongers guilty of "forcing and perverting Scripture" (84n.), Cabbalists such as Abraham Abulafia come in for special abuse in the *Tale*. Abulafia went beyond those who saw that the written Torah, though fixed and permanent, permitted various vocalizations and hence various meanings; he recommended that its letters be rearranged as well.[19] Such interpretation "tertio modo, or totidem literis" (83) was a practice of thirteenth-century Spain, however, not eighteenth-century England; and Cabbalism, one would have thought had long been defunct. Bolingbroke, however, thought otherwise: "The Jewish rabbins have done by the Old, and our Christian rabbins by the New and Old Testament both, what Peter did by his father's will in our friend Swift's *Tale of a Tub*. The text was against him, but by a new combination of the same words or syllables or letters he made it speak for him and support his claim. It had been well if Martin and John and the rest of Peter's brethren . . . had adhered to the text in the plain and obvious meaning of it, instead of imitating the very men whom they have opposed and whom they laugh at. But they have done otherwise."[20] It seems to be Bolingbroke's view, and one he thinks he shares with Swift, that all interpretation—any commentary that exceeds or otherwise alters "the plain and obvious meaning"—is cabbalistic and absurd.

No one proposed that biblical commentary be made a capital crime; but out of the religious strife that characterized the Interregnum and Restoration grew a widespread suspicion that interpretation itself was the root cause of dissention, and that it might be somehow curbed, either by certain sorts of censorship or, better still, by showing it to be superfluous in the first place. In the chapter that follows, Locke is taken as representing this anti-hermeneutic animus; but it was hardly peculiar to him. The plainness doctrine elaborated in Locke's *Reasonableness of Christianity* had, in various forms, been basic to Protestantism since Luther. Designed to obviate or at least circumscribe interpretation, the principle of plainness suggested that interpretation was typically unnecessary and often wilful perversion. The Protestant Dryden puts the case most succinctly:

> The welcome news is in the letter found;
> The carrier's not commission'd to expound.
> It speaks itself, and what it does contain,
> In all things needful to be known, is plain.[21]

In Swift's *Tale* as well, the father's will is depicted as consisting "wholly in certain plain, easy directions" (190). What is plain cannot be explained; to expound it is to obscure it. The text that "speaks itself" is silenced by comments and glosses, drowned out by others' voices. In fact, because clarifying the clear is utterly superfluous, such interpretation can only be self-serving subterfuge. The charlatan Peter, Bolingbroke charges, made the text "speak for him"; such ventriloquy is "employed by those who seek to impose their own inventions under some other and better authority than their own."[22] Insofar as interpreting the plain and literal is needless or worse because it generates only misinterpretation, pluralization, and consequently factionalization, interpretation can and should cease.

This, we must remember, is the fool's hermeneutic, and of course it is not entirely foolish or wholly anti-interpretive. To say with Dryden and many others that the plain text "speaks itself" implies that it obviates interpretation, to be sure, but only interpretation as knavishly conceived. The "sola" in Luther's often repeated formula "scriptura sola" means without the mediation, or interference, of patristic interpretation. It need not mean, however, without *any* interpretation. The Protestant Bible is a *self*-interpreting text. It has interpretations, therefore, but these interpretations cannot be differentiated from the text. This principle is not peculiar to Protestant or specifically to biblical hermeneutics. Every text is self-evident. That is, any interpretation that *is* an interpretation must be of the text, must belong to it and be the text's own interpretation, its self-interpretation. The fool's monistic interpretation of interpretation means not just that every text is plain and can have no (knavish) interpretations but also—what amounts to the same thing—that no text can be distinguished from the interpretations of it, since the genuine ones are its own interpretations, and anything else is not an interpretation at all.

On the other hand, whatever the plainness of the gospels—and it was convenient to forget that Jesus spoke to the people in parables so that "hearing they may hear, and not understand" (Mark 4:12)[23]— the Pauline epistles were notoriously obscure. They could not be excluded from the category of "things needful to be known," yet could not be called "plain"; and interpreting them was not only permissible but mandatory. In his *Letter to a Young Gentleman Lately Entered into Holy Orders,* Swift recommends that "many terms used

in Holy Writ, particularly by St. Paul, might with more discretion
be changed into plainer speech" (9:66). Locke likewise admits that,
"though I had been conversant in these epistles, . . . yet I found that
I understood them not—I mean the doctrinal and discursive parts of
them."[24] So he wrote a paraphrastic commentary. From Locke's
position that certain important parts of the Bible are opaque, it is
only a small (though decisive) step to the Catholic Dryden's thesis
that Scripture as a whole

<blockquote>

                               is mute,
And is itself the subject of dispute. . . .
All vouch the words their int'rest to maintain,
And each pretends by those his cause is plain.
Shall then the testament award the right?
. No that's the Hungary for which they fight;
The field of battle, subject of debate;
The thing contended for, the fair estate.[25]

</blockquote>

Here we return to the knave's position. Unless someone can speak
for Scripture and through it, it does not speak at all. The Bible is a
mute text whose meaning is accessible only indirectly, through an
interpreter.

To a fool, interpreting a mute text is always nonsense or sham—
like taking *Reynard the Fox* "to be a complete body of civil knowledge," *Whittington the Cat* to contain "a defence of the Gemara of the
Jerusalem Misna," or even *The Hind and the Panther* to be a "complete
abstract of sixteen thousand schoolmen from Scotus to Bellarmine"
(68–69). If a text has no plain meaning, the fool thinks it has no
meaning and, Bolingbroke explains, it should be considered as senseless as the Chinese table of Fohi: "This table consists of several lines,
some shorter, some longer, and placed in a certain order like that of
a diagram or scheme, serving, as they imagine, to the design or
demonstration of the most sublime knowledge. The learned men
among them have been employed several thousand years in attempting to draw some of this sublime knowledge out of the table. . . .
[These] Chinese critics have been employed just as reasonably as the
Christian expositors of mysteries, neither fully nor plainly revealed
by revelation itself."[26]

But Dryden was no fool. By a mute text, he meant not a meaningless one but rather one that calls for interpretation. Because it
does not "speak itself," it requires another's speech; because it does

not interpret itself, moreover, it necessitates an interpretation other than itself. In both respects, the mute text justifies the knavish interpretation of interpretation that insists on the duality of the text and the interpretation of it. The knave's distinction between surface and depth figures that duality, the principle of essential difference between interpretation and text and the creativity of interpretation that is its consequence. There is nothing peculiarly Catholic about this principle. An interpretation that is an interpretation and not a duplicate of the text must differ from it. The fool is right that anything beyond what is plain and apparent must be invented. Any interpretation of the text identical to it, however, would simply be the text or a duplicate of it; the copy of a mute text would itself be mute, and hence pointless. Any requisite interpretation—any interpretation necessitated by the muteness of the text—justifies its existence by its inventiveness and difference, by exceeding what it interprets. The knave's dualist interpretation of interpretation implies not just that every text means more and other than it is willing or able to say, but also—what amounts to the same thing—that every text must be distinguished from interpretations of it, since the only genuine interpretations are different from the text, and a copy is not an interpretation at all.

Because of their insistence on this difference, the knaves are at a distinct disadvantage in explaining what makes an interpretation right or wrong. The fools, by contrast, have no problem: an interpretation that belongs to the text is right, one that differs from it wrong. The coincidence of the self-interpreting text with its interpretations not only explains the text's identity and self-sameness over time but legitimates the notion of a uniquely correct interpretation. Without the fool's notion of the one right reading—that is, without the possibility of interpretive consensus—there seem to be only two prospects, both dismal. One is the advent of a hermeneutic dictator powerful or persuasive enough to "reduce the notions of all mankind exactly to the same length and breadth and height of his own" (166).[27] The other is the fission of the one catholic and universal Church into "six and thirty factions" (70). "Every sect will wrest a several way / (For what one sect interprets, all sects may)," as Dryden warns.[28]

"The infinite variety of opinions in matters of religion," Jeremy Taylor writes, "as they have troubled Christendom with interests, factions, and partialities, so have they caused great divisions of the heart and variety of thoughts and designs among pious and prudent men. For they all, seeing the inconveniences which the disunion of persuasions and opinions have produced, directly or accidentally, have thought themselves obliged to stop this inundation of mischiefs."[29] Among those who wanted to stem this flood without permitting what Taylor called "the liberty of prophesying" was Swift himself. In *Sentiments of a Church of England Man* he warns against the "danger of schism" and the "evil of dissension" (2:6, 11). Since "difference in opinions has cost millions of lives" (11:246), unanimity—even if coerced and consequently hypocritical—seemed preferable to toleration of diversity to those like Swift, Bolingbroke, and many others who opposed repealing or weakening the Test Act. "[One] cause of the multiplication of extravagant opinions and sects," Bolingbroke argues, is "the arbitrary practice of giving different senses to the same passages of the Bible," a practice originating in the patristic tradition of assigning "a grammatical, a literal or historical, an allegorical or figurative, an anagogical or divine, and a tropological or moral sense. Some or all of these may be applied to the same sentence, nay to the same word." Such interpreters pluralize meaning; but instead of many meanings, they are ultimately left with none. "They interpret the same passages of Holy Writ" in "many different, remote, and inconsistent senses, such as destroy one another."[30]

Unless truth itself is inconsistent and self-contradictory, the very plurality of incommensurate interpretations betrays their falsehood. When Gulliver told the king of Brobdingnag that "there were several thousand books among us written upon the art of government; it gave him (directly contrary to my intention) a very mean opinion of our understandings," because the laws of Brobdingnag "are expressed in the most plain and simple terms, wherein those people are not mercurial enough to discover above one interpretation" (11:135–36). More than one true interpretation, indeed, there cannot be.

Catholics, of course, could identify the uniquely correct interpretation as that of the uniquely authorized interpreter speaking *ex cathedra*. All interpretation, however—Protestant and Catholic, religious and secular alike—required some principle whereby to limit the interminable proliferation of interpreters and interpretations or, more simply, to distinguish understanding from misunderstanding. On the island of the magicians, Gulliver tells us, "Having a desire to see those ancients who were most renowned for wit and learning, . . . I proposed that Homer and Aristotle might appear at the head of all their commentators; but these were so numerous that some hundreds were forced to attend in the court and outward rooms of the palace. I knew and could distinguish those two heroes at first sight. . . . I soon discovered [however] that both of them were perfect strangers to the rest of the company" (11:197). It might seem as if the ancients' renown were registered by the number of their commentators, but that is not the joke here.[31] Rather, the commentators are so numerous precisely because they are strangers to the authors. If they were familiar with him, there would be not many interpretations but one, that of the author himself. As the putative basis of hermeneutic nonproliferation and correctness, the author interpreting his own works is as infallible as the Pope.

"Nothing is more frequent than for commentators to force interpretation which the author never meant," the *Tale*'s commentator remarks (186n.). The classic criterion of unforced understanding is to "understand what the author aims at" (159n.). To understand a text is to understand its author, and this means in part that the paradigm case for hermeneutics is not the subject–object confrontation between interpreter and text but instead the I–Thou relationship of people understanding one another.[32] "When I am reading a book, whether wise or silly," Swift once remarked, "it seems to me to be alive and talking to me" (4:253). This extraordinarily pregnant notion of reading as dialogue is perhaps most fully realized in the novel, especially in Fielding and Sterne, both of whom considered writing "but a different name for conversation."[33] In the ideal intimacy of interpersonal understanding, in fact, the written text or other mediation becomes transparent and drops out, allowing the complete fusion of mind with mind. "When I read a volume," says Hume's Demea, "I enter into the mind and intention of the author; I become him, in a manner, for the instant, and have an immediate feeling and conception of those ideas which revolved in his imagination while employed in that composition." This "entering into the mind" of another, Hume elsewhere calls "sympathy," and the intentionalist criterion of understanding as a union of minds makes interpretation a special kind of sympathetic transposition, as we will see in chapter four.

As Demea proceeds, however, he shows why this model for reading humanly authored books is not applicable to the book of nature or its author: "So near an approach we never surely can make to the Deity. His ways are not our ways. His attributes are perfect but incomprehensible. And this volume of nature contains a great and inexplicable riddle, more than any intelligible discourse or reasoning."³⁴ As a criterion for understanding nature, intention is an inappropriate model; for understanding God, sympathy is an arrogant one. The consequence is either a bifurcated hermeneutic (such as Vico's) suited to the bifurcated world, human and natural, or else a suspicion that just as the criterion of intention was proving inapt for interpretation of the book of nature, it might be equally unsuited to other books as well.

Swift, however, complained bitterly that Wotton and others who read the *Tale* as a satire on religion had "overlooked the author's intention" (7). Even today, determining his meaning is no easy matter, and the difficulty of discovering what Swift intended, we might be tempted say, is due in part to his success in concealing it. "He too was a mysterious writer," Guthkelch and Smith admit, "quite as mysterious as any of the writers he satirized" (liii).³⁵ Just as plausible as the knave's supposition that Swift deliberately concealed his intentions, however, is the fool's suspicion that he really had none— that is, that he intended an effect, a diversion, an amusement, not a proposition or concept or meaning.

Whatever the case, readers of the *Tale* often find themselves in the position of the commentator who admits, "I cannot conjecture what the author means here or how this chasm could be filled, though it is capable of more than one interpretation" (179n.). That the commentator is probably the author himself and that he at least seems to be saying that he doesn't know what he means, though he may not mean what he is saying, complicates matters even further. It is nevertheless clear that as the author recedes, interpretations multiply, and that without him it becomes much harder to sort out the right from the wrong ones.

The fools, we have seen, have no difficulty defining what misinterpretations are; as proponents of plainness, however, they have a great deal of difficulty in explaining why there are so many of them. What could account for such epidemic blindness and perversity? The knaves, by contrast, have considerable difficulty specifying what distinguishes right interpretations from wrong ones, but none at all explaining why there are so many. As hermeneutic dualists, they see that interpretations differ from each other because it is in the very nature of interpreted meaning to differ from the author's intention and the text that embodies it. In *Tale of a Tub,* text and meaning are clearly distinguished: the father's will is one thing, the coats another;

the New Testament one thing, the "doctrine and faith of Christianity" another (73). They are different. The difference is not signalled as problematical; nor is the fact that there are three coats. Nevertheless, it is with the death of the Father—the disappearance of the author which is the very occasion of the will—that its meanings start proliferating.

"It were much to be wished," Swift writes, "and I do here humbly propose for an experiment, that every prince in Christendom will take seven of the deepest scholars in his dominions and shut them up close for seven years in seven chambers with a command to write seven ample commentaries on this comprehensive discourse. I shall venture to affirm that whatever difference may be found in their several conjectures, they will be all, without the least distortion, manifestly deducible from the text" (185). One might well interpret this passage of the *Tale* as saying pretty much the same thing as Dryden does in mock bewilderment:

> Strange confidence, still to interpret true,
> Yet not be sure that all they have explain'd,
> Is in the blest original contain'd.[36]

Yet Dryden's sarcasm doesn't seem so funny to the knave who knows that in interpreting, confidence is always misplaced. Insofar as difference from the text is among the defining characteristics of interpretation, the business of interpretation is by nature uncertain. The notion of infallible interpretation (whether by the author or the Pope) is self-contradictory, for the possibility of mistake belongs to the very nature of interpretation. Nor does Dryden seem so funny to the fool, who works with a one-dimensional model of understanding, rejects the figure of "containing and contained" as a knave's mystification, and thus finds nothing odd about a true interpretation not "contain'd" in the original.

Perhaps, then, instead of reading Swift's proposal of the seven scholars' seven commentaries ironically with Dryden, we might read it unironically with Bolingbroke. This proposal, we learn in the 1720 note, "alludes to the story of the seventy interpreters" (185). The Greek Old Testament is called the Septuagint because it was reputed to be the work of seventy translators who produced, independently, seventy translations that agreed word for word. As I show in chapter three, when Bolingbroke refers to this story in his *Letters on the Study and Use of History,* he does so to ridicule the notion of miraculous unanimity. Though elsewhere he denigrates the practice of "giving different senses to the same passages," in the *Letters* it is the idea of consensus that strikes him as funny. Once we begin to think of making a mute text speak by translating it—that is, once we adopt translation, rather than incision and exposure, as the model of interpretation—it becomes easy to explain how *Tale of a Tub* might have seventy times seven interpretations, all of which are manifestly deducible from the text, though not one of them is contained in it.

Since Bolingbroke is thinking of translation as bridging not linguistic but temporal boundaries, the new element in his model of interpretation as translation is time, and it is no accident that he develops it in the course of his *Letters on History*. Here the knave's vertical dualism of surface and depth metamorphoses into a horizontal pluralism of past, present, and succeeding futures. The history of interpretations of the *Tale* itself suggests that the pluralization of meaning derives not just from simultaneous multiplicity, as reflected in hermeneutic sects and factions, but from successive proliferation as well. As Swift suspected, the *Tale* has, like other books, met with "numberless commentators, whose scholastic midwifery has delivered them of meanings that the authors themselves, perhaps, never conceived and yet may very justly be allowed the lawful parents of them: the words of such writers being like seed, which, however scattered at random, when they light upon a fruitful ground, will multiply far beyond either the hopes or imagination of the sower" (186). This passage, too, can easily be read ironically, as satire of those who ignore the author's intentions and multiply the sense by discovering meanings never meant. Readers who detect this irony while also picking up the echo of Jesus's parable of the sower might well, with Wotton, condemn such merriment as blasphemous, or at least tasteless.

Read in the fool's way, however, the significance of the passage and the parable has to do with the historical generation of meaning. Jesus explains his words as follows: "He that received seed into the good ground is he that heareth the word, and understandeth it; which also beareth fruit, and bringeth forth, some an hundredfold, some sixty, some thirty" (Matt. 13:23). Here understanding is figured as growth, and growth as multiplication. No longer associated with sectarian division, the process of interpretive application in which the one word emanates many is as natural as that whereby the one seed grows and in fertile ground multiplies many times over.

The appearance of this organic figure in the *Tale* could be considered casual did it not also occur as one of the miraculous virtues in the three brothers' coats: "They will grow in the same proportion with your bodies, lengthening and widening of themselves, so as to be always fit." Swift explains the allegory of growth thus: "By the wisdom of the divine founder [the coats are] fitted to all times, places, and circumstances" (73). One coat, many times and situations—it might seem that Swift is not far from Taylor, who concludes that Scripture "itself affords of liberty and variety."[37] Taylor's "eclectic theology," as he calls it, is based on the unhistorical premise that at all times the single text possesses an immanent plurality of meaning, and so justifies hermeneutic liberty. Such tolerant eclecticism sits uneasily with Swift, however, and the notion of richness, complexity, or any kind of simultaneous multiplicity tends to gloss over not only the problem of the unity of the text, but also the problem of history, which receives such intensive consideration in the *Tale*.

"Nothing," Swift writes, "is so very tender as a modern piece of wit and which is apt to suffer so much in the carriage. Some things are very witty today or fasting or in this place or at eight a clock . . . any of which, by the smallest transposal or misapplication, is utterly annihilate" (43). This observation, however caricatured, comprises the rationale for historicism in a nutshell, and its methodological consequence is that:

> Whatever reader desires to have a thorough comprehension of an author's thoughts cannot take a better method than by putting himself into the circumstances and postures of life that the author was in upon every important passage as it flowed from his pen; for this will introduce a parity and strict correspondence of ideas between the reader and the author. Now, to assist the diligent reader in so delicate an affair, as far as brevity will permit, I have recollected that the shrewdest pieces of this treatise were conceived in bed in a garret; at other times (for a reason best known to myself) I thought fit to sharpen my invention with hunger; and in general, the whole work was begun, continued, and ended under a long course of physic and a great want of money. (44)

Nothing is so ephemeral as modern wit, and only such ephemerality raises the issue of historical relativism. Prince Posterity serves and so preserves the ancients, but Father Time consigns the moderns to oblivion. The moderns therefore require historical inquiry. Since occasional productions can be understood only through the occasions that produced them, preliminary to understanding intention is understanding the "circumstances and postures of life." Historical transposition is prior to sympathy. "Will's Coffee-house," Swift's note generously informs us, "was formerly the place where the Poets usually met, which though it be yet fresh in memory, yet in some years may be forgot, and want this explanation" (64n.). The ancients are historic, the moderns merely historical. The one invites imitation and emulation, the other invites footnotes. Lacking the perennial universality of the ancients, the works of the moderns cannot, without absurdity, be understood by reference to times other than their own, whether later or earlier. "To judge . . . of Shakespeare by Aristotle's rules," Pope objects in the preface to his edition, "is like trying a man by the laws of one country who acted under those of another."[38]

Yet this injustice raises doubts about the ancients as well. If Aristotle's poetics cannot be justly applied to Shakespeare, this means that the ancient is no more universal than the modern. "Those rules of old, discovered not devised," as Pope described them, can no longer claim to be "nature methodized"; nor can anything else. After the knave Bentley exposed the Phalaris fraud, it began to be a matter of "grave dispute whether there have been ever any ancients [at all]" (125).[39] Modern ephemerality becomes paradigmatic of all things human. There are no timeless ancients whose works are universally applicable and directly accessible (that is, plain). All must be interpreted—historically.

If the historian tries to transport himself back to the past, Peter, in the tale of the three brothers, tries to transport the past forward to the present. What necessitates Peter's interpretive accommodations, his historicism-in-reverse, is that his father's will is a document meant not only to be interpreted and understood but also to be used and applied. Even more than the classics, which served not merely as objects of scholarship but also as models of life, Scripture involves an intrinsic claim to immediate relevance such that it is not only a repository of historical knowledge—knowledge about what is past—but also a guide to action here and now.

In accommodating the past to the present, Peter's hermeneutic chicane, though obviously self-serving, still constitutes an act of reverence. Rather than merely ignoring the will's dictates, he attempts to apply them: he tries to reconcile strict observance of a "very precise" will with "a strict observance after times and fashions"

(80). Neither is dispensable. If his misinterpretations are self-interested, they are not wrong *because* self-interested. A more faithful application of the word would not be any less faithful to the world. Scripture epitomizes the holiness of every text that must be preserved inviolate in the process of exegesis; the interpreter has no authority to "add to or diminish" it. Yet, at the same time, its very claim to applicability—to be Scripture— means that its eternal truths must be brought to bear in the temporal world of "human fashions," which are "of very short duration" (84) and so epitomize the "transitory state of all sublunary things" (66).

Though Scripture remains forever one and the same, it claims to apply to the manifold of human history, and so in even the most faithful application there persists a tension between the one and the many, between the self-same text and the self-differing, historical world. Application will always have the appearance of denying one or the other, either foolishly reducing the reality of historical change by making it conform to a self-identical text or, as in the case of Peter, knavishly fragmenting and multiplying the self-identity of the text by making it conform to the reality of historical change.

This brings us to the crux of the hermeneutic problem: namely, that the coats, as we read in the *Tale,* are of themselves "fitted to all times, places, and circumstances" (73). Theirs is a specifically historical universality; the coats are not just "wash and wear." Rather than just being appropriate to all situations in general, they adapt themselves to meet each changing situation individually. This notion of self-altering coats puts Peter's critics in a quandary. Even if we admit that Peter deliberately misreads the will and alters the coats to fit new fashions, how can such perverse misinterpretations be distinguished from correct, true interpretations? How can Peter's alterations be distinguished from those intrinsic to the coats themselves? The coats, the father tells his sons, "grow in the same proportion with your bodies, lengthening and widening of themselves, so as to be always fit" (73). Thus the fact of alteration offers no sure sign that the coats have been violated since they alter (of) themselves. In history, texts may remain the same, but their meanings are always growing and changing. What, then, makes one change adventitious and mistaken, another organic and immanent?

Peter claims the "power to make and add certain clauses for public emolument, though not deducible, *totidem verbis,* from the letter of the will, or else, *Multa Absurda Sequerentur*" (90). However patently self-serving it may be, however it seems in substance to contradict the provision that nothing be added or diminished from the will, Peter's claim is quite justified: the necessity of avoiding absurdity does indeed give him the power to make additions and changes. This is especially clear if we think of the will as a legal document, rather than a scripture. "A system of human law and human policy," Bolingbroke asserts, "is the product of human understanding, and therefore incomplete and imperfect, liable to different constructions at all times, and fit to be altered at some. But this cannot be said, without blasphemy, of the Christian dispensation."[40] If Scripture represents the impermissibility of altering the text, law represents the impossibility of not altering it.[41]

In his *Commentaries on the Laws of England* Blackstone explains why Peter can legitimately claim the power "to make and add certain clauses." Under the heading of interpreting laws "according to the effect," Blackstone writes: "As to the effects and consequence, the rule [of interpretation] is that where the words bear either none or a very absurd signification if literally understood, we must a little deviate from the received sense of them. Therefore the Bolognian law, mentioned by Puffendorf, which enacted 'that whoever drew blood in the streets should be punished with the utmost severity,' was held after long debate not to extend to the surgeon who opened the vein of a person that fell down in the street with a fit."[42] The necessity for equitable interpretation, as we will see in chapter five, gives judges the discretionary power to avoid absurdity and actually to "correct" laws by adapting them to fit circumstances unforeseen by legislators. But how, asks the fool, can an interpretation that alters a law be an interpretation of it? How, asks the knave in return, can an interpretation which does not alter the law be faithful to it?

Blackstone freely admits that "there can be no established rules and fixed precepts of equity laid down." There can be no laws governing the interpretation of laws. That way lies mere regress. What is left, however, if there are no rules by which to tell right from wrong interpretation, to distinguish a correction of the law from a perversion of it, or to differentiate an alteration that belongs to a self-altering law from one that does not? Just this lack of rules prompts Hume to affirm in consternation that "jurisprudence is . . . different from all the sciences; and that in many of its nicer questions there cannot properly be said to be truth or falsehood on either side. . . . The preference given by the judge is often founded more on taste and imagination than on any solid argument."[43] But for the saving qualifiers, this argument denies the possibility of justice. By founding juridical interpretation on taste, Hume means to identify legal judgment with aesthetic preference as merely subjective and arbitrary. Anything goes, and the notion of misinterpretation disappears.

Swift, by contrast, is certainly not willing to give it up, no less in his own case than in that of Scripture. He charges in the "Apology" that the *Tale* has been misinterpreted by readers who "have neither candour to suppose good meanings nor palate to distinguish true ones" (5). It is an offhand remark, and Swift does not elaborate or explain it, although he does say again later that such misinterpretations would never enter the head "of any reader of taste and candour" (12). These are somewhat surprising faculties to identify with interpretation, perhaps. By "candour," of course, Swift means not forthrightness but charity, also called *equitas hermeneutica*. More to the point here, Swift pairs the charity that "supposes good meanings" with the palate, the good taste, that can "distinguish true ones." Swift understands " taste" not in Hume's way, as subjective preference, but as the faculty that discerns interpretive truth. In this respect he is like Burke, who, as I show in the final chapter, stigmatizes rule-governed politics as tasteless and indeed, for that reason, false.

To say that taste, whether political or literary, determines what constitutes a true interpretation registers the fact that there are no rules,[44] no sure, certain criteria distinguishing true from false interpretation. This hardly means that anything goes, however. The absence of rules defining misinterpretation no more implies that there are no misinterpretations than the absence of rules governing beauty implies that nothing is ugly. To say with Swift that taste governs interpretive truth implies that meaning is mutable yet cannot be reduced to the merely fashionable, something that endures yet cannot be reduced to stasis and fixity. Finding a meaning is more like finding a balance than finding a thing, discovering a point of equipoise between the past text and the present application, which point is the understanding itself. Since there can be no law for the interpretation of laws, a judgment of taste is always needed to balance the twin claims of past and present without reducing either.

In this context, we can view Martin as the man of hermeneutic good taste, who neither affects to despise present fashion, like Jack, nor capitulates to its dictates, like Peter. With Jack, Martin "flayed off" (139) some of the fashionable decorations with which Peter had ornamented the coats; but others he left. "Where he observed the embroidery to be worked so close as not to be got away without damaging the cloth, or where it served to hide or strengthen any flaw in the body of the coat, contracted by the perpetual tampering of workmen upon it, he concluded the wisest course was to let it remain, resolving in no case whatsoever that the substance of the stuff should suffer injury; which he thought the best method for serving the true intent and meaning of his father's will" (136—37). What method is this, that of the knave or the fool? Something of both, it seems.

Martin flays, strips, and exposes false surface appearances like any knave. Like any fool, however, he also wants to "sodder and patch up flaws and imperfections" (174). He knows full well that the remaining embroidery is adventitious, tacked on in the course of accommodating the coat to once-current fashions. Some of these additions, however, have become oddly intrinsic: "worked so close" as to become indivisible from "the body of the coat." In history some supplement becomes inseparable from substance. The tasteful decoration, though mere ornament, nevertheless belongs to the coat; otherwise it would not be tasteful. Application of doctrine becomes the doctrine itself; the tasteful interpretation is text—not apocryphal but canonical text, and therefore not secondary or adventitious at all.

But this is merely to say that the coat grows, lengthening and widening of itself. Taste on the part of the interpreter corresponds to innate growth on the side of what is interpreted. Through the history of apt applications to novel circumstances, through tasteful alterations that are new but not forced, the text continually becomes itself, comes into its own. A growing text, which contains an immanent principle of self-difference, is at once *alter et idem;* it stays the same by altering. Such a text renders untenable the dichotomy of fools and knaves, for even the true interpretations differ from the text and from each other. Yet the differing interpretations, being true, nevertheless belong to and are indistinguishable from the very text in itself.

I

Locke on

Human Understanding

"Ino sooner perceived myself in the world but I found myself in a storm," Locke wrote in 1660.[1] Then at the dawn of his intellectual life, two facts were already clear to him as to everyone else: first, the fragmentation of religious, civil, and intellectual life in England; second, the "Furies, war, cruelty, rapine, confusion" which those schisms had caused.[2] Even though the Restoration promised a remission of the storm, it was evident that the fabric of common life and thought was in shreds: fractious parties in the government, contending schools within the academies, fanatical religious sects, each in self-certain possession of the whole truth, each righteously clamoring for the power to annihilate the others. The fragile sense of national unity that came with the Restoration could thus be only short-lived. Peace and quiet were what Englishmen most wanted, and the question early and late in Locke's career was how to achieve it.

Having been born into this incoherence, and consequently never yearning for some golden age of unanimity, Locke accepted difference as a given. Between social groups he discerned "no common criteria in terms of which differences [could] be resolved";[3] so he formulated social goals that took the form less of agreement than peaceful coexistence amidst disagreement. In the early authoritarian tracts on government, his position was not that disagreements should be resolved but that dissent should be suppressed. Such suppression was necessary, he thought, precisely because resolving even trivial disputes was inconceivable. "He must be a stranger to England that thinks that meats and habits, that places and times of worship etc. would not be sufficient occasion of hatreds and quarrels among us."[4] Since "matters of indifference" were deemed by the disputants to be worth killing and dying for, people had to be ruled by power. Consensus was not an option.

Though in these early pieces, Locke "draws his sword in the same side with the magistrate, with a design to suppress, not begin a quarrel,"[5] it was evident even to him that violent suppressions contribute to public quiet no more than the violent disputes they were intended to pacify. He acknowledges that in defending force he is entering "a field of battle and not so much proposing a thesis as raising a war-cry."[6] Thirty years later Locke reversed himself, of course, and disavowed enforced unanimity; but he is constant in asserting the irreducibility of difference. In the *Essay Concerning Human Understanding,* he asserts it on the basis of a skeptical line of argument: "It is unavoidable to the greatest part of men, if not all, to have several *opinions* without certain and indubitable proofs of their truth. . . . The necessity of believing without [certain] knowledge, nay often upon very slight grounds, in this fleeting state of action and blindness we are in should make us [hesitant to] constrain others."[7] The premise of inevitable plurality here is the same as in the authoritarian tracts. Only the suggested response varies.

This premise and response are most fully elaborated in the *Letter on Toleration* and its sequels. Here too fragmentation is a given; the sole issue is how to avoid its bloody consequences. Because differences should not be suppressed and because they cannot be resolved, Locke argues, they must therefore be tolerated. "It is not the diversity of opinions, which cannot be avoided, but the refusal of toleration to those that are of different opinions . . . that has produced all the bustles and wars that have been in the Christian world upon account of religion."[8] Since difference is unavoidable, the only practical possibility is to try to prevent the disputes it occasions, and toleration, in Locke's view, is the best means of doing so.

In advocating toleration, it is important to realize, Locke was raising yet another war cry, not merely championing manifest truth and justice. Though it seems to us a self-evident virtue, it was not so for Locke's original audience, to many of whom it was a dubious and unacceptable principle of social intercourse. Far from universal, toleration was then (and remains now) a partisan principle, for two reasons: not everyone embraced Locke's position—witness the controversy surrounding the *Letter*—and, more important, no one ever advocates universal toleration. There is always something or someone, always some group of subversives and anarchists (or Catholics and atheists, for Locke), which threatens peace or tolerance itself and thus proves intolerable.[9] Moreover, negative tolerance, as in Locke's version, is merely intolerance shorn of its violence. For the victims of persecution this is, to be sure, a very great gain, and no one would want to underestimate the importance of reducing violence and oppression.

Yet, though it is undoubtedly a landmark of civilized society, toleration is a social and political rather than cognitive value. It promotes peace, not truth; and for it to become even a social value, three, related things must be assumed. We have already met with two of them in Locke's thought: first, finite beings have no choice but to base their conduct on opinions that, however probable, lack certainty; second, uncertain opinions are inevitably plural. The third assumption underwriting tolerance as a virtue is that unity and plurality are signs, respectively, of truth and falsehood. There is "one truth," Locke writes,[10] and "there are great numbers of *opinions* which, . . . both for their absurdity as well as oppositions to one another, *it is impossible should be true*" (I. 3. 21). Likewise, there is "one way to heaven";[11] "these [religious] divisions and systems were made by men, and carry the mark of the fallible on them."[12] Again, "Since the law of nature is everywhere one and the same, but traditions vary, it follows either that there is no law of nature at all, or that it cannot be known by means of tradition."[13] Tolerance becomes a virtue, then, on the basis of three assumptions: the plurality of opinions, the unity of truth, and the inaccessibility of that unitary truth. Together, these prescribe what is finally a negative response to difference: you differ from me; one of us is therefore wrong; but it is impossible to be certain which one, so I must not harm you.

Locke's political, religious, and philosophical writings, I will argue, are based on an unrecognized possibility, of which his enlightened advocacy of toleration is symptomatic. The unimagined alternative to both tolerance and intolerance, the principle uniting social with cognitive values, the locus of the blind spot governing Locke's thought, I contend, is precisely human understanding—that is, understanding and interpreting what other human beings think and say and write.[14] To take understanding in the latter sense, as both a social virtue and an epistemological necessity, is to assume (by contrast with Locke) that human understanding is dialogical, and that refraining from understanding others does not make possible a cognitive life of one's own but precludes knowledge entirely. Locke's monological epistemology assumes the divisibility of dialogue and truth; that is, it assumes that the cognitive subject can—indeed, must—acquire knowledge alone.

Like other aspects of Locke's thought that we will be examining, tolerance—no less than intolerance—obviates substantive dialogue, dialogue in which people come to an understanding. He does not assume, of course, that people are bound always to disagree, but rather that when and where people do concur about some truth, it is because they have reached it independently, not because they have talked about it. Toleration is an adequate response to difference only if talk is ultimately pointless, and the pointlessness of dialogue seems to be a direct corollary of Locke's epistemological individualism. Exaggerating to make the point clear, we can say that grounding his philosophy is the monological premise that, on any given question, it is difficult—perhaps impossible—and in principle unnecessary to understand what other people think. One's own understanding, however limited its range, can get no help from others and can manage well enough on its own. "So much as we ourselves consider and comprehend of truth and reason, so much we possess of real and true knowledge. The floating of other men's opinions in our brains makes us not one jot the more knowing, though they happen to be true" (1. 3. 24).

In what follows, I concentrate on the anti-dialogical—and, more broadly, anti-hermeneutical—elements in Locke's thought. In practice, of course, he read and talked and argued with his friends and opponents, as every thinker must; but here I am concerned not with his practice but with his philosophy, and virtually nothing in the latter renders dialogue or interpretation fundamental to knowledge. Quite the contrary; the distinctive aspects of Locke's philosophy are those which typify (indeed, generate) the widespread eighteenth-century reaction against interpretation in all its venues: scholastic, sectarian, juridical, historical, and literary. Since the anti-interpretive elements in Locke's thought, though predominant, are at times counterbalanced by other, more favorable comments, my concentration on the former runs the risk of being unfairly selective. Nevertheless, a sympathetic study of eighteenth-century hermeneutics must open with a less than sympathetic account of Locke, since he, more than any one else, represents the impediments which hermeneutic self-consciousness had to overcome.

"I have long since learned not to rely on men," Locke writes; "these bubbles however swollen and glittering, soft and inviting, are not fit to be leaned on, and whoever shall make them his support shall find them nothing but a little gilded air."[15] What specific personal disappointments, if any, lie behind Locke's general distrust of his fellowmen is difficult to say; and for our purposes it does not matter, since it is in any case clear that his was a principled distrust. In "this great Bedlam England,"[16] Locke professed himself unwilling to rely on other people's rationality, even their sanity. The famous chapter on "The Association of Ideas" added to the fourth edition of the *Essay* opens with the following observation: "There is scarce any one that does not observe something that seems odd to him and is in itself really extravagant, in the opinions, reasonings, and actions of other men." This extravagance, he goes on to say, "is really madness; and there is scarce a man so free of it" that if he persisted, he would not be "fitter for Bedlam than for civil conversation" (2. 33. 1–4). Even if the same is true of oneself, it is better to go wrong with one's own madness than be the dupe of another's.

In all his writings, from the earliest to the most mature, it is evident that for Locke this Crusoe-like self-reliance in the last instance obviates the need to understand other people. "In our inquiry after knowledge, it . . . little concerns us what other men have thought. . . . If a traveller gets a knowledge of the right way, it is no matter whether he knows the infinite windings, byways, and turnings where others have been misled; the knowledge of the right secures him from the wrong, and that is the great business. And so methinks it is in our intellectual pilgrimage through this world. It is an idle and useless thing to make it our business to study what have been other men's sentiments in things where reason only is the judge."[17]

Whether the question at hand is religious, political, or philosophical, Locke always looks in the same direction for answers—and it is not to others. On the question, Who will judge when political repression suffices to justify a revolution?, he replies, "I myself can only be judge in my own conscience."[18] With respect to responsibility for the individual's eternal welfare, Locke writes similarly: "The care . . . of every man's soul belongs unto himself, and is to be left unto himself."[19] And the constant theme of the *Essay Concerning Human*

Understanding is that men must think and know for themselves (1. 4. 23.). To locate whatever truth is to be had by finite creatures within themselves, to make its discovery a mute, solitary process, is to reverse the valence of difference itself, so that it no longer needs to be resolved. Locke's monological injunction to intellectual independence transforms difference from an evil to be avoided into a value to be embraced. In response to social and intellectual fragmentation, he advocates fragmentation to the ultimate degree, down to the indecomposable epistemological unit: the isolated, indivisible individual.[20]

It is true that in both the *Second Treatise* and the *Essay,* Locke appears to subscribe to the orthodox view that God made man social—by inclination and necessity. Yet, while never withdrawing his assent, Locke scarcely embraces—indeed, he denies—its consequences. If human beings are naturally social, there remains no possibility of a dichotomy between the natural and the social—no possibility, that is, of one of the basic dualisms of Locke's political theory. Insofar as the *Second Treatise on Government* opposes the state of society to that of nature and posits the priority of natural atomism over artificial communality, to that extent Locke implies the priority of the individual over the social. The contract theory of interpersonal relations depends on this priority: first the person, then the relation. Unlike human beings traditionally conceived, persons are not naturally social animals. Of their own nature they are sufficient unto themselves even if they can enter into artificial compacts with others.

Even after voluntarily joining the social and interpersonal sphere, moreover, individuals retain their status as the authority of last instance. Ultimately, people answer only to God—that is, to no one on earth but themselves—not only with regard to spiritual concerns but also with respect to thoughts and deeds. In this respect, as well as in his discussion of personal identity, Locke holds a legal—or what he calls a "forensic"—conception of personhood: the person is that isolated being which can be held individually accountable, which not only judges things in freedom, independently of others' opinions, but for that very reason can be tried and found guilty. For every belief and act, each person has a moral and intellectual responsibility, a personal responsibility, that cannot be avoided and cannot be shared. Whatever a person does and thinks, it does and thinks alone.

Instead of social duties, a person has rights—notably to life, liberty, and property. Each of these is an individual right; and the last, property, is therefore most problematical, since Locke makes it the basis of justice. Whereas justice can be conceived as a social value—say, as an extension of the golden rule—Locke makes property-based justice an exclusively personal and almost anti-social value.[21] "Children," he writes in *Some Thoughts Concerning Education,* "cannot well comprehend what injustice is till they understand property and how particular persons come by it."[22] By "injustice," Locke means depriving propertied individuals of what they have, not depriving the unpropertied of what they do not have. Justice, the right to acquire and retain property, is not a civil obligation but a personal right.

In one sense, "property" means that which is proper to a thing, its own quality or characteristic. In the related sense that concerns Locke, it means that which is proper to a person. Properties, like rights, are either natural or acquired; and in the *Second Treatise* Locke memorably contends that people have a natural right to acquired property. Labor is a natural right, a right over one's own body; and labor, we recall, is the act of appropriation or enownment whereby Locke explains how things like land and wind and sea originally proper to no one become the property of someone, one's own.

Owning is the personal right to essentially unlimited self-expansion, for if life and liberty belong to what the individual is, property pertains to what it can be. By owning and accumulating properties, the individual is indefinitely enlarged. Whatever it owns becomes its own, its property, itself. Capable of appropriation without limit, the atomic individual is no longer a part within a social unit but potentially the whole. Even if the larger social whole in some sense exists, the *polis* is not an end in this politics. Rather, fulfilling one's obligations to the polis is a means to individual ends: to insuring that one can retain the property one has and accumulate more. Owning expands one's own by appropriating what was other; thus the right to own always in principle pits the self against the other, for the other represents the barrier to, as well as the possibility of, further enownment. Since property is a natural right in Locke's view, antagonism to the other is inherent in—proper to—the person.

Moreover, just as labor appropriates physical things, so too it makes ideas one's own property.[23] Locke repeatedly exhorts his reader to the labor of thought and castigates its opposite, laziness of mind. Such laziness explains the commonest of errors: namely, participation in the communal tradition. "The lazy and inconsiderate part of men, making far the greater number, [take] up their notions by chance, from common tradition and vulgar conceptions, without much beating their heads about them" (1. 4. 15). The tradition of innate ideas is Locke's specific target here, but the mode of argument is typical. Enownment is verification. Mental labor makes an idea at once both one's own and true; hence laziness is doubly damaging.

In the religious sphere mental indolence takes two forms. The distinctively Protestant form of laziness consists in the pretense of direct inspiration: "Immediate revelation being a much easier way for men to establish their opinions and regulate their conduct than the tedious and not always successful labour of strict reasoning, it is no wonder that some have been very apt to pretend to revelation" (4. 19. 5). Here, the absence of labor explains why enthusiasm can generate no cognitively significant ideas. Only ideas appropriated through cognitive labor—only ideas that are one's own property— have authority as knowledge. This principle is no less evident in the opposite form of religious laziness: namely, the "implicit faith" of Catholics, who rest content with mediate knowledge. "Some (and those the most) taking things upon trust misemploy their power of assent, by lazily enslaving their minds to the dictates and dominion of others in doctrines which it is their duty carefully to examine" (1. 4. 21). "If I must believe for myself, it is unavoidable that I must understand for myself. For if I blindly and with an implicit faith take the Pope's interpretation of the Sacred Scripture without examining whether it be Christ's meaning, 'tis the Pope I believe in, and not in Christ."[24] The value of thought as knowledge is measured by the degree to which it results not from lazy enslavement but free labor. That is to say, cognitively significant thought is property.

The labor of appropriation is required not just for religious but for all ideas. "Reading furnishes the mind only with materials of knowledge; it is thinking makes what we read ours. . . . [Some writers] would be of great use if their readers would . . . [turn] them into knowledge; but that can be done only by our own meditation; . . . and then, as far as we apprehend and see the connection of ideas, so far it is ours."[25] "In the sciences, every one has so much [knowl- edge] as he really knows and comprehends. What he believes only and takes upon trust are but shreds which . . . make no considerable addition to his stock who gathers them. Such borrowed wealth, like fairy-money, though it were gold in the hand from which he received it, will be but leaves and dust when it comes to use" (1. 4. 23).

Borrowed intellectual wealth, by this argument, is not shared property (that is a mere contraction). It is either worthless "fairy-money"—that is, not wealth at all—or else it is merely raw material to be appropriated by labor. By reading thoughtfully and critically, ideas that once belonged to others are appropriated—or, perhaps more exactly, expropriated. In critical reading, others' ideas become our own; thus there is no debt to be repaid, no property of others that must be returned. Briefly put, borrowing truth, unlike borrowing things, is impossible. Locke is not here questioning the value of understanding what others think; rather, he suggests that if and when their ideas are genuinely understood, they are no longer theirs but our own. Thus, if understanding means understanding other people's ideas as others', then understanding in that sense never occurs.

This argument bears on Locke's notorious unwillingness to pay his intellectual debts by acknowledging them.[26] But more important than what now appears to be a personal failing is that Locke is here formulating a new corollary of the right of intellectual property: namely, the principle of originality.[27] Judged by this monological principle, intellectual borrowing, even if possible, is undesirable. In the final book of the *Essay* Locke concludes: "It is sufficient for me if, by a discourse . . . wholly new and unborrowed, I shall have given occasion to others . . . to seek in their own thoughts for those *right helps of art,* which will scarce be found, I fear, by those who servilely confine themselves to the rules and dictates of others" (4. 17. 7). Originality is not creation *ex nihilo,* to be sure; it requires materials, specifically (for Locke the empiricist) those supplied by experience. Origination is the labor of appropriation that makes property of those materials, the enownment that makes of them something one's very own. Rather than creating without materials, then, originality is creation without borrowing. An original is not only not an imitation; it is not an interpretation. It is the specific kind of ideative production that is the antithesis of, and only possible without, understanding others.

Scripture is the great exception when it comes to Locke's doubts about the need for understanding. Yet even with respect to the Bible he was not always willing to argue from the need for understanding to its possibility. "Though everything said in the text be true, yet the reader may be—nay, cannot choose but be—very fallible in the understanding of it" (3. 9. 23). Locke often suggests that it is the imprecision of scriptural language which occasions the reader's difficulties. Since "revealed truths, which are conveyed to us by books and languages, are liable to the common and natural obscurities and difficulties incident to words, methinks it would become us to be . . . less magisterial, positive, and imperious in imposing our own sense and interpretations [on them]" (3. 9. 23). Though Scripture is beset with "unavoidable difficulties of speech," Christians cannot desist from the attempt to understand it; hence, Locke concludes, "it would become us to be charitable one to another in our interpretations or misunderstandings" of it (3. 9. 22, italics omitted).

This is the skeptical argument for religious tolerance that we touched on earlier. But although tolerance is Locke's best-known response to the conflict of interpretations, it is not his most typical. Of its very nature, interpretation always leaves room—room for alternative interpretations and so for disagreement. To minimize the conflict that arises from such plurality, Locke advocates tolerance; but his more radical solution is to eliminate the alternatives and thus the room for disagreement itself. Why and how Locke does so, even in the case of Scripture, we can begin to see by glancing at the two *Treatises on Government*. Condemning Filmer's reliance on "scripture-proofs" in rationalizing political subjugation, Locke writes in the *Second Treatise* that "learning and religion shall [always] be found to justify all that [a tyrant] shall do to his subjects."[28] Since interpretation can justify anything, his conclusion seems to be, it justifies nothing. When the intent is to disprove Filmer's interpretation of Scripture, as in the case of the *First Treatise,* Locke of course offers counter-interpretations in rebuttal; but when the intent is positive and constructive, as in the *Second Treatise,* the argument is discursive and demonstrative, not primarily interpretive.

Similarly, in the legal sphere, Locke contends that "a barefaced wresting of the laws" to the tyrant's advantage is a hermeneutic act of war which legitimizes insurrection.[29] In the context of his suspicion of juridical interpretation, it is particularly telling that he advocates no autonomous judiciary. Three elements are necessary, he says, if a government is to preserve property and thus fulfill its chief end: "an *established,* settled, known *law,*" "*a known and indifferent judge* with authority to determine all differences according to established law," and "a power to back and support the sentence." Yet, when he enumerates the powers of government in the next paragraph, there are only two: "*the legislative and executive power.*"[30] The interpretive branch has disappeared into the executive.[31]

This is perfectly consistent with Locke's general desire to suppress interpretive difference by minimizing interpretation wherever possible. Long before the Glorious Revolution in support of which the *Two Treatises* were published and even before the Exclusion controversy concerning which they were written,[32] Locke had recognized the danger of interpretation and sought to reduce its provenance. His early "Essay on Infallibility" (1661) is in large part an anti-Catholic tract, but its import is not limited to an exhibition of Locke's religious partisanship. Papal infallibility is merely the most palpable manifestation of the authority of interpretation in general, and Locke's early antagonism to it is paradigmatic for his entire career. This essay expresses the hermeneutic threat most pointedly: "While in any state and society of men the right of making laws is the highest and greatest power, certainly next and almost equal to this is the authority of interpreting these laws. For what is the point of drawing up dumb, silent statements of laws if anybody may attach a new meaning to the words to suit his own taste, find some remote interpretation, and twist the words to fit the situation and his own opinion?"[33]

As here posed, this is merely a rhetorical question, and Locke makes no attempt to answer it. He implies that laws are needed that are not silent and dumb—that is, laws that express their own meaning and so require no interpretation; but he does not here betray any awareness that such an ideal cannot be realized.[34] As we will see in chapter six, Aristotle and Grotius, and Blackstone after them, explain why laws cannot be made completely explicit—that is, why they are always in need of interpretation—but Locke does suggest a drastic remedy for interpretive license. A kind of argumentative overkill is evident in the "Essay on Infallibility"; for to prove it unnecessary "that an infallible interpreter of Holy Scripture be granted in the Church,"[35] Locke contends that it is unnecessary to have any interpreter at all. This thesis he demonstrates by dividing the question. Scriptural passages are of three kinds, he contends, and the issue is which kinds require interpretation. First, there are passages in Scripture irrelevant to one's conduct; there is thus no point in interpreting them. Second, there are divine mysteries beyond human understanding; these are therefore impossible to interpret. Third are unambiguous passages defining our principal duties, and these, being clear, do not require interpretation. Since these three divisions comprehend the Bible in toto, Locke concludes that interpretation of Scripture is in no case necessary or possible.

If certain passages even of Scripture are irrelevant to conduct and hence not worth interpreting, the same is all the more true of the writings of secular authors, who have no claim to authority.

> [T]here being no writings we have any great concernment to be very solicitous about the meaning of but those that contain either truths we are required to believe or laws we are to obey and draw inconveniences on us when we mistake or transgress, we may be less anxious about the sense of [ancient] authors, who, writing but their own opinions, we are under no greater necessity to know them, than they to know ours. . . . [T]herefore in the reading of them, if they do not use their words with a due clearness and perspicuity, we may lay them aside, and, without any injury done them, resolve thus with ourselves, *Si non vis intelligi, debes negligi.* (3. 9. 10).

To the uncharitable, this contention may well seem a thinly veiled defense of intellectual laziness—if a book cannot be understood, it's not worth understanding—but the argument in fact belongs to Locke's general attempt to obviate interpretation per se.

Admittedly Locke adds: "I say not this, that I think commentaries needless." Yet such mild concessions seem pale and disingenuous when juxtaposed with his contemptuous dismissals elsewhere. "What have the greatest part of the comments and disputes upon the laws of God and man served for, but to make the meaning more doubtful and perplex the sense?" (3. 10. 12). "Many a Scripture or clause in the code at first reading has, by consulting commentators, quite lost the sense of it" (3. 9. 9).

Whatever sense is to be obtained from a text must be gleaned directly from the text itself. In his *Thoughts Concerning Education,* Locke approvingly cites La Bruyère's admonition: "The study, says he, of the original text can never be sufficiently recommended. . . . Draw from the spring-head, and take not things at second hand. . . . Acquaint yourself fully with the principles of the original authors; bring them to a consistency; and then do you yourself make your deductions. In this state were the first commentators, and do not you rest till you bring yourself to the same. Content not yourself with those borrowed lights. . . . Their explications are not yours. . . . On the contrary, your own observations are the product of your own mind."[36] Even interpretation, we see, must be original. To understand others' ideas, like anything else, it is advisable to avoid others' ideas. Even if occasionally helpful, the commentators' assistance is at worst positively prejudicial to understanding. "Supposing that Hippocrates or any other book infallibly contains the whole art of physic, would not the direct way be to study, read, and consider that book . . . rather than [consult the commentary of anyone] who, though they espouse [Hippocrates'] authority, have already interpreted and wiredrawn all his text to their own sense—the tincture whereof I have imbibed, I am more in danger to misunderstand his true meaning than if I had come to him with a mind unprepossessed."[37] Here, as always for Locke, others' understandings are a primary obstacle to one's own.

Warnings against interpretation pertain to texts more infallible than Hippocrates, of course. Locke condemns Christians who "help to cozen themselves by choosing to use and pin their faith on such expositors as explain the Sacred Scripture in favour of those opinions that they beforehand have voted orthodox and bring to the Sacred Scripture not for trial but confirmation."[38] As the essay introducing his *Paraphrase and Notes on the Epistles of St. Paul* indicates, Locke recommends consulting not the expositors but "understanding St. Paul's epistles by consulting St. Paul himself." Locke claims no special revelation, to be sure, no private access to the apostle. The consultation he means is with the text alone. Locke is invoking the principle of intrinsic interpretation: that meaning is immanent in the text.

This principle is by no means original to Locke. The Preface to *The Reasonableness of Christianity* opens with the following apology: "The little satisfaction and consistency that is to be found in most of the systems of divinity I have met with made me betake myself to the sole reading of the Scriptures . . . for the understanding of the Christian religion."[39] Behind the somewhat awkward phrase "sole reading," one hears the Latin "sola scriptura," which had been the fundamental principle of Protestant hermeneutics since the Reformation. It means that the text is sufficient to its own understanding and should therefore be approached directly, without priestly mediation. "For the reformers the important principle," G. R. Evans writes, "is that the Bible is . . . its own interpreter, proving, judging, illuminating itself. Luther insists that Scripture itself is clearer than all the commentaries of the Fathers."[40] The seemingly innocent and disinterested principle of "sole reading" is therefore thoroughly partisan. To "consult St. Paul himself" is not to avoid "systems of divinity" but to embrace the system of Wycliffe and Luther.[41]

Locke does not consider the possibility that to read Scripture alone is merely to read it with an unacknowledged mediator. Rather, he integrates the principle of "sola scriptura" into his own programmatic reaction against interpretation per se. Bitterly familiar with the disruptions that conflicting interpretations had caused the "peace of the Church" and the nation, Locke envisioned a solution that required neither reconciling interpretive differences nor even tolerating them. As he had said in the "Essay on Infallibility," "The most certain interpreter of Scripture is Scripture itself."[42] The principle of "sola scriptura" obviates the need for others' interpretations; its corollary, the notion of a self-interpreting text, obviates the need for one's own interpretation as well. What Locke writes on St. Paul's epistles is not, in his view, an exposition or commentary. It is not Locke's interpretation, but rather a paraphrase of St. Paul himself, and thus in one sense not an interpretation at all.[43]

To conceive of the possibility of avoiding interpretation, understanding and interpreting must be regarded as distinct activities. In Locke's view, interpreting is not always necessary for understanding; in fact, it is a positive evil whenever understanding is possible without it. This distinction is typical of pre-Romantic hermeneutics, and it bears a closer look. One of Locke's alternative phrasings of "sola scriptura" suggests what is involved in segregating interpretation from understanding: "The light which Scripture affords itself," Locke writes, "is commonly the clearest discoverer of its own meaning."[44] What distinguishes this particular phrasing is Locke's metaphor of understanding as light—clichéd even then, no doubt, but nonetheless significant. For, unlike the "candle of the Lord" metaphor which Locke inherited from the Cambridge Neoplatonists, in this instance the light radiates from the text, not from the reader. "Sola scriptura" here verges on the modern principle of the textual immanence of meaning. The self-interpreting, self-illuminated text is intrinsically meaningful.

"Plain" is Locke's preferred epithet for describing self-interpreting texts. The plain needs no elucidation, no light shed on it from without, for it is of itself visible.[45] Locke applies this epithet to his own work in describing the "historical, plain method" of the *Essay;* and in *The Reasonableness of Christianity* he applies it to Scripture with monotonous insistency: "This will be plain to anyone who considers . . . ," "That this is the meaning of the place is plain from . . . ," "Can there be anything plainer than . . . ?"[46] Texts whose meaning is plain "certainly have little need of an interpreter, since they are so clearly transmitted that if any interpretation were added, it would in turn inevitably require another interpretation."[47] Interpreting what is already clear by phrasing it in language that is ipso facto less clear can only darken the sense.[48]

For the plain, which is itself a source of light, what is needed is precisely not interpretation but rather disinterpretation, as it were, a disencumbering of the light of the interpretive concealments that obscure it. Christ's purpose in the Sermon on the Mount, Locke writes, was "clearing the precepts of the law from the false glosses which were received in those days."[49] And in the *Essay Concerning Human Understanding* Locke sets himself the same task: of "clearing ground a little and removing some of the rubbish that lies in the way to knowledge."[50] This is not a casual metaphor. Locke's purpose is to disclose what is of itself visible, and since the self-evident is not susceptible of proof, "clearing" is the only service that understanding is capable of rendering it. The self-evident can only be dis-covered: that is, allowed to shine by its own light. "Truth certainly would do well enough if she were once left to shift for herself. . . . Errors indeed prevail by the assistance of foreign and borrowed succours. But [truth makes] her way into the understanding by her own light."[51] Error, interestingly, shines by reflected or borrowed light, the light of interpretation.

If truth is visible by its own light, understanding it requires nothing more than opening one's eyes. Understanding is distinct from interpretation because it does not need to do anything. Just as "in bare naked *perception,* the mind is, for the most part, only passive" (2. 9. 1), so also in the cognitive perception of the self-evident, understanding is not an action but a passion. Intuitive truth, Locke writes, "is irresistible, and, like bright sunshine, forces itself immediately to be perceived as soon as ever the mind turns its view that way" (4. 2. 1). Undoubtedly Locke recognizes active powers in the mind; but such passages as these, which characterize understanding as cognitive perception, imply that self-evidence—that is, the light of truth—is a force to which the mind submits. Understanding is less something the mind does than something it suffers. Thus, if interpretation is a name for the *activity* of understanding, then Locke's emphasizing the fundamentally *passional* nature of understanding is another way of saying that understanding is divisible from interpretation and that interpretation is, ideally, dispensable.

Second, to characterize understanding as cognitive perception implies that understanding the truth is a passion no less solitary and monological than sensory perception. Understanding needs nothing from others' understandings. "Knowing is seeing, and, if it be so, it is madness to persuade ourselves that we do so by another man's eyes."[52] The same epistemological solipsism here expressed in Locke's posthumous *Conduct of the Understanding* appears as early as his *Essays on the Law of Nature*: "By saying that something can be known by the light of nature, we mean nothing else but that there is some sort of truth to the knowledge of which a man can attain by himself and without the help of another."[53] The "light of nature," like the other variants of the truth-as-light metaphor, signifies the independence of truth from dialogue and mutual understanding. Truth-as-light signifies not merely the self-evidence of truth but the self-sufficiency of the *ego cogito* in perceiving it.

Locke's very turn to epistemology, not just his particular theses about knowledge, is an expression of that confidence in cognitive autonomy and self-sufficiency. "I thought that the first step towards satisfying several inquiries the mind of man was very apt to run into was to take a survey of our own understandings, examine our own powers, and see to what things they were adapted. Till that was done, I suspected we began at the wrong end. . . . Men, extending their inquiries beyond their capacities . . . raise questions and multiply disputes, which never com[e] to any clear resolution" (Intro., 7). "['T]is the affectation of knowing beyond what we perceive that makes so much useless dispute and noise in the world" (2. 1. 19). Once the survey is complete, the boundaries of understanding charted, and the limits of its capacity determined, it will be apparent that some questions lie beyond the possibility of resolution. Controversies about matters that could be argued forever will be perceived as pointless and therefore cease. To survey the limits of understanding, then, does not so much satisfy inquiries and settle disputes as obviate them. About things that lie beyond understanding, as well as things that are self-evident, it is pointless to talk.

Interminable disputes are ipso facto meaningless, and therefore what Locke seeks above all might be called "termini": the means of concluding arguments, finishing debates, ending controversies. Echoing Ecclesiastes, Locke complains: "In the interpretation of laws, whether divine or humane, there is no end; comments beget comments, and explications make new matter for explications" (3. 9. 9).

If interpretation is the prototype of the interminable, the terminus that ends debate must be conceived either as something that is not itself an interpretation or that can have no interpretation. A terminus, simply, is either first or last.

Sometimes it takes the form of a court of ultimate appeal. If the enthusiasts, for instance, assume that "there be nothing but the strength of our persuasions whereby to judge of our persuasions," Locke searches for a way out of that circle, "something extrinsic to the persuasions themselves" whereby to assess them. "*Reason,*" he concludes, "must be our last judge and guide in every thing" (4. 19. 14). To say that reason is "last" means that reason is not itself a persuasion; it thus terminates the endless circle of persuasions about persuasions and interpretations of interpretations. It is the floor which shows that the abyss is not infinite. "Most men cannot . . . be at quiet in their minds without some foundation or principle to rest their thoughts on," Locke writes (1. 3. 24, italics omitted), and he is manifestly such a man himself, for his work is informed with the faith that "[T]here are fundamental truths that lie at the bottom."[54]

These foundations can be conceived as ultimate in the sense of last, but they are also basic, primordial, or, as Locke prefers to say, "original." It is primarily in the first, or beginning, that Locke seeks an end. We have already touched on Locke's notion that all readers should endeavor to make themselves a "first commentator"[55]—that is, situate themselves at the beginning, prior to interpretation. Similarly, Locke speaks of "the first beginners of languages" (3. 1. 5) and argues that "anyone who is willing to look back and trace a tradition to its very source must necessarily come to a stand somewhere and in the end recognize someone as the original author of this tradition."[56] The tabula rasa is especially important in this regard, for what this metaphor implies is that "*perception* [is] the first step and degree towards knowledge" (2. 9. 15). The tabula rasa makes it possible for there to be a cognitive first. Behind the mistaken belief in innate ideas, Locke contends, lies "this fallacy, that men are supposed not to be *taught* nor to *learn* anything *de novo*" (1. 1. 23). One overarching intention of the *Essay Concerning Human Understanding* is to refute that supposition: in cognition, Locke argues, as in everything else, there is always a first.

Locke urges epistemology as "the first step." This is not merely a methodological prescription but a substantive one. To take the understanding of understanding itself as the beginning presupposes that understanding is—or at least can be—evident to itself. Otherwise, Locke would find himself in the position of the "poor *Indian* philosopher (who imagined that the Earth wanted something to bear it up)" and so proposed "an elephant to support it, and a tortoise to support his elephant" (2. 13. 19). If the understanding of understanding is to be a beginning, then, and not merely a step backward into endless regress, it must be the case that self-understanding is terminal: self-evident. Truth can be safely situated in the solitary ego only if self-certainty is the absolute foundation upon which all other certainties are erected, the indisputable that terminates all disputes.

Locke's thesis of self-certainty, and his monological epistemology generally, rests on two arguments: that there is no idea in my mind of which I am not conscious and that my ideas are exactly what I think they are. In the early *Essays on the Law of Nature,* Locke had concurred with the scholastic axiom that "nothing indeed is achieved by reason . . . unless there is first something posited and taken for granted."[57] If so, reason is helpless without tradition and the whole host of ideas that precede and enable rational thought. In the *Essay Concerning Human Understanding,* by contrast, Locke derives knowledge from the senses alone, not from precedent knowledge; thus he must refute "that *mistaken axiom that all reasoning [is] ex praecognitis et praeconcessis*" (4. 2. 8). Since I am not aware of any preconceptions when I reason, conclusive refutation of this axiom requires postulating that "no proposition can be said to be in the mind which it never yet knew, which it was never yet conscious of" (1. 2. 5). Understanding needs materials, of course, but in that respect alone it is not self-sufficient. The condition of our having ideas is experience, not prior ideas—that is, ultimately, others' ideas.

Locke's desire to assert the individual's cognitive self-sufficiency explains why he spent so much energy on the question of innate ideas. From the first publication of the *Essay,* it seemed to many readers that Locke had wasted his time disproving what no one in fact believed.[58] Admittedly, a mistaken notion of what the "historical" method required in investigating human understanding led him to confuse temporal with logical priority. Though on occasion he admittedly pursued such red herrings as the issue of prenatal knowledge, nevertheless, the basic question that Locke was addressing was crucial. The doctrine of innate ideas implies that all understanding depends on prior understanding, and that understanding is therefore interpretive. This doctrine Locke must deny. Without this denial, every idea comes to be seen as an interpretation of a previous idea, whether I am aware of the precedent idea or not—and with that admission, interpretation can no longer be eliminated, separated from understanding, or even limited and localized. Quite the contrary, it becomes intrinsic to all understanding whatever. The first premise of self-certainty, then—that there is no idea in my mind of which I am not conscious—rules out the possibility that my ideas may be interpretations of other, precedent ideas of which I am unaware, and thus Locke preserves the faculty of understanding as an autonomous origin.

The second premise of self-certainty—that my ideas are exactly what I think they are—depends on a notion evidently borrowed from Descartes. "[W]e have an intuitive knowledge of our own existence and an internal infallible perception that we are" (4. 9. 3). Locke defines "intuition" as that knowledge which the mind has "without the intervention of any other *idea*" (4. 2. 1). Intuition, then, is immediate knowledge, not inference; it is not mediated by any other idea intervening between it and its object. Positively defined, it is knowledge of the thing itself and hence infallible. Negatively defined, intuition is nonsemiotic cognition, knowledge that is not mediated by signs, so not an interpretation.

Locke extends the province of intuition well beyond one's own existence, for not only *that* I think but *what* I think is a matter of intuitive knowledge. For him, unlike Descartes, what we know intuitively are above all, our own ideas, since they and they alone, in Locke's view, are known without the mediation of any intervening ideas. Our knowledge of our ideas is not interpretive, and so we have privileged access to them. The knowledge that "the mind has of its own *ideas* . . . is the utmost light and greatest certainty we, with our faculties and in our way of knowledge, are capable of" (4. 2. 1). Intuition of our own ideas is indubitable, because an idea is "whatsoever is the object of the understanding when a man thinks, . . . whatever it is which the mind can be employed about in thinking."[59] There can therefore be no distinction between what a person's ideas are and what he thinks they are, and thus no error is here possible.

If there could be a distinction, I would be just as liable to mistakes about my ideas as about anything else, and such fallibility would show that my knowledge of my own thoughts is not intuitive but interpretive. If, for instance, Locke had followed through with the notion that "the actions of men [are] the best interpreters of their thoughts" (1. 3. 3), he would have come to the surprising conclusion that I have no privileged access to the contents of my mind: my ideas as manifested in my actions are no more open to me than to others, who have in principle just as much access to my actions as I do.

All this Locke must deny in order to retain the locus of certain knowledge within the individual. "A man cannot conceive himself capable of a greater certainty than to know that any *idea* in his mind is such as he perceives it to be" (4. 2. 1). That is to say, human understanding can be in doubt and error about anything else, but with respect to its own ideas, it is infallible—or at least, we cannot help acting as if we were infallible about them. Our intuitive knowledge of our own ideas consists not of interpretations but of the very things themselves, and on the infallibility of self-knowledge "depends all the certainty and evidence of all our knowledge" (4. 2. 1). All certainty depends on the conclusion that I, and I alone, am infallibly certain of my ideas, and of them alone. If they too must be interpreted, all certainty disappears; knowledge dissolves into judgment, and epistemology into hermeneutics.

Insofar as the immediate object of understanding is its ideas, the thesis of self-certainty implies that understanding is inherently infallible.[60] "The faculty of reasoning," Locke writes, "seldom or never deceives those who trust to it."[61] If reason never deceives, it is not the case that to err is human. Error is essentially accidental and in principle avoidable. This is not to say that Locke is under any sanguine delusion about the impediments to understanding. Much of the *Essay* is preoccupied with the causes of misunderstanding, and the *Conduct of the Understanding* is virtually organized as a list of them: haste, superficiality, anticipation, partiality, habit, presumption, and, most important, prejudice and language. Error has causes, but truth merely has conditions, and the main condition of truth for Locke, as we have seen, is clearing away the rubbish, removing the causes of error—which, if they can in fact be removed, must be accidental and extrinsic. The corollary of the notion that truth shines by its own light is that the understanding is intrinsically receptive to it.

Locke recommends eliminating prejudice, for example, in this way: "Everyone is forward to complain of the prejudices that mislead other men or parties, as if he were free and had none of his own. This being objected on all sides, it is agreed that it is a fault and a hindrance to knowledge. What now is the cure? No other but this, that every man should let alone others' prejudices and examine his own."[62] Because he regards understanding as inherently infallible, Locke fails to notice that his advice is circular. Just as the contract theory of the origin of government assumes the very legal system it is designed to explain, so the recommendation that everyone examine himself impartially presupposes the very freedom from prejudice it is designed to effect.[63] Locke does not perceive that only others can perceive our prejudices, because he presupposes that misunderstanding is abnormal and exceptional: fallibility—about ourselves and indeed about everything else—is not inherent but adventitious to human understanding.

If error, like blindness, is accidental, if knowing comes as naturally to the understanding as seeing to the eye, and if truth shines by its own light and need only be disencumbered to be understood, then whatever intervenes and mediates between the subject and its object not only fails to make knowledge possible but impedes it. Language is by far the most important among such mediations, and with it we will conclude. In examining the extent and certainty of knowledge, Locke writes:

> I found it had so near a connexion with words that, unless their force and manner of signification were first well observed, there could be very little said clearly and pertinently concerning knowledge, which, being conversant about truth, had constantly to do with propositions. And though it terminated in things, yet it was for the most part so much by the intervention of words that they seemed scarce separable from our general knowledge. At least [words] interpose themselves so much between our understandings and the truth which it would contemplate and apprehend that, like the *medium* through which visible objects pass, the obscurity and disorder do not seldom cast a mist before our eyes and impose upon our understandings. (3. 9. 21)

Here Locke articulates the two contrary conceptions of language between which he feels obliged to choose. If truth appears only in propositions, it appears only in language; but if truth is obscured by the medium of words, it appears only apart from language. Locke chooses the latter.[64] Since he holds that immediate—that is, unmediated—intuition is possible, it follows that the fog of words that "interpose themselves" between the mind and its object interferes with understanding. Language is the prototype of the intervention between subject and object that precludes a definitive, terminal intuition, necessitates ongoing interpretation, and thus epitomizes what makes knowledge uncertain. Words, therefore, are to be defined and clarified where necessary but avoided entirely if possible.

Locke does sometimes write as if wordless knowledge were indeed possible. For example, he urges his readers to distinguish things "from the marks men use for them"; if, instead, they continue to confound things "with words, there must be endless dispute, wrangling, and jargon" (2. 13. 27). On one reading this is simply sound advice: it is always helpful to clarify one's language and so obviate needless disagreements.[65] But whereas language is sometimes the cause of disputes, it is always their condition. Thus an even more efficient way of precluding disputation than defining words is to dispense with language altogether.[66] "Learning [that is, being learned or well-read]," Locke states, "is distinct from knowledge, for knowledge consists only in perceiving the habitudes and relations of ideas one to another, which is done without words."[67] Knowledge and truth are essentially nonverbal in Locke's view; hence language is strictly secondary to cognition.

Given this secondariness, Locke can insist that we "distinguish between the method of acquiring knowledge and communicating it" (4. 7. 11). Grounding his programmatic reaction against interpretation, no premise is more crucial (or more questionable) than this: that there is a profound difference between knowing and saying what one knows.[68] For it is this distinction that grounds epistemological individualism and makes understanding what other human beings have thought and said at best secondary and at worst a superfluous impediment to genuine knowledge. If, *pace* Locke, thought were (as Plato said) the dialogue of the soul with itself, there would be no absolute difference between talking to oneself and talking to others, between thinking our thoughts ourselves and "communicating our thoughts with others," or between my understanding my own talk and others understanding it. Had Locke pursued the alternative conception of language, had he fully admitted that language is "scarcely separable" from thought and truth, this admission would have metamorphosed his monological epistemology into a dialogical hermeneutics, for understanding oneself would then be "scarcely separable" from understanding others.

If language is not accidental to thought and if there is therefore no essential distinction "between the method of acquiring knowledge and communicating it" (4. 7. 11), then dialogue and coming to an understanding with others become a condition of knowledge, not an occasion of communication subsequent to it. Once there is no longer an absolute difference between our ideas and our words for them, it is no longer true that "the scene of *ideas* that makes one man's thoughts cannot be laid open to the immediate view of another" (4. 21. 4). For if to think is to speak to oneself, then to speak to another is to lay open the very things themselves, to display one's thoughts immediately and exactly as they are to another. If language is not a mere instrument of thought,[69] our ideas and thoughts—our innermost selves—are in principle accessible to others.

With that concession, however, the monological individualism which undergirds the *Essay Concerning Human Understanding* wobbles ominously. If knowledge, including self-knowledge, is not ultimately private and ineffable, then the inward theater of ideas, allegedly "invisible and hidden from others" (3. 2. 1), cannot be conceived of as a wordless dumb show; it is rather a verbal drama, and for that reason essentially open to others. But this breakdown of the division between inner and outer, self and other, is perfectly alien to Locke. He never conceives of the possibility that the inmost privacy which is the individuality of the individual is only accidentally inaccessible; that the autonomous, insular "person" is chimerical; that human understanding, even of the material world, is fundamentally indivisible from understanding other human beings; and that the perennial effort to get beyond interpretation is therefore inevitably doomed to failure.

2

Toland on Reason

Wat is at stake in *Christianity Not Mysterious*? What in this once incendiary tract still remains a live issue, a matter for thought? Whether Toland is properly called a Deist, a Socinian, a pantheist, or a rationalist is still of interest to historians of ideas. So too for thinking Christians, the main issue of this little book—whether reason is the rule or merely the instrument of faith—is scarcely dead. Yet Toland has something to say even to readers who consider themselves neither historians nor believers. Though apparently contributing to the Trinitarian–Unitarian controversy, Toland barely mentions that dispute.[1] His topic is something that is prior to the derivation of any particular doctrine from Scripture—namely, the scope and nature of understanding as such. Locke and others had affirmed that Scripture was plain in all essential points. What could this mean but that essentially it was "not mysterious"? Along with many others, Locke had denied that reason and revelation were inherently incompatible. Toland merely took this denial in its positive form: even divine revelation is understandable, and if so, nothing is intrinsically mysterious. Everything is at least potentially accessible to human understanding. For us today, Toland's interest lies in his insight into what it means to understand not just Scripture but any book whatever—even *Christianity Not Mysterious*.

Its thesis, broadly and simply stated, is that to understand something means to make sense of it. Toland defines the nature of understanding as reason, and what is understandable he call "reasonable." Lest this thesis seem innocuously truistic, we should recall that upon first publication in 1696, *Christianity Not Mysterious* was condemned and burned by the hangman. "What reason did not dictate, reason cannot explain," Samuel Johnson wrote.[2] The attempt to make a text reasonable is a prescription for misinterpretation if the text to be understood is not amenable to reason; and such, Toland's opponents claimed, is the case with Scripture. To the orthodox, Scripture was above reason; to the heterodox, below it; and for both, interpretive rationalization therefore amounted to misinterpretive perversion. Despite his critics on the right and left, however, Toland sketched out a conception of understanding that is not only plausible but, I hope to show, in certain respects right; thus his interest lies not merely in his being symptomatic of eighteenth-century polemics but in what he can contribute to our own understanding of understanding.[3]

Toland's conception of interpretation is superior at points even to that of Spinoza's better-known and more influential *Tractatus Theologico-Politicus* (1670). Toland certainly read and assimilated its famous eighth chapter "On the Interpretation of Scripture." He took from it what he could and incorporated it into his own book. So it comes as no surprise that his contemporaries considered him a Spinozan. Despite all the manifest borrowing, however, Toland deviates from the *Tractatus* to an extent that justifies our considering Spinoza as one of the targets of *Christianity Not Mysterious*.[4] This is not to contest the scholarly consensus[5] that Toland conceives of himself as replying mainly to Protestant divines and perhaps specifically to Stillingfleet's sermon "Christianity Mysterious, and the Wisdom of God in Making it So" (1694). Stillingfleet and others of like mind saw no problem with the nature of understanding generally. But for Toland, understanding as such is a question, and it is in his subterranean debate with Spinoza that he most suggestively explores it. Toland essentially adopts and vindicates the position which Spinoza assigns to Maimonides and rejects. Read as a challenge to Spinoza from the right, Toland's hermeneutics appears radically conservative. In its radicality, it is opposed to conservatives[6] such as Stillingfleet; but in its conservatism, it provides a genuine, if tacit, critique of the Cartesian hermeneutics—now called the hermeneutics of suspicion—

which Spinoza first articulated. Before pursuing Toland's critique of Spinoza, however, we need to consider those aspects of the skeptical theory that Toland shares with him.

First, both advocate objectivity in interpretation and ground the possibility of objective interpretation on parallel distinctions. Toland distinguishes sharply between "means of information" and "grounds of persuasion," or assent: "The means of information I call those ways whereby anything comes barely to our knowledge, without necessarily commanding our assent. By the ground of persuasion, I understand that rule by which we judge of all truth" (14).[7] The skeptical thrust of this distinction becomes evident when we see that for Toland no source of information (even if divine) of itself verifies the information it conveys or has inherent authority to command our assent. Unless revelation conforms to reason, it cannot be accepted as true or even revealed. Spinoza posits a similar distinction: "Revelation and philosophy stand on totally different footings"; whereas philosophy pursues knowledge, "revelation has obedience for its sole object" (9).[8] The conservative interpretation of Spinoza's distinction is that it protects religion from the cavils of philosophy; it precludes privileging the learned and democratizes salvation. Yet it is also possible to see that in distinguishing between revelation and philosophy, Spinoza deprives revelation of its truth claim, assigning truth to philosophy only, thereby giving it absolute priority over revelation. Knowledge precedes obedience; information precedes assent. These distinctions, if they can be maintained, make objective interpretation possible.

In elucidating what he calls "the best method" of interpretation, Toland distinguishes it from the backwards method of orthodox divines: "The order of nature is in your systems of divinity quite inverted. They prove the authority and perfection before they teach the contents of Scripture; whereas the first is in great measure known by the last. How can any be sure that the Scripture contains all things necessary to salvation till he first reads it over? Nay, how can he conclude it to be Scripture, or the Word of God, till he exactly studies it? This confusion I have carefully avoided" (xxvii). Here Toland is elaborating and extending one version of "sola scriptura," the founding principle of Protestant hermeneutics that we touched on in the previous chapter. Scripture is of itself intelligible, and only of itself. Toland accepts only internal evidence for the authority of Scripture, that deriving from the book itself, not that of external tradition. For Toland, therefore, it is not possible to prove the authority of Scripture *before* understanding its contents. Hermeneutics comes first. Since the only acceptable evidence that Scripture is the Word of God is to be found in the book itself, one must begin with understanding; and that means without any presuppositions about its divine origin. Such conclusions can only come afterward. In opposition to the confused, inverted method of the divines, Toland's rational method of interpretation prescribes a specific sequence and order: study before concluding; read before evaluating.

So conceived, rational interpretation is objective—that is, understanding is different from judgment, and understanding should and can precede judgment. The most general and important judgment that must be deferred pending understanding is that concerning Scripture's truth claim. The perceived need for objective interpretation follows from the recognition that not everything written is true, and thus no method of understanding can begin by assuming the truth of the text to be interpreted. In formulating the structure of objective interpretation, Toland is clearly drawing on Spinoza. The aim of the *Tractatus* is (inter alia) to refute those who posit "beforehand, as a foundation for the study and true interpretation of Scripture, the principle that it is in every passage true and divine. Such a doctrine," Spinoza continues, "should be reached only after strict scrutiny and thorough comprehension of the Sacred Books" (8). This principle of "comprehension" before "doctrine" reflects not just the distinction between philosophy and revelation, but the hierarchy of philosophy over revelation that the distinction enables and conceals.

Objective interpretation is, strictly speaking, agnostic, since it claims not to know whether Scripture is true or not. But there is more to this than skepticism, for, as Todorov has observed, "the unformulated presupposition of [Spinoza's] approach is that the Scriptures cannot speak the truth."[9] If Scripture cannot be proved true ex post facto, as even many believers secretly feared, then, if it is not assumed true beforehand, it will never be judged true at all. This means that objectivity—the mandate that judgement be postponed—is merely a cover for (deistic or atheistic) prejudice, since the judgment against the verity of Scripture is written into the method itself. Bracketing the truth of the text as an a priori hermeneutic principle is tantamount to rejecting it absolutely. If Scripture is true, it will be understood to be true only if it is judged to be so beforehand, dogmatically. The "dogmatic" hermeneutics that Spinoza opposes, then—and Toland too, insofar as he follows him—holds that interpretation and evaluation are indivisible: judgment about the truth of a text is a condition of understanding it, not just a consequence of it.

Second, for the objectivist the prime source of interpretive error is accommodation—that is, in Toland's words, when "the Holy Scripture is put to the torture to countenance . . . scholastic jargon" (xii). In explicating 1 Corinthians 2:7, "But we speak the wisdom of God in a mystery," Stillingfleet exemplifies this fault:

> If we would take a survey of the nature of wisdom according to the sense of the ancient philosophers, we shall find Aristotle in the sixth [book] of his *Ethics* defining it [as] . . . the understanding and knowledge of things in their nature the most excellent and valuable. Where though it ought to be supposed that Aristotle carried his notion no higher nor farther than the things of nature and that St. Paul pointed chiefly at things revealed and supernatural; yet I cannot see but that the terms made use of by that great philosopher in the definition . . . do with full propriety and fitness fall in with the account here given of this divine wisdom by our apostle in the text.[10]

Spinoza considered such humanistic accommodations of philosophy and revelation as category mistakes motivated by hypocrisy. Against those who never tire of "professing their wonder at the profound mysteries of Holy Writ," Spinoza objects, "I cannot discover that they teach anything [in the name of mystery] but speculations of Platonists and Aristotelians, to which (in order to save their credit for Christianity) they have made Holy Writ conform" (7). Toland writes in much the same vein: "They make the *Scriptures* speak either according to some spurious *philosophy,* or they conform them right or wrong to the bulky systems and formularies of their several communions" (5). "The Jewish rabbis, divided at that time into Stoic, Platonic, and Pythagorean sects, etc., did, by a mad liberty of allegory, accommodate the Scriptures to the wild speculations of their several masters" (xxi). Toland does not consider such accommodation peculiar to Jewish commentators, of course. "You'll find the grossest mistakes and whimsies of the Fathers to have been occasioned by the several systems of philosophy they read before their conversion and which they afterwards foolishly endeavoured to reconcile with Christianity" (126).

Such "reconciliation" becomes the prototypical error under the regime of Protestant hermeneutics, because the force of "sola" in the famous formula is to insist that unmediated (that is, nontraditional) understanding is always possible. "They come nearest the thing," Toland agrees, "who affirm that we are to keep to what the *Scriptures* determine about these matters; and there is nothing more true, if rightly understood" (5). Scripture is autonomous, and to interpret it as if it were heteronomous, dependent on another text (for example, Aristotle) for its elucidation, is to guarantee that it will be misunderstood.

Toland does not explain why the Church Fathers were so foolishly and perversely accommodationist, but the reason is clear in Spinoza. It is because they considered Scripture true. Their attempt to reconcile Scripture with philosophy follows from their accepting Scripture's truth as a foundation for understanding it. This explains the connection between Toland's rejection of accommodation and his assertion that understanding a text must precede judging its truth. Reading for truth at the outset, as Toland suggests, means allegorizing—that is, interpreting the mysterious in terms of the familiar, the unknown in terms of the known. Interpreting the truth always involves two texts: the text to be understood and a second, norm text already known to be true. Understanding the truth of the text to be understood means demonstrating its commensurability with the norm text. The reader who takes an allegorical approach does not try to find something while looking for nothing. He knows that he cannot seek the truth of the text under scrutiny unless he already knows what he is looking for—the truth—and the norm text provides him with the necessary foreknowledge. To know in advance what one is looking for, however, is to be prejudiced; and for skeptical and objectivist hermeneutics, prejudiced understanding must be assumed to be misunderstanding.

Further, since the truth of the norm text goes unquestioned so long as it is producing interpretive expectations, allegorizing involves dogmatizing. Understanding a text as true always consists in subordinating it to some unquestioned dogma, whether explicit or unannounced. Often the norm text was Scripture itself, and other works were either harmonized with it or rejected. But when the Bible itself was at issue, as for Spinoza and Toland, only two options were left open. The first was Stillingfleet's: like any other book assumed to be true, Scripture must be read through other unquestioned texts.

The second was Spinoza's: if the truth even of Scripture can be questioned, no text can be treated as indubitable. Once no text is permitted to function as an indubitable norm text, then not just reading a book through some particular norm text but reading through any such text is an invitation to error. Hence, reading for truth, which always involves such reading-through, itself becomes the cardinal sin for skeptical hermeneutics. Nothing is more conducive to error than reading for truth. Thus Spinoza insists: "We are at work not on the truth of passages, but solely on their meaning" (101). This distinction, carried to its logical conclusion, marks the beginning of critical and the end of charitable interpretation as hermeneutical principles.

Reading exclusively for meaning is the only way to read the text "sola," for meaning per se belongs to the autonomous individual text, whereas truth is shared and common among texts. The text whose meaning is unique might conceivably mean anything at all; and it can be read objectively—that is, permitted to mean anything whatever—only if it is not restricted to meaning the truth. The sole way to avoid dogmatizing—employing suspect norm texts as if they were infallible—is to bracket truth. Skeptical interpretation produces the "text itself" by suspending its truth claim. The autonomous text is necessarily fictive.

We can see more clearly what is at issue here by contrasting the Spinozan ideal of interpretation with its opposite. According to the skeptical model (suited for reading as if the text were false), understanding consists in isolating the text to be understood, respecting its autonomy, and protecting it from the encroachments of all reputed norm texts. On this model, accommodation is the archetypal error. By contrast, according to the dogmatic model (suited to reading for truth), understanding consists in showing that all true texts are one, since, as Toland says, "truth is always and everywhere the same" (xx). Here accommodation—assimilating one true text to another—is understanding itself. The difference between the skeptical and the dogmatic models is not merely that they have different objects, meaning and truth; it is also that whereas the skeptical, or critical, model supposes that it is possible to read for meaning without reading for truth, the dogmatic, or charitable, model supposes that this distinction is impossible, since reading for truth is the condition of understanding any meaning at all.

An additional area where Toland and Spinoza share common

ground concerns the question of whether understanding Scripture is different in kind from understanding anything else. This involves two subsidiary questions: whether it is different from interpreting nature and whether it is different from interpreting other books. With respect to the first, both men occupy a position that might be called "hermeneutic monism": "The method of interpreting Scripture," Spinoza asserts, "does not widely differ from the method of interpreting nature—in fact, it is almost the same" (99). Similarly, Toland holds "that reason is the only foundation of all certitude, and that nothing revealed, whether as to its manner or existence, is [any] more exempted from its disquisitions than the ordinary phenomena of nature" (6). Before asking what *interpretatio naturae* could be that would make it essentially the same as *interpretatio biblicae,* we need to consider the argument common to both statements, that everything understandable is of the same kind. Underwriting this hermeneutic monism is a postulate of ontological monism that Toland and Spinoza share with many both before and after them, from Augustine to the physico-theologists Ray, Durham, and Paley. For us today the postulate of ontological monism is particularly striking, because in our time the opposite, the dichotomy between nature and culture, is so common as to be a cliché. For us, words and deeds are interpretable, but not things. Only cultural phenomena have meaning and so can be understood; nature is to be explained, and with the task of explanation hermeneutics has nothing to do. By contrast with this dualism, ontological monism does not call for two different kinds of cognition, applicable to two different ontological spheres, but only one. Toland calls it "reason," and his thesis is that reason's scope is unlimited. As he says in the above passage, nothing is exempt from its disquisitions. Nothing rational, whether natural or supernatural, lies beyond the bounds of rational understanding. This is the ontological version of hermeneutic monism.

The textual version that depends on it is a good deal more familiar. Perhaps the first advocate of "the Bible as literature," Toland urges us to "read the sacred writings with that equity and attention that is due to mere human works; nor is there any different rule to be followed in the interpretation of Scripture from what is common to all other books" (49).[11] Here hermeneutic monism corresponds to the principle of textual monism. Unlike the ontological version, textual monism is something new—in part, no doubt, because the idea that all texts are of one kind is heretical. We can understand how the orthodox would view Toland's nondifferentiation of sacred and human writings as a denial of revelation. Yet he nowhere makes this denial explicit; and though this silence hardly proves him orthodox on the issue of inspiration, it need not be understood merely as politic discretion.

For his purposes, Toland need not deny that Scripture is revealed, only that the distinction between divine and human authorship matters in interpretation. The postulate of textual monism (which denies the significance of different kinds of authors) registers a shift in emphasis from author to reader. Regardless of whether books are divisible into those divinely and those humanly authored, all readers are human, and it is by readers' rules and readers' reason that books must be understood. "Since by revelation men are not endued with any new faculties, it follows that God should lose his end in speaking to them if what he said did not agree with their common notions" (133). Any revelation that is not open to human understanding ipso facto reveals nothing and so is not revelation at all. This is to say that the scope of reason is not limited by its supposed impotence to understand divine revelation. A mystery is simply something not yet understood. Whatever lies not just in fact but in principle outside the bounds of rational interpretation is not suprarational mystery but simple nonsense. There is nothing rational that cannot be understood by reason. Revelation is either intelligible, hence rational, or nonsensical, hence not of divine origin.

This emphasis on the primacy and reliability of human reason Toland shares with Spinoza. "As the highest power of Scriptural interpretation belongs to every man," Spinoza writes, "the rule for such interpretation should be nothing but the natural light of reason which is common to all" (119). And again, "I think I have now set forth the true method of scriptural interpretation, and have sufficiently explained my own opinion thereon. Besides, I do not doubt that everyone will see that such a method only requires the aid of natural reason" (113). Toland undoubtedly would have said the same of his own method. Both have what seems to us a touchingly naive faith in methodical reason. Spinoza speaks of being able to "advance without danger of error" (99), and Toland says, "It is impossible for us to err as long as we take evidence for our guide" (19). Natural reason is an innate source of interpretive infallibility, a pope within.

But for Toland rationality is not a characteristic of method alone.

It belongs symmetrically to both sides of the process: the interpreting subject employs reason to discover the reasonableness of the interpreted object. Here, in this second respect, Toland breaks with Spinoza. To oversimplify, a main difference between their two approaches is that although both begin with a distinction between reason and revelation, Toland reduces Scripture to reason, Spinoza to revelation. Toland sets out to prove, as his subtitle indicates, "that there is nothing in the gospel contrary to reason nor above it"; thus there is a consistency between means and end, text and exegesis. Scripture is essentially the same kind of book as any other—even *Christianity Not Mysterious*. But for Spinoza, by contrast, the method of understanding is radically asymmetrical to its object, since it involves a rational method of interpretation employed on an essentially nonrational object. "Scripture," he asserts, "very often treats of matters which cannot be deduced from principles known to reason, for it is chiefly made up of narratives and revelation. The narratives generally contain miracles—that is, . . . relations of extraordinary natural occurrences adapted to the opinions and judgement of the historians who recorded them. The revelations also were adapted to the opinions of the prophets, . . . and in themselves surpassed human comprehension. Therefore the knowledge of all these—that is, of nearly the whole contents of Scripture—must be sought from Scripture alone, even as the knowledge of nature is sought from nature" (100).

When Spinoza equates the method of interpreting Scripture with that of interpreting nature, then, he does so not because Scripture and nature are equally intelligible. For him, ontological monism means that both are equally unintelligible—that is, neither the book of nature nor the book of books is interpretable by "principles known to reason."[12] Hence Spinoza's principle of intrinsic interpretation— "The contents of scripture must be sought from scripture alone"— implies not only that Scripture, like all books, has an inside and an outside, but also that, being nonrational, Scripture is to be understood with reason in abeyance, because reason is itself outside, hence prejudicial. One implication of this line of argument, as Leo Strauss has shown,[13] is that the principle of intrinsic interpretation derives not from the plainness doctrine but, just the opposite, from the intrinsic unintelligibility of the text to be interpreted. Spinoza's skeptical method is designed for a book that doesn't make sense. This means that it is emphatically not designed for the *Tractatus,* which excepts itself from the objects it deals with, as *Christianity Not Mysterious* does not.

At this point we need to examine more concretely what Spinoza means by textual interpretation and what it has to do with *interpretatio naturae.* Two passages explain the parallel: "As the interpretation of nature consists in the examination of the history of nature and therefrom deducing definitions of natural phenomena on certain fixed axioms, so scriptural interpretation proceeds by the examination of Scripture and inferring the intention of its authors as a legitimate conclusion from its fundamental principles" (99). "We must begin from the most universal proposition, inquiring first from the most clear scriptural statements what is the nature of prophecy or revelation and wherein it consists; then we must proceed . . . at last to the meaning of a particular revelation" (106). By interpretation, then, Spinoza means deduction: inferring particulars from universals, axioms, or principles. Thus any kind of interpreting presupposes such principles, and the only question is where they come from. Because nature cannot be understood a priori, one must start inductively, from the history of nature—that is, from particular events of nature itself. Similarly, since "Scripture very often treats of matters that cannot be deduced from principles known to reason" (100), the presuppositions necessary to interpret it cannot come from reason. Thus, Spinoza argues, they must derive from Scripture itself. Some passages—the "most clear"—are chosen to serve as "fundamental principles" that Scripture means to inculcate not just in their immediate context but everywhere throughout the Bible. These key passages, therefore, can serve as the standard of correct understanding for other passages that are less clear.[14]

Understanding still involves interpretation, but Spinoza thinks that his intrinsic method allows Scripture to be self-interpreting. Such interpretation still involves accommodation, but it is the accommodation of one part of Scripture to another, not to an extrinsic norm text. If Scripture were wholly beyond reason, of course, if it were wholly nonrational and unintelligible, then no particular passages would be understandable enough to serve as universals. But Spinoza always leaves a window of comprehensibility. "*Nearly* the whole contents of Scripture" is above human comprehension; "Scripture *very often* treats of matters" beyond reason. Without exceptional passages of plain sense, intrinsic interpretation would be impossible.

Just as Spinoza did not think all Scripture obscure, so he did not consider all books unintelligible, and this is of some importance. The textual version of hermeneutic monism that we found in *Christianity Not Mysterious* is absent from the *Tractatus*.[15] We have seen that Spinoza identifies the interpretive method appropriate to Scripture with that appropriate to nature; but because he bases this identification on their common a priori unintelligibility, he cannot extend his textual hermeneutics to books in general. For not all books are hermetic. Spinoza distinguishes between "hieroglyphic" books such as Scripture and "perceptible" books such as Euclid's geometry. Corresponding to the two types of texts, apparently, are two kinds of understanding. Concerning the first, Spinoza writes: "The universal rule . . . in interpreting Scripture is to accept nothing as an authoritative scriptural statement which we do not perceive very clearly when we examine it in the light of its history" (101). Very briefly summarized, historical interpretation involves acquainting oneself with the language in which Scripture was written, composing a topical concordance gathering all passages on each subject, and surveying the life and times of the authors, paying attention to the textual history of their works. Testifying to Spinoza's brilliance is that three centuries of philology have found little to add to his conception of historical interpretation.

Yet it must strike us as curious that the historical understanding which, until recently at least, has been considered universally necessary applies in Spinoza's view only to Scripture and other hermetic texts. What Spinoza calls "perceptible" books do not require historical interpretation at all: "Euclid can easily be comprehended by anyone in any language; we can follow his intention perfectly, and be certain of his true meaning without having a thorough knowledge of the language in which he wrote. . . . We need make no researches concerning the life, the pursuits, or the habits of the author . . . [nor into] the vicissitudes of his book nor its various readings nor how nor by whose advice it has been received. What we here say of Euclid might equally be said of any book which treats of things by their nature perceptible" (113). Whereas the subject matter of geometry is of itself intelligible, Spinoza says that "nearly the whole contents of Scripture" are not.[16] The narratives of miracles and the prophecies were accommodated to their original audience—not to us. We must therefore interpret such texts historically, because they don't make sense.

Spinoza does not envision two kinds of interpretation, then, one for hieroglyphic, the other for perceptible texts. In his view, Euclid doesn't require any interpretation at all. This has several important consequences: first, the real exemplar of a text intelligible in itself is Euclid. Only a "perceptible" text can be understood "sola scriptura": intuitively, directly, and without commentary. As for Descartes, so far Spinoza, Euclid is the real scripture. Second, there is in fact only one kind of interpretation for Spinoza, and that is historical. When historical interpretation is unnecessary, all interpretation is unnecessary. That is to say, insofar as there exist self-interpreting texts, interpretation is necessary only on specific occasions, not always or everywhere; hence interpretation and understanding are not at all the same.

This second point is of fundamental significance. It is not just that historical hermeneutics is a special hermeneutics, its provenance limited to a particular kind of book. It is that for Spinoza hermeneutics per se is limited, needed only occasionally. When Toland writes, by contrast, that there is no "different rule to be followed in the interpretation of Scripture from what is common to all other books" (49), we see how great is the gulf that divides him from Spinoza. For though Toland's intention may well be that Scripture be read like secular books, he necessarily also implies that secular books should be read like Scripture. What is necessary for the Bible is necessary for all other books as well, and that is rational interpretation. Interpretation is universally, not merely occasionally, necessary to understanding. Whereas Spinoza implies that some kinds of texts can be understood without being interpreted, Toland denies that such texts exist. If *Christianity Not Mysterious* is an "epochal little book," as Reedy contends,[17] it is because it inaugurates the epoch of universal hermeneutics. Differing from Locke as well as Spinoza, Toland perceives, a hundred years before Schleiermacher, that interpreting *is* understanding, not just an aid to it. Understanding always involves interpretation, comparison, accommodation, application.

We have examined in some detail what Spinoza means by interpretation. It is time to turn to Toland. Reason, we know, is what defines both understanding and all its objects for Toland. Yet he warns us that "the word *reason* is become as equivocal and ambiguous as any other" (8), and we should not assume that, despite his careful definitions, he means something simple and straightforward. Reason is a slippery notion at best, and we need to look closely at what Toland says about it.

He begins, like Locke,[18] by distinguishing reason from intuition. Intuition, or self-evidence, occurs "when the mind, without the assistance of any other idea, immediately perceives the agreement or disagreement of two or more ideas, as that two and two is four" (11). Reason, by contrast, is not immediate but rather the perception of the relation between two ideas by means of intermediate ideas. What first needs to be emphasized is that intermediacy is the *specifica differentia* of reason, and it is this intermediacy which makes reasoning interpretive. In a syllogism, the minor premise acts as the intermediate idea between the major premise and the conclusion. Locke equated logic with semiotic, for all intermediate ideas act as signs. If deductive logic is its prototype, the act of reasoning consists in interpreting signs. But inductive reasoning, too, is inferential, and in that respect it is not unlike reasoning by analogy or metaphor, which is also "understanding as." Excepting intuition, all knowing, Toland concludes, involves an interpretive knowing-through.

Thus he defines reason as "that faculty of the soul which discovers the certainty of anything dubious or obscure, by comparing it with something evidently known" (12). Given this conception of reason, I will argue, the Spinozan ideal of objective interpretation proves to be unworkable. Reasoning, Toland says, consists in comparing something with an intermediate idea. Insofar as reasoning is distinguished from intuition, moreover, it is not like comparing twice two with four but more like comparing apples and oranges. It compares something with something else, something other. Thus rational interpretation of a text, say, always involves comparing it with another, different text. Rational understanding, then, occurs when the one text is found to be commensurate with the other. The interpreter does not first understand one text, then accommodate it to the other. The act of accommodation is the act of understanding.[19] The Spinozan variant of intrinsic interpretation—that is, interpreting one part of a text by appeal to another—does not eliminate the need for a second text but merely locates otherness within the text to be understood. Understanding cannot get along without some other text. That is to say, understanding never begins from nothing—with the text *sola*—but is always interpretation through something prior; it always presupposes this other, because understanding *is* accommodation to this other. To exclude the other and so preclude accommodation is to prevent understanding.

Nor can understanding avoid dogmatizing the other text. "No particular hypothesis whatsoever has a right to set up for a standard of reason to all mankind," Toland asserts; "and so far am I from aiming at any such thing that it is the very practice I oppose in this book" (126). The similarity to Newton's famous "Hypotheses non fingo" is clear enough; but now we can discern the difference as well.[20] Toland does not disavow hypothesis per se in the name of immediate access (reason is not intuitive and so not immediate); what Toland disavows is any "particular hypothesis." Insofar as reason consists in comparison, it needs something else with which to compare the text to be understood, and that other text will (consciously or not) function as a criterion of clarity, reason, and truth. It is not just accommodation to a prior text, then, but accommodation to dogma that explains the nature of understanding: it involves assimilation to some "standard of reason" that cannot be called into question in the process of understanding, because it is the condition of that understanding itself.[21]

We can see why this happens by considering how the meaning of reason has changed in Toland's phrase "standard of reason." In the definition cited previously, reasoning is comparing; here, as a standard, reason is that to which something is compared. The action of comparing ideas is presumably neutral with regard to the outcome of the comparison: sometimes the two ideas square with each other, sometimes not. This methodological neutrality underwrites reason's claim to objectivity. As mere juxtaposition, reason is a method, a content-free form of thought. In the phrase "standard of reason," however, it is not a mere form, but just the opposite, a content. Here is another example: "All the doctrines and precepts of the New Testament (if it be divine) must . . . agree with natural reason" (46). Here again "reason" names not a neutral method of knowing but a criterion of acceptability by which scriptural doctrines are judged. The equivocality of "reason," its ambiguity between form and content, is particularly important, since it explains the symmetrical nature of interpretation in *Christianity Not Mysterious*. Reason characterizes both the method of understanding and its result because the method influences the outcome. Reasoning is a making reasonable. Toland expressly denies "that we may use reason as the instrument, but not the rule of our belief" (5). Reason is not just the means but the end which the means accomplish. Using reason-the-instrument consists in accommodating the text to reason-the-rule.[22] When the text conforms to the rule—that is, when the text is rationalized—we understand. There can, then, be no distinction between "studying" and "concluding." Rationalizing the text—discovering how it makes sense—is not subsequent to understanding but understanding itself. This is to say that interpretation consists in comparison to reason-the-rule; and such rules of reason, Spinoza rightly discerned, are ultimately indistinguishable from prejudices. Interpretation is always prejudiced by presuppositions about what makes sense (presuppositions it gets from other texts), and it cannot avoid such prejudices without preventing understanding.[23]

Such talk of prejudice seems far removed from Toland's understanding of reason.[24] All the charges that Protestants had levelled against the Roman Pope could be transferred to the Protestant pope within;[25] yet Toland does not do this, because he begins with a Cartesian and Lockean notion of "evidence" that guarantees interpretive infallibility: "It is impossible for us to err as long as we take evidence for our guide" (19). Here the word *evidence* has the technical sense of that which is its own proof, that which is intuitively certain. Evidence is the bedrock of the self-interpreting upon which certain interpretation rests. Self-evident conclusions, Toland implies, cannot be mistaken. Reason, we have seen, "discovers the certainty of anything dubious or obscure, by comparing it with something evidently known" (13). The rule of reason to which reason compares dubious and obscure ideas, then, is self-evident truth. To accommodate the obscure not just to the familiar but to the self-evident guarantees that the interpretation will be true.

Toland expands the realm of self-evidence, moreover, when he writes, "We cannot otherwise discern [God's] revelations but by their conformity with our natural notices of him, which is in so many words to agree with our common notions and our own ordinary ideas" (30). Here "common" and "ordinary" seem closer to commonsensical, customary, and traditional. The point is that if skeptical hermeneutics takes everything that seems self-evident as if it were dubious, Toland's dogmatic hermeneutics takes ordinary ideas as if they were self-evident. Not all of them, of course, but always some common notions are and must be accepted as obviously true, because assimilating the dubious to the true grounds interpretive truth.

The idea of a true interpretation requires elaboration. For Toland's notion of reason as comparison, we have seen, understanding is accommodation, and accommodation consists in assimilating one text to another that is (taken to be) self-evident. The significance of this conception is that it annihilates the distinction between "means of information" and "grounds of persuasion," understanding and assent. But isn't it possible just to understand something without believing it? Spinoza thought so. Since "making sense" equates finding a sense and assessing it to be reasonable (that is, to make sense), and so confuses means and ends, Spinoza warns his readers against using their reason: "We must take especial care when we are in search of the meaning of a text not to be led away by our reason . . . in order not to confound the meaning of a passage with its truth" (101).

In Boyle's "Discourse of Things above Reason" (1681), Pyrocles makes the same distinction as Spinoza: "I presume you need not be told that to explain the sense of a proposition and to make out the truth of it (*unless in common notions or things evident by their own light*) are always two things, and oftentimes two very distant ones."[26] It is the exception that interests us here, because Toland, by contrast with Spinoza, bases his hermeneutic on it. On some occasions—namely, in understanding the common and the self-evident—it is not possible to understand without believing or to segregate meaning from truth. In such cases, to understand is to affirm. Moreover, insofar as "rational" interpretation always assimilates the dubious to something taken to be self-evident, it always precludes any distinction between understanding and judging. As a rational interpretation rationalizes the text, so a true interpretation, for Toland, is primarily an interpretation of its truth. Here the symmetry of Toland's hermeneutics is clearest: a true interpretation is that which discovers the truth of what it interprets.

An example of Toland's mode of interpreting Scripture will make this clearer. In defending the competence of reason to understand revelation, he needs to refute opponents who cite Romans 8:7: "The carnal mind is enmity against God; for it is not subject to the law of God, neither indeed can be." Toland interprets this text thus: "If these words be spoken of reason, there can be nothing more false; because reason does and ought to subject itself to the divine law. . . . The carnal mind then in this place is not reason, but the carnal desires of lewd and wicked men" (128). If the verse is interpreted in such a way as to contradict self-evident truth (here, that reason subjects itself to divine law), then the verse is false. But since Scripture cannot be false, the interpretation must be so. Conversely, the truth of the interpretation is guaranteed by the truth of Scripture.

We are dealing with a very basic question here: How do you know when you have understood? Toland answers, when it makes sense, when it can be integrated with known truths. This answer assumes, however, that the text is true. For Spinoza, as we have seen, this assumption is unacceptable, because much of Scripture is in fact false, and he needs to devise another way of defining true interpretation that does not rely on its making sense: namely, that an interpretation is true when a definite procedure or method has been strictly followed. Of the historical method, Spinoza asserts, "By working in this manner everyone will always advance without danger of error, . . . and will be able with equal security to discuss what surpasses our understanding and what is known by the natural light of reason" (99). Only Spinoza's notion of correctness is universal, for it applies even to texts that are false or nonsensical. For any and all texts, it is the method that validates the interpretation. *True* means correct, error-free; it is a formal quality. For Spinoza, truth pertains to the process of interpreting alone; for Toland, by contrast, truth characterizes not just the interpretation but the text. "If we would know whether Moses believed God to be a fire or not," Spinoza warns, "we must on no account decide the question on grounds of the reasonableness or the reverse of such an opinion" (102). His object is what "Moses believed," which belief may be true or not; but whatever the case, we can interpret the prophet's beliefs correctly by following a prescribed method.

"In order not to confound the meaning of a passage with its truth," Spinoza writes, "we must examine it solely by means of the signification of the words" (101). To this Toland replies, "The question is not about the words but their sense" (33). For him, the thing to be understood is not what Moses believed (which, of itself, is of little consequence) but the real nature of God. I call Toland a "conservative" because, first and foremost, rational interpretation is concerned not just with the correctness of the interpretation but with the substantive veracity of the text, the truth of what it has to say about the subject matter.

The radicalness of Toland's position emerges when we take his thesis a step further: it is on the truth of the text that not only interpretive correctness but the very possibility of understanding depends. Or, negatively put, if the reader does not presuppose the text's truth,[27] understanding it will be impossible: "Those who stick not to say they could believe a downright contradiction to reason, did they find it contained in the Scripture, do justify all absurdities whatsoever" (30). Now Spinoza does not profess to believe everything he finds in Scripture (as the divines did), but he does profess to find contradictions to reason there. Toland's argument is that if so—if Scripture is not limited to the reasonable—then there is no way to tell what it might mean, for it might mean anything at all, or even nothing at all. If, to interpret objectively, the reader can give God "no privileges above the maddest enthusiast or the Devil himself" (33)—if the author cannot be presumed sane, reasonable, and truthful—then his meaning is utterly unpredictable, and any particular meaning that the reader assigns is likely to be nothing but the projection of his own prejudices.

At issue is the viability of the doctrine of "sola scriptura," understood as the proposition that meaning is immanent in the text. Father Simon, Counter-Reformation textual editor of the Bible, had contested it on the grounds that interpreters cannot rely on the words of Scripture alone, because the Bible is so textually problematical that the words are themselves unreliable.[28] Toland more radically suggests that, even if all textual problems could be solved, one still could not guarantee the correctness of one's interpretation by confining oneself to "the signification of the words," as Spinoza recommends, for words alone cannot determine meaning.[29] If "the words of Scripture . . . may signify everywhere whatever they can signify," Toland writes, then "anything may be made of everything" (xxv). Without presuppositions limiting what the words can signify, their meaning becomes completely indeterminate and indeterminable.

In this debate, the question of figurative expression is decisive. Hence it is of utmost importance to determine which passages of Scripture are literal. We recall that Spinoza's program of intrinsic interpretation—that is, comparing obscure passages with clear ones—required that some passages be univocal, literal, and plain. But the problem, as the tradition of allegorizing had amply demonstrated, is that any passage whatsoever can be taken figuratively.[30] As the advocate of intrinsic interpretation, Spinoza must show that it is possible to distinguish literal from metaphorical statements without considering the truth or reasonableness of the statements under scrutiny. Toland must show that this is impossible and so determine whether any particular passage is figurative or not and hence cannot find any determinate meaning at all.

For illustration, we can return to the passage where Moses says God is a fire. How do we know that this is metaphorical? And if it is—fire means anger—is *that* statement literal or is it metaphorical too? Toland adopts the standard Socinian position:

> The question is not about the words, but their sense, which be always worthy of the author and therefore, according to the genius of all speech, figuratively interpreted when occasion requires it. Otherwise, under pretence of faith in the word of God, the highest follies and blasphemies may be deduced from the letter of Scripture, as that God is subject to passions. . . . And if a figure be admitted in these passages, why not, I pray, in all expressions of the like nature, when there appears an equal necessity for it? (33—34)

The "occasion requires" that a passage be interpreted figuratively when literal interpretation makes it foolish or blasphemous, false or nonsensical. If the literal sense is reasonable, then the passage is literal; if unreasonable, the passage is figurative. That is, in Toland's view, reasonableness is the test of metaphorical expression, for the premise of rational interpretation is that ultimately everything makes sense.

Spinoza, by contrast, must determine whether the passage is metaphorical quite apart from whether it makes sense. Here he is at his best:

> As Moses says in several other passages that God has no likeness to any visible thing, whether in heaven or in earth or in the water, either all such passages must be taken metaphorically, or else the one before us [that is, God is a fire] must be so explained. However, as we should depart as little as possible from the literal sense, we must first ask whether this text, God is a fire, admits of any but the literal meaning— that is, whether the word fire ever means anything besides ordinary natural fire. If no such second meaning can be found, the text [that says God is a fire] must be taken literally, however repugnant to reason it may be; and all the other passages, though in complete accordance with reason, must be brought in harmony with it. . . . However, as we find the name fire applied to anger and jealousy (see Job 31:12), we can thus easily reconcile the words of Moses, and legiti-

mately conclude that the two propositions, God is a fire and God is jealous, are in meaning identical.

Further, as Moses clearly teaches that God is jealous, and nowhere states that God is without passions or emotions, we must evidently infer that Moses held this doctrine himself or, at any rate, that he wished to teach it; nor must we refrain because such a belief [in God's emotions] seems contrary to reason, for, as we have shown, we cannot wrest the meaning of texts to suit the dictates of our reason or our preconceived opinions. The whole knowledge of the Bible must be sought solely from itself. (102–03)

Does Spinoza himself succeed here in determining what Moses believed per se without accommodating the text to his own reason—that is, to his preconceived opinions and the norm texts they derive from? It seems not when he says, "We should depart as little as possible from the literal sense." This is an a priori hermeneutic principle, derived perhaps from Reformation hermeneutics, but not from Scripture (Paul says that "the letter killeth"). Spinoza might well reply, however, that while he dogmatically accepts the primacy of the literal, he makes no assumptions about which passages in particular are literal. That is determined intrinsically.

The intrinsic facts are: Moses says that God has no likeness to any visible thing and that God is a fire. Since these are mutually inconsistent, Spinoza concludes that either one or the other must be taken metaphorically. Now this conclusion is questionable, since it follows only if one posits a second a priori hermeneutic principle: the self-consistency of the text. This principle is by no means obvious, and Spinoza himself questioned its applicability to the various prophets: "As the prophets differed in matters speculative among themselves . . . we must not, on any account, infer the intention of one prophet from clearer passages in the writings of another" (106). He does not doubt the principle of consistency in the case at hand, however, since what Moses believed is being determined from Moses alone. Yet here too it is no less questionable. Samuel Johnson once wrote, "Inconsistencies cannot both be right, but imputed to man, they may both be true."[31] There is no intrinsic reason to suppose Moses self-consistent. Everyone contradicts himself occasionally, and if the interpreter's aim is solely to determine what Moses believed, that end does not justify assuming the self-consistency of his beliefs. Spinoza's asumption is justified only on the basis of a third a priori hermeneutic principle—indeed, Toland's principle—that the object of interpretation is not Moses' beliefs per se but what is reasonable and true; for beliefs need not be consistent, but reason must be.[32]

That Spinoza fails to live up to his own methodological ideals does not necessarily discredit them in principle, however. Could not Spinoza have dispensed with the third principle, reason, and so achieved a less biased, more objective determination of Moses' meaning per se? The answer to this question, we can now see, is No. If we do not posit Moses' truth and reasonableness, we cannot assume his self-consistency; so when he says in one place that God has no likeness to any visible thing and in another that God is a fire, we have no justification for concluding that one of the two passages is metaphorical. Both may be figurative; both may be literal, even though that would make them contradictory. Without rationalizing, there is indeed no way of distinguishing the literal from the metaphorical; and if, using the intrinsic method, anything may be made of anything, then, as Toland insists, the method is incapable of finding any determinate meaning at all.[33] The only way to understand a text at all is to posit its truth at the outset.[34] That is to say with Hans Frei, "Theory of meaning is equivalent to theory of knowledge, and to understand is identical with being able to distinguish between what is true and what is false."[35]

If so, all interpretation is rational interpretation. Reasoning is comparing, and comparing with the reasonable.[36] We might say that since intrinsic interpretation has been shown to be impossible, the standard of reason to which the text is compared must necessarily be extrinsic. Interpretation consists in comparing the text to be understood with another text, an external text. But if intrinsic interpretation is impossible, the word *extrinsic* loses its polemical edge for lack of an opposite. Extrinsic interpretation is interpretation per se, and the metaphor of outside and inside, container and contained, becomes inappropriate. To accommodate the text to be understood to another is to understand the text *itself.*

If to understand is to assimilate the obscure to the clear, the dubious to the evident, the strange to the familiar, however, doesn't this amount to the uncontested triumph of dogmatic hermeneutics? When Toland asserts that "we cannot in this world know anything but by our common notions" (30), doesn't this imply, in Spinoza's words, that we "wrest the meaning of texts to suit the dictates of our preconceived opinions" insofar as we understand at all? If this is so, we must wonder how it is possible to learn something uncommon from reading, something hitherto unknown; and if such learning is not possible, what is the purpose of reading at all? This question reopens the question of mystery, its existence and function in interpretation. We have been considering reason and the reasonable in some detail; it is time to turn in conclusion to what does not make sense.

Translated into secular terms, "mystery" names the element of unfamiliarity in any text, its positive and valuable resistance to assimilation, and the promise that it has something to teach that the reader does not already know. "Mystery" requires not that the text be interpretively accommodated to the reader, but that the reader adapt himself to the text—that is, learn something. Insofar as Toland's hermeneutics implies that all interpretation is self-confirmation and that the reader's preconceptions cannot be challenged by the text, it ironically exposes the unconscious bondage that underlies "free thinking." One of Toland's fundamental insights is that some dogmatism, some accepting of something as unquestionably true, cannot be avoided, since it is the condition of understanding. But if his description of understanding as the accommodation of the dubious to the evident precludes understanding anything new, it is prima facie false. The fact is that Toland does better with the objective than the subjective side of understanding. Unlike Spinoza, he does not specify how the interpreter can break out of the prison house of his dogmas and prejudices, but he does explain why no text obviates the effort to understand—that is, why no text is ultimately mysterious—and in so doing, sketches the outlines of a reply to Spinoza in the first respect as well.

Toland defines *mystery* in two, antithetical ways: "First, it denotes a thing intelligible of itself, but so covered by figurative words, types, and ceremonies that reason cannot penetrate the veil nor see what is under it till it be removed. Secondly, it is made to signify a thing of its own nature inconceivable, and not to be judged of by our ordinary faculties and ideas, though it be never so clearly revealed" (67). Mystery, then, is either something intelligible but concealed or something unintelligible even though revealed. The first we might call "contingent mystery," what we do not understand because of some obstacle that could in principle be removed, the second "essential mystery" what we can never understand even if all obstacles are removed. Toland's thesis is that all real mystery is of the first kind and that the second is nonexistent and contradictory, a mere ruse of priestcraft.

Especially in New Testament usage, he argues, *mystery* means not what is of itself unintelligible but rather what was unknown or unclear until the Advent. *Mystery* in this sense is what was to be revealed, and Christ's preaching and passion have revealed it. "He fully and clearly preached the purest morals; he taught that reasonable worship and those just conceptions of heaven and heavenly things which were more obscurely signified or designed by the legal observations. So, having stripped the truth of all those external types and ceremonies which made it difficult before, he rendered it easy and obvious to the meanest capacities" (158). At the death of Christ, the veil of mystery was rent, and thereafter what before was hermeneutically obscure became intelligible not just to priests but to all. Everything is revealed, everything is in principle open to common human understanding.[37]

This means that even if everything must be accommodated to the interpreter's prejudices, nothing is of such a nature that it can ultimately defy understanding. The outlines of Toland's reply to Spinoza's charge follow from this conclusion. Though we always "wrest" the meaning of texts to suit our "preconceived opinions," it does not follow that we are trapped in what we already know. Whatever its mypoia and limits at any particular moment, human understanding is ultimately open to everything without exception. Whatever dogmas are involved, they ultimately make understanding possible, not preclude it. They do not even preclude understanding of the new and the strange, because if the novel must be accommodated to the familiar in the process of understanding, by the same process our common ideas, suppositions, and beliefs are accommodated to the uncommon thing we are trying to understand. In accommodating the text to the interpreter's preconceptions, the latter too are "wrested."

Mystery in the sense of something real and true but intrinsically unintelligible, Toland shows, has served to excuse laziness and justify abandoning the attempt to understand prematurely: "It cannot be imagined how much the notion of mystery contributes to the obscurity of Scripture in most translations. When an able linguist meets with a difficult passage, he presently takes it for a mystery, and concludes it is to no purpose to be at more pains about what is in itself inexplicable" (141). To eliminate this excuse, therefore, Toland demonstrates that mystery is not a possible outcome of understanding. His argument is disarmingly simple: "Of what is not knowable we have no idea, so it is nothing to us" (78).[38] As far as we know, everything that is, is knowable; the contrary supposition (we know of unknowable things) is merely paradoxical.[39] Since, therefore, nothing that is cannot be understood, it is no longer possible to conclude "I understand it, and it is a mystery," for that is to say "I understand it, and it is not understandable." The consequence of abolishing mystery as a possible outcome of understanding is not so much to affirm whatever dogmas the interpreter happens to have as the opposite: a continual incitement to interpretive labor. It means that the effort to understand the obscure is always worthwhile.

In practice, the fact that nothing is inexplicable means that we have no choice but to read as if the text makes sense at some level. This implies, for example, that "the Word of God must be everywhere uniform and self-consistent" (130). As the phrase "must be" indicates, Toland is describing not a fact but a supposition, an a priori principle of understanding—namely, that of charitable interpretation: that one must read *as if* the text were completely intelligible. One form of unintelligibility is self-contradiction; thus the principle of charitable interpretation enjoins us to read as if the text had no internal contradictions, not even merely apparent ones. Surprisingly, Toland allows no distinction between what seems self-contradictory to us and what really is not so. "A seeming contradiction is to us as good as a real one; and our respect for the Scripture does not require us to grant any such [contradictions] in it, but rather to conclude that we are ignorant of the right meaning when a difficulty occurs, and so to suspend our judgments concerning it till with suitable helps and industry we discover the truth" (34–35).

Once the possibility of inferring from an apparent contradiction or other unintelligibility in a text that "it is a mystery—" has been taken from us, we must conclude that "we are ignorant": we must inform ouselves further, seek "suitable helps," work with more "industry." This is hardly the posture of a self-satisfied dogmatist. Toland shifts the locus of opacity from the object to the subject: "If after all [our efforts] we should be at a loss about the meaning of any expression, we ought rather to charge it upon distance of time and the want of more books in the same tongue than to attribute it to the nature of the thing" (152). Unintelligibility is a failure of interpretation, not a feature of the text, and it is a contingent failure. Understanding is always possible. We do not understand many things, of course; but there is nothing that we cannot understand with sufficient effort and opportunity. Toland's hermeneutics urges us to the task.

3

Bolingbroke on History

Perhaps any attempt to take Bolingbroke's ideas seriously today must begin with apology and concession. The man now strikes us as so unprincipled that serious analysis of his stated principles seems pointless and misguided.[1] Many of his political ideas were less matters of commitment than instruments of convenience. Bolingbroke seems to have been no more sincerely a patriot in his leadership of the Patriot opposition than he was a traitor in his collusion with the Stuart Pretender. Deist defender of the State Church, partisan opponent of parties, a Tory more Whiggish than Walpole when occasion demanded, Bolingbroke served expediency in word and deed.[2] His *Remarks on the History of England,* for example, forages over the entirety of British history for anything useful in denigrating Walpole or glorifying the Opposition. In Bolingbroke's hands the past became ordnance with which to wage the political wars of the present, and in war all's fair. The sincerity of his polemical ends cannot be doubted; but in choosing means to achieve them—in testing his facts, weighing his arguments, and examining his principles—Bolingbroke was, by general admission, less than fastidious.

The *Letters on the Study and Use of History,* our focus here, seem genuinely disinterested by comparison with the polemical *Remarks;* yet even these cannot be taken at face value. Written in 1735 during Bolingbroke's second, "voluntary exile" in France after a particularly disheartening Opposition defeat, the *Letters* concern themselves less with history than with philosophy of history,[3] an abstract topic suited to a man who has abstracted himself from the fray. Yet, when Bolingbroke describes his subject as "a thread of thought long ago laid aside" (173),[4] the reader recalls that what had interrupted Bolingbroke's thought was the renewed political activity of the middle years, which rekindled his hopes for power, hopes now extinguished for a second time. His picking up his thread of thought again—that is, the very act of writing the *Letters on History*—itself testifies to the frustration and disappointment of a man whom history had passed by. Bolingbroke desperately wanted to be not a philosopher of history or even a student of it but instead the subject of history, a historic figure, the prime minister advising "the prince," not a writer of epistolary essays on abstruse topics to Lord Cornbury, a political nobody.

Even if we manage to read the *Letters on the Study and Use of History* as philosophy of history, rather than sublimated despair, what we find is that they are not wholly coherent, original, or consistent. The last two letters, which sketch the history of Europe from 1659 to 1688, have to do with history, not "the study and use" of it; moreover, they occupy as much space as the other six letters combined and seem not to belong to the design of the work at all.[5] Further, Letter 5 opens by mentioning that "a long interval" has elapsed since the previous letter, and Bolingbroke wanders about rather aimlessly while trying to resume his argument. The structural incoherence evident here and elsewhere, among and within individual letters, may in part result from their being written in a conversational and informal genre. As Bolingbroke remarks in his *Letters to Pope,* "I dare not promise that the sections or members of these essays will bear that nice proportion to one another and to the whole which a severe critic would require. . . . These epistolary essays, therefore, will be written with as little regard to form and with as little reserve as I used to show in the conversations which have given occasion to them" (3:45). All this admitted, however, Pope's own epistolary essays exhibit no such disregard of form. Bolingbroke's lack of finish, rather than intrinsic to the genre, betrays the studied carelessness that disdains the vulgar rules of orderly exposition.

More significant than such formal lapses is the fact that Bolingbroke's philosophy is in substance "entirely derivative" from the Greek and Roman rhetoricians and their Renaissance heirs, on the one hand, and from Locke, Bayle, and Rapin, on the other.[6] The philosophies of history deriving from these two sources, ancient and modern, are not entirely compatible, as we will see. However easily pigeonholed in his political roles—and sometimes he seems to go out of his way to stereotype himself—Bolingbroke in his role as philosopher of history can be categorized neither as a Renaissance nor an Enlightenment thinker. More ambivalent about skeptical, critical inquiry even than Toland, he occupies a liminal position, straddling the crevasse between two distinct historical epochs and "two great and contradictory traditions of historical scholarship."[7] In the battle between the ancients and moderns, Bolingbroke seems, with utter nonchalance, to have taken both sides.[8]

Whatever our discomfort, he himself registers no consciousness of inconsistency, no sense of self-contradiction in his philosophy of history at all; and that very obliviousness has seemed to call for explanation—indeed, to invite detraction. Leslie Stephen asks "whether this brilliant statesman and philosopher was anything but a showy actor declaiming popular platitudes without understanding them."[9] D. G. James alleges that Bolingbroke "is quite determined not to acknowledge that there are, in these matters, problems to be solved; he will not *think*."[10] Less strident, Isaac Kramnick speaks merely of the confusions in Bolingbroke's thought: "These confusions cannot be explained away. They exist."[11]

In what follows, I do not propose to clear up Bolingbroke's confusions. To resolve his apparent contradictions in real concurrence strikes me as impossible and in some respects undesirable. Admittedly, one might well wonder whether Bolingbroke would seem quite so self-contradictory if European history were periodized differently; that is, if his thought were not perceived as split between two periods. But for us who see the Enlightenment as beginning sometime between 1678 and 1751, during Bolingbroke's lifetime, his thought exhibits an insistent and troubling bifurcation. Without trying to make a virtue of incoherence, I want to argue, nevertheless, that the distinctiveness and hermeneutic interest of Bolingbroke's philosophy of history derives in large part from its hybrid—even mongrel—quality. Rather than expressing a position, the *Letters* register a contest, or rather a number of contests. The book raises a whole range of questions rather than answering them. In fact, however unwittingly, Bolingbroke raises a broader, more comprehensive spectrum of questions than might have been possible had he produced a fully coherent, systematic philosophy, of either the humanist or Enlightenment type.

Kramnick regrets that "in his philosophy of history, Bolingbroke could not shed the humanist ideal and give himself completely to the more modern tendency of his thought."[12] Readers still committed to the humanist ideal will decline to share Kramnick's regret, of course; yet even those of "more modern tendency" may be unwilling to conceive Bolingbroke's humanism as simply a reactionary vestige, ultimately without claim to serious attention. If we are not to sacrifice Bolingbroke's disorderly richness to the demands of logical consistency (or, worse, to our own prejudices), the ancient tendencies evident in the *Letters* must be taken seriously, along with the modern. What I propose then is neither to lament Bolingbroke's untidiness nor to ignore his inconsistencies, but rather to magnify them and organize them as fully as possible. I conceive the manifest contradictions in the *Letters* as belonging to an incipient and unresolved dialectic, one that outlines a task of integration for historical hermeneutics still incomplete today.

Example is the hinge of the *Letters'* implicit dialectic. In Bolingbroke's best-known phrase, borrowed from Dionysus of Halicarnassus's commentary on Thucydides, "History is philosophy teaching by examples" (177). Bolingbroke was hardly the last to affirm the humanist tradition of exemplary history expressed in this maxim. Yet it has already become moribund by 1735,[13] and a century later it was pretty much dead, at least for philosophers and historians. Specifically, the proposition that history is philosophy teaching by examples has three implications which the nineteenth century came to question and reject. First, it implies that philosophy can be learned by examples; this Kant denied.[14] Second, it implies that history teaches lessons; this Hegel denied.[15] Third, it implies that history is philosophy; this Ranke denied.[16] Indeed, after Ranke there was nothing left of the humanist maxim.

Yet, before then, in the eighteenth century, at least one more interpretation of this maxim was possible: example is neither history nor philosophy exactly, or it is both in some sense, or it is the link between them. This interpretation, unclear though it is, seems to me to be close to Bolingbroke's understanding of the matter. Example serves as the focal point of an implicit synthesis, in part because it appeals to what Bolingbroke calls "the whole man." Whereas philosophical precepts address the understanding alone, example engages all the diverse capacities that constitute the complete human being. "The wisest lessons go but a little way to convince the judgment and determine the will unless they are enforced [by examples]," Bolingbroke asserts. Example "makes a kind of appeal . . . to our senses, as well as our understandings." Further, "example appeals not to our understanding alone, but to our passions likewise, . . . [and] sets passion on the side of judgment." In its reference not only to understanding but to judgment, will, sense, and passion all at once, "example . . . makes the whole man of a piece; which is more than the strongest reasoning and the clearest demonstration can do" (178). Example appeals to a synthesis of human faculties, a totality of which the bare precepts of philosophy fall far short.

For Bolingbroke, to say that "history is philosophy teaching by examples" undeniably does imply in a certain sense that "history is philosophy." Most important, it implies that history is worth knowing. Knowledge of past events is useful in the present, and knowledge that comprehends both past and present can be called "general." Since "philosophy" is a common collective term for general knowledge, historical examples that illustrate general precepts are in that sense philosophical. "We must apply ourselves to [history] in a philosophical spirit and manner," Bolingbroke writes; "we must rise from particular to general knowledge" (191).[17] On this view, history achieves dignity and significance insofar as it approximates the generality of philosophy; for philosophical generality represents the standard of cognitive value to which history, like all knowledge, aspires.

Yet for Bolingbroke historical examples cannot be wholly equated with philosophy, let alone reduced to a kind of poor man's philosophy, because they are in certain ways superior to it. "Such is the imperfection of human understanding, such is the frail temper of our minds," Bolingbroke observes, "that abstract or general propositions, though ever so true, appear obscure or doubtful to us very often, till they are explained by examples" (178). On the one hand, this assertion affirms that the abstractions of philosophy represent the standard of intelligibility. Were human understanding perfect— open to truth in its unembodied form—philosophical universals would suffice, and the concreteness of history would be superfluous for the purposes of knowledge. The need for examples, then, testifies to the imperfection of human understanding and to our humanity per se, which is finite, not divine.

On the other hand, as this sentence unfolds, a curious reversal occurs: disembodied abstractions no longer represent the norm of intelligibility. Viewed strictly within the bounds of a human world in which human understanding knows nothing higher and is therefore itself the standard, the need for examples no longer betrays the limits of human understanding, but rather exposes the limits of philosophy, conceptuality, and generality. Philosophy remains "obscure and doubtful" until it is "explained by examples," which serve to illustrate, elucidate, and illuminate what would remain dark without them. In a human world, the general cannot be the self-sufficient standard of intelligibility, since it stands in need of the concrete, of history. Here below, philosophy aspires to the clarity of examples, not vice versa. Examples are irreducible to philosophy in Bolingbroke's exposition, then, precisely insofar as they function to remedy the obscurity of philosophical precepts, and are therefore superior to them.

Given the intrinsic obscurity of abstract ideas, concreteness is a condition of understanding; hence concrete experience remains a permanent prerequisite for knowledge. "Human knowledge is so entirely and solely derived from actual being," Bolingbroke writes in his heavily Lockean philosophical papers, "that without actual being, we should not have even one of those simple ideas whereof all the complex ideas and abstract notions . . . are composed" (3:105). Historical examples are one source of "actual being," one object of experience. Though remote in time and space, as well as mediated through language and narrative, historical examples nevertheless qualify as perceptual experience in that, by contrast with abstract precepts at least, examples make "a kind of appeal . . . to the senses" (178). To do so, they must be "related in their full extent and accompanied with such a detail of circumstances and characters as may transport the attentive reader back to the very time, make him a part of the councils and an actor in the whole scene of affairs" (223). Readers so transported see the event as if they were present, as if it were not a narrative at all, but an image, a picture, an object of perception.[18] "Scipio Africanus had always in his hands the works of Xenophon," Bolingbroke recalls from Cicero. "The images of virtue, represented in [Xenophon's] admirable picture the Cyropaedia, were . . . worthy to be imitated by Scipio" (180).

Lacking such images, "monkish annalists and other ancient chroniclers" do not deserve the name of historians, because they do not "write history in that fulness" necessary for it to become a picture (225). Unlike the chronicler, who offers vague images, the historian as such "depicts" history, pictures it, and so makes it available to experience. Unlike the philosopher, who offers no images at all, the historian of exemplary acts makes virtue visible. Relying on the same Platonic and Ciceronian traditions as Bolingbroke, Fielding states the matter succinctly: "Example is a kind of picture in which virtue becomes as it were an object of sight."[19] In this way the classical tradition of example fed into the empiricist view of history as one kind of the experience that necessarily grounds all specifically human knowledge.

It was the historical agent's experience, not the reader's experience, that was the concern of empiricism, however. "Original records" and "authentic memorials" are "the sole foundations of true history" (198), Bolingbroke asserts; and better still than documents and vestiges are firsthand accounts. The empiricist emphasis on the epistemological primacy of the agent's experience privileged eyewitness narratives as not only authentic but authoritative. Thus Bolingbroke speaks of Davila's history as being confirmed by "the authority of the first duke of Epernon, who had been an actor, and a principal actor too, in many of the scenes that Davila recites" (229). It follows that the most authoritative histories are those, like Clarendon's *History of the Rebellion,* written by participants, or at least by someone "placed so many centuries nearer [than ourselves] to the original truths" (196).

History-as-memoire ideally obviates any need for hypothesis and a priori philosophizing. As Bolingbroke was explicitly aware, however, the best biographies are not necessarily autobiographies. The empiricist criterion becomes suspect to the degree that the best histories are not in principle those written by observers. "In matters of history we prefer very justly contemporary authority; and yet contemporary authors are the most liable to be warped from the straight rule of truth in writing on subjects which have affected them strongly" (217). "There are thousands of eye-witnesses ready to attest the truth of all the miracles supposed to have been wrought" at the tomb of the Abbé of Paris (214). This is a standard Pyrrhonist argument; but more broadly, even when there is no question of mass deception or delusion, eyewitness accounts betray an irremediable narrowness of perspective. "The events we are witnesses of," Bolingbroke remarks, "appear to us very often original, unprepared, single, and unrelative" (186), though in truth they are neither unique nor spontaneous nor isolated phenomena. That is to say, however objective, eyewitnesses never quite see what they are looking at.

Direct experience is intrinsically partial and therefore prejudiced. "The people of each country are apt to prefer themselves to those of every other and to make their own customs and manners and opinions the standards of right and wrong, of true and false" (182). More experience cannot of itself counteract this partiality; the "prejudices that we are apt to contract in our education . . . experience for the most part rather confirms than removes, because it is confined like our education" (183). Rather than more experience, the remedy for the immanent provinciality of experience is history; and this means that history cannot, in Bolingbroke's view, be identified wholly with personal experience. Philosophical precepts, Bolingbroke writes, have the disadvantage of "coming on the authority of others"; by contrast, examples "come upon our own authority, we frame the precept after our own experience" (178). Yet historical examples, in an important sense, cannot be "our own."

Bolingbroke divides examples into two kinds: "the force of examples is not confined to those alone that pass immediately under our sight; the examples that memory suggests have the same effect" (178). Given this distinction, remote examples alone qualify as specifically historical. Only experiences not one's own, only history, can rectify the deficiencies of experience. "The school of example," Bolingbroke asserts, "is the world; and the masters of this school are history and experience. I am far from contending that [history] is preferable to [experience]. . . . But this I say, that the former is absolutely necessary" (179). Far from being identified with personal experience in the empiricist manner, history is here contrasted with it. History as such is not experiential but reported, not immediate but remote, not one's own but another's—and is necessary and valuable for precisely those reasons. "Mere sons of earth," Bolingbroke concludes, "if they have experience without any knowledge of the history of the world, are but half scholars in the science of mankind" (179).

Whereas Locke postulated the exhaustiveness of self-reflection (there is nothing in my mind I have no consciousness of), Bolingbroke's defense of history presupposes the inadequacy of one's own experience to the purposes of self-understanding. "All history that descends to a sufficient detail of human actions and characters is

useful to bring us acquainted with our species, nay, with ourselves,"
he contends (229). Mediated through an understanding of the past,
self-knowledge on this view results not from introspection and firsthand experience, but from interpretation. Moreover, Bolingbroke's
defense supposes the insufficiency not just of self-presence, but of
any present to its own understanding: "As experience is conversant
about the present, and the present enables us to guess at the future;
so history is conversant about the past, and by knowing the things
that have been, we become better able to judge of things that are"
(194). If the study of history really is necessary, as Bolingbroke wants
to claim, this must be because experience cannot of itself achieve full
understanding of "things that are." This requires a detour through
the past; it requires abstracting oneself from the intrinsic narrowness
of experience and rising from the particular to the general. In pro-
viding the means of self-abstraction, history serves as a means of
philosophizing.

What I have been suggesting so far is that, in Bolingbroke's exposition, historical examples embody an implicit synthesis in being
at once particular and general. Unlike precepts, examples are concrete; unlike experiences they are abstract; and in specifiable ways,
each aspect of their nature remedies the deficiencies of the other. The
"force of example" to which Bolingbroke so frequently refers exhibits a similar, related ambiguity. On the one hand, he urges his readers
to understand the "spirit and force" of historical examples (178).
Here the word *force* refers to an example's general sense, as opposed
to the particulars of what happened, just as one might speak of the
force of an argument, as opposed to its details. In such usage *force*
means import or significance. Exemplary history is philosophical in
that it has force, spirit, meaning. The "study and use of history"
consists in performing the hermeneutical task of determining that
meaning. The first point I wish to make, then, is a simple one: as
the title and argument of the *Letters* indicates, Bolingbroke conceives
the "force of example," the meaning of history, as something to be
studied and used.

On the other hand, if one sense of Bolingbroke's phrase "force of
example" corresponds to that of a phrase such as "the force of an
argument," his second, more typical usage corresponds instead to
that of "a forceful argument." In the latter, *force* signifies not just a
meaning but a power, something less studied than felt. In terms of

the quasi-mechanist psychology of the tabula rasa, examples have "a force sufficient to make due impressions on our minds" (219). They have an impact, leave a mark. Such locutions emphasize the power of example to induce an effect, specifically on the understanding and will.

On the understanding, example has the effect not just of conveying information but altering the way in which information is processed and evaluated. By accustoming "ourselves early to contemplate the different nations of the earth, in the vast map which history spreads before us, in their rise and their fall, in their barbarous and civilised states, in the likeness and unlikeness of them all to one another and of each to itself," we are less apt to make here and now "the standards of right and wrong, of true and false" (182). First, then, "history purges the mind of those national partialities and prejudices that we are apt to contract" (183). Involving more than just becoming better informed, such broadening constitutes an alteration in the moral character. It is a "use of history" in the sense of a beneficial result; but the purgation of prejudices through historical examples, we need to remember, is the effect of a force, not just a "use" in the sense of using history in some instrumental way.

Echoing Cicero's phrase that history is *"magistra vitae,"* Bolingbroke writes that "history prepares us for experience, and guides us in it" (183). In referring to its preparatory status, Bolingbroke means that history is typically studied in school, before the student is "actually on the stage" of the world (182). More fundamentally, however, the effect of example here consists in the kind of reverse accommodation that Toland talks too little about; for here the object assimilates the interpreting subject: history prepares us for experience in that it molds the mind. In the forge of history the student receives a certain "cast of thought" and "temper of mind." Historical study not only informs, but also forms the reader, giving "a certain turn to our ways of thinking," affecting the way things are experienced, and determining whether they count as experiences at all. "We shall gather or not gather experience, be the better or the worse for this experience, when we come into the world and mingle among mankind, according to the temper of mind and the turn of thought that we have acquired beforehand and bring along with us." Thus Bolingbroke concludes that historical study early in life "will tincture all our future acquisitions" (182). It does not just purge the mind of

prejudice. Prior to experience and coloring it, history instills beneficial prejudices, beneficial in a way that empirical epistemology
could never conceive—but (as Burke was to insist) still prejudices.

The force of example also has a corollary effect on the will. "We
ought always to keep in mind," Bolingbroke admonishes his readers,
"that history is philosophy teaching by examples how to conduct
ourselves in all the situations of private and public life" (191). It is
not just a matter of acquiring knowledge, but of applying it; so, in
preparing us for experience, "the study of history will prepare us for
action" (194). In respect to action too, the "application of examples"
(192) means at least two things. One is instrumentalist and consists
in deducing the precept—discovering the abstract meaning—embodied in the example and then applying it to one's conduct. But beyond
this, the "force of example" signifies not just its abstract meaning
but its motivating energy, its power to spur action. [20]

"The citizens of Rome," Bolingbroke recalls, "placed the images
of their ancestors in the vestibules of their houses, so that whenever
they went in or out, these venerable bustoes met their eyes, and
recalled the glorious actions of the dead, to fire the living to excite
them to imitate and even to emulate their forefathers. . . . Now these
are so many instances of the force of remote example" (179). Like
such images and as an instance of them, [21] exemplary history "fires"
and "excites" its readers. "Example sets passion on the side of judgment." It arouses the passion of desire, especially the desire for fame.
Yet passion in the other sense is also involved, insofar as the "force
of example" is something to which one submits. It works to "convince the judgment and determine the will" (178). Rather than being
a voluntary act, in understanding the exemplary something happens
to the student, involuntarily and irresistibly. Thus Bolingbroke
speaks of the "magic of example," an occult force that disdains the
barriers of time and distance (179). Not only does example illustrate
precepts; the force of embodied example magically induces one to
embody them. "Example secures the observance of those precepts
which example insinuated" (178).

"The power of example is so great," Samuel Johnson warned, "as
to take possession of the memory by a kind of violence, and produce
effects almost without intervention of the will." [22] Bolingbroke writes
in the same vein: "We are obliged to apply to ourselves what we see
happen to other men" (178). This obligation is not moral but rather
natural: "We are naturally apt to apply to ourselves what has hap-

pened to other men, and . . . examples take their force from hence"
(211). At a minimum, this force means that human beings have an
aptitude to learn not only from their own past experience but from
other people's. It means, further, as Aristotle observed, that the
mimetic instinct is somehow natural to human beings: perhaps all
learning is at bottom miming. Less innocuously, Bolingbroke means
that the inclination to imitation, being natural, is an irresistible impulse, and so the force of example can on occasion override reason
and sanity. "The Athenians are said to have been transported into a
kind of martial frenzy by the representation of a tragedy of aeschylus,
and to have marched under this influence from the theatre to the
plains of Marathon" (212).

On the one hand, then, "force of example" signifies the meaning,
import, or significance that the reader can put to good use; on the
other, it points to its effect, which is action. The latter distinguishes
Bolingbroke's from Hume's view of history as spectacle. "To see all
the human race, from the beginning of time, pass, as it were, in
review before us," Hume writes, "what spectacle can be imagined,
so magnificent, so various, so interesting? What amusement, either
of the senses or imagination, can be compared with it?"[23] By contrast
with Hume's aesthetic conception of history, Bolingbroke argues
that example "guides conduct" and irresistibly "determines the will";
he conceives history not as a picture but a power.

What unites Bolingbroke's two senses of *force,* as meaning and
power, is application. Whether voluntarily and consciously or involuntarily and unconsciously, applying consists in past history influencing present action. Bolingbroke's criticism of the *vita contem-
plativa* is directed at both philosophers and antiquarians, because
both, for different reasons, take insufficient account of history's application in action. "We should neither grope in the dark nor wander
in the light," Bolingbroke often repeats (219, 195, 222, 229). Philosophy conceived as merely speculative knowledge, including the
knowledge of abstract ethical rules, cannot of itself motivate people
to act. Hume elaborated more fully on the impotence of knowledge
as such, but Bolingbroke affirms much the same thing: "The wisest
lessons in favour of virtue go but a little way to convince the judgment and determine the will unless they are enforced by [example]"
(178). One reason for the inefficacy of lessons is that "longum iter
est per praecepta," as Bolingbroke insists in the words of Seneca. A
philosophically authorized decision comes only after a "long deduc-

tion of reasoning." Abstract arguments take the long way round, by contrast with examples, which are understood with the swiftness of intuition.

Antiquarianism ironically has the same effect as philosophy, deferring the use of history in action. Bolingbroke avows a "thorough contempt for the whole business of these learned lives; for all the researches into antiquity, for all the systems of chronology and history. . . . I had rather . . . make as many anachronisms as a Jewish chronologer, than sacrifice half my life to collect all the learned lumber that fills the head of an antiquary" (175–76). This kind of thing can easily be mistaken for an arrogant self-justification of laziness. For the humanist, however, antiquarianism is more than a waste of time; it is a waste of life, where life means action, specifically ethical and political action.

Bolingbroke is addressing Cornbury in particular and statesmen in general, and in so doing, he opens himself to the charge of elitism,[24] of directing his philosophy of history only to those in public office and ignoring the unempowered. Yet he states that, "in a free government, the public service is not confined to those whom the prince appoints to different posts in the administration under him; . . . there the care of the state is the care of multitudes" (237). All are called to be statesmen under a free government; all are citizens involved in political action; hence all stand in need of useful history— the kind that antiquarians fail to offer. Bodin epitomizes their fault. "Seneca speaks of men who spend their whole lives in learning how to act in life, 'dum vitae instrumenta conquirunt.' . . . This method of Bodin would . . . leave us no time for action, or would make us unfit for it. A huge common-place book, wherein all the remarkable sayings and facts that we find in history are to be registered, may enable a man to talk or write like Bodin, but will never make him a better man, nor enable him to promote, like a useful citizen, the security, the peace, the welfare, or the grandeur of the community to which he belongs" (195).

What antiquarians forget is that history is addressed not to historians but to citizens. In other words, historical study is not its own end but is rather subservient to the general aims of life. The antiquary's curiosity scatters and divides those aims by separating knowledge from life. Bolingbroke describes curiosity as a passion like lust: wanton, promiscuous, and indiscriminate, because it has no purpose in life other than to satisfy itself. To its shame, historical curiosity is autotelic. "Nature gave us curiosity to excite the industry of our minds; but she never intended it should be made the principal, much less the sole object of their application" (177). "He who improperly, wantonly, and absurdly makes it so indulges a sort of canine appetite: the curiosity of the [antiquary], like the hunger of the [dog], devours ravenously and without distinction whatever falls in its way; but neither of them digests. They heap crudity upon crudity, and nourish and improve nothing but their distemper" (219). This metaphor of understanding as digestion and assimilation, lifted almost verbatim from Locke,[25] suggests that the failure of the antiquary is a failure to assimilate his learning, apply it to himself—indeed, to make it part of himself. History is not the only study susceptible of such abuse. "An application to any study that tends neither directly nor indirectly to make us better men and better citizens, is at best but a specious and ingenious sort of idleness, to use an expression of Tillotson: and the knowledge we acquire by it is a creditable kind of ignorance, nothing more" (177).

In denigrating antiquarian curiosity as "knowledge that is ignorance," Bolingbroke points to a humanist distinction scarcely intelligible today: namely, that between fact and truth.[26] In one of the forms Bolingbroke gives it, this distinction remains accessible today: "Certain Greek authors . . . examined very accurately whether Anacreon loved wine or women best, whether Sappho was a common whore, with other points of equal importance. . . . But ten millions of such anecdotes as these, though they were true, . . . would be of no value in my sense, because of no use towards our improvement in wisdom and virtue" (223). Conceived as a distinction between fact and value, the distinction between fact and truth remains intelligible. We understand that not everything true is useful, because we understand the notion of pure research, which separates truth from utility, and we think of application and use in the technological way, as something subsequent to knowledge, hence not identical with it. Nevertheless, what Bolingbroke means by "study" is not pure research, and what he means by "use" is not exhausted by applied science. What does it mean, then, to distinguish truth from fact?

In condemning antiquarian curiosity for issuing in "knowledge that is ignorance" because it is useless, Bolingbroke suggests not just that wisdom consists in useful knowledge. More radically, in the humanist tradition, wisdom is a kind of knowing that is using; applying is understanding, not merely something that follows it as a secondary act. We saw above that, according to Bolingbroke, philosophy needs to be explained by examples; general rules and laws are clearer in the concrete than in the abstract. From this familiar principle follows a startling implication: since the abstract needs to be applied in order to be understood, application cannot be conceived merely as a consequence of understanding but must also be considered a condition of it. If so, it is not true that one must understand first, in order to apply later. Wisdom is applying.

Bolingbroke's critique of antiquarianism extends this insight into the relation between application and understanding a step further. When Bolingbroke asserts, "History is not an object of curiosity" (219), he means, first, that history is not just something to look at, like a curio in a museum case, but is also an instrument with a use. More radically, however, history cannot be an object of detached curiosity because, unlike an instrument, it possesses its own force, separate from the person who wields it. The mummies reach out of their cases to grab you by the throat. Historical examples have the power to make an impression, leave a mark on the person who is studying them, and thereby destroy all pretense of detachment. Application in this sense is not something one does to or with history. Effective history is not something one uses; rather, historical examples prevent one's *not* using them. They not only seize the judgment but determine the will. Facts—inert bits of information—cannot be true, for historical truth is a power; and to understand it, therefore, is to register its force in action. From the viewpoint of the humanist tradition, when antiquarianism or any kind of autotelic history prescinds the knowledge of history from its power—from action, use, and application—the result of not pure knowledge but, quite the opposite, ignorance.

Against this humanist background we can appreciate how fully Bolingbroke reverses himself when he affirms, side by side with effective history, the antithetical Enlightenment ideal of critical history, where the emphasis is on convincing the judgment prior to determining the will. "History must have a certain degree of probability and authenticity," Bolingbroke asserts, "or the examples we find in it would not carry a force sufficient to make due impressions on our minds" (219). Here the force of history, no longer irresistible, is conditional on the process of verification. Bolingbroke explains, "I have observed already that we are apt naturally to apply to ourselves what has happened to other men, and that examples take their force from hence, as well those which history, as those which experience, offers to our reflection. What we do not believe to have happened, therefore, we shall not thus apply; and for want of the same application, such examples will not have the same effect" (211). The effect of history depends on its credibility, and credibility on the judgments of critical self-consciousness.

Some histories do meet the criterion of probability in Bolingbroke's view. He steers a middle course between the learned credulity of the antiquarians and the learned skepticism of the Pyrrhonists. Rather than believing all of history or none of it, Bolingbroke speaks (in Locke's words) of the "degrees of assent that we may give to history" (213). Bolingbroke's moderation or his opponents' extremism aside, all are unanimous in conceiving history as subject to assent, and assent as something "we may give" or withhold. "What we do not believe to have happened, therefore, we shall not thus apply" (211). For critical history, application is not an effect of history on the historian, but rather, vice versa: the deliberate judgment of an epistemological subject, a voluntary act of mind that can be performed or not.

Critique, as its etymology indicates, works by dividing. Reason establishes "strict rules of criticism" that distinguish "the truth of fact" from fables with only "the appearance of truth" (212). Fact is a critical concept, in that it is primarily defined negatively, by what it is divided from: fact is not fable, not fiction, and so forth. "Criticism separates the ore from the dross," Bolingbroke asserts almost tautologically (217). Critique refines and purifies. Since the resultant facts have passed the necessary epistemological tests, they provide reliable foundations upon which the various edifices of belief can safely be erected. The Church is the most important such structure. "A religion founded on the authority of a divine mission, confirmed by prophecies and miracles, appeals to fact: and the facts must be proved as all other facts that pass for authentic are proved. . . . History alone can furnish the proper proofs, that the religion they teach is of God" (231). We read nothing of the force of example in such passages; instead, history needs to be proved, and then itself functions as proof. It has an entirely epistemological status.

Though Bolingbroke had affirmed against the antiquarians that "history is not an object of curiosity," in embracing critical history, he too makes it an object of knowledge. Consequently, in moving from effective history, where history is a force, to critical history, where history consists of information, the power switches sides, from history to the critic. For critique doesn't just divide; it is a creative power. "Original records" and "authentic memorials" are admittedly "the sole foundations of true history" (198), but they never amount to more than *materia historica;* they are not histories themselves. Documents are found; histories are made—by historians, as is especially patent when they are critical historians. Critique establishes "the truth of facts," in Bolingbroke's words, the truth of made things. This is one meaning of Vico's famous dictum *Verum est factum.* The true, the intelligible, is what we have made. Whereas for effective history the historian more or less passively registers the power of example, critique situates creative power in the hands of the historian, and the force of history is thereby brought under the historian's control. Through critique, subjective self-consciousness escapes the force of history and exerts its own power over it.

Bolingbroke acknowledged that the power of reason over history is easily exaggerated. It is not quite true that "what we do not believe to have happened . . . we shall not apply" (211). "Doubts concerning the truth of history," he admits, "have hindered [no one] from applying the examples he has met with in it and from judging of the present and sometimes of the future by the past" (219). "We must content ourselves to guess at what will be by what has been; we have no other means in our power, and history furnishes us with these" (189). To a certain extent, the use of history—reading the present and future from the past—is an acritical act. Action is the best index of belief, and we always act as if tomorrow will be very much like yesterday. Such beliefs as these, Reid and the common-sensists later pointed out, are either not subject to doubt or not affected by it. Ascribing human behavior exclusively or even primarily to critical—that is, potentially dubitable—beliefs has the effect of overintellectualizing human motives and thereby inflating the importance of critical self-consciousness.

Since it overestimates the powers of reason, critical history must describe Don Quixote as mad. "In Amadis of Gaul," Bolingbroke remarks, "we have a thread of absurdities that are invented without any regard to probability and that lay no claim to belief." If, nevertheless, "Don Quixote believed" (212) then, that must be because he was mad, for only "enthusiasm and frenzy can give credit to such histories." Critical history needs to call the Don's belief madness, because otherwise his story would demonstrate that in fact credibility has no necessary reference to probability, thereby falsifying critique's fundamental rationale. Yet, ascribing his behavior to madness gets us no further than ascribing it to a miracle and is really no explanation at all.

Exemplary history has the advantage here. By showing that examples of themselves elicit imitation and so effect action, exemplary history captures the acritical, passional side of historical study. Exemplary history is rhetorical in conception, in that it diverts attention from the historical object (typical of critical history) toward its effect, what happens to the reader.[27] In his essay "On Luxury" Bolingbroke tells the story of the Sybarite people who were so artistic that even their horses moved to music. Learning this, their enemies from Cretona brought harps and pipes onto the field of battle. When the instruments were played, the Sybarites' horses began to dance, and three hundred thousand of their warriors were killed. Bolingbroke concludes: "Though this story seems a little fabulous, it contains at least a very good moral" (1:477). When history becomes exclusively rhetorical—that is, effect-oriented—whether the narrative is factual or fabulous matters not at all, so long as it achieves its effect.

At the conclusion of Charlotte Lennox's *The Female Quixote,* the heroine is informed by her physician that all the romances she has been imitating are not meant to be believed.

> Surely Sir, replied Arabella, you must mistake their design; he that writes without intention to be credited must write to little purpose; for what pleasure or advantage can arise from facts that never happened? What examples can be afforded by the patience of those who never suffered or the chastity of those who were never solicited? The great end of history is to shew how much human nature can endure or perform. . . . The first confutation stills our emotions, and however we were touched before, we then chase it from the memory with contempt.

"Facts that never happened" are not facts, to be sure; but truths that never happened may still be true, as the doctor replies to Arabella: "Truth is not always injured by fiction. . . . The fables of Aesop, though never I suppose believed, yet have been long considered as lectures of moral and domestic wisdom, so well adapted to the faculties of man that they have been received by all civilized nations."[28] This defense of Aesop's fables as nonfactual truth is not so

far removed from Aristotle's defense of poetry as "a more philosophical and a higher thing than history: for poetry tends to express
the universal, history the particular" (*Poetics* 9. 3). Nor is Aristotle
far removed from Bolingbroke's own contention that exemplary
history is philosophical, because it contains "abstract or general propositions." The consequence, however, is that in this respect exemplary history cannot distinguish itself from poetry.

Here critical history has the advantage. "What may have happened," Bolingbroke asserts, "is the matter of an ingenious fable;
what has happened is that of an authentic history" (212). This distinction of history from fable bears further thought. We can see that
it means making history an object of knowledge rather than a force;
it means that history becomes nonrhetorical—that is, object- as opposed to effect-oriented. More fundamentally, however, in dividing
history from fable, critique separates signified from signifier, the past
from the stories about it, narrative from narrated, word from thing.
What makes critique critical is precisely these distinctions, and they
in turn define critical history as against exemplary history. The latter
does not differentiate between *récit* and *histoire;* histories are about
history, because history is (itself) a book. No longer is knowledge
essentially nonverbal, as in Locke; nor does language advene to
history ex post facto.

Evidence that Bolingbroke conceives history as a book is not far
to seek. "History is the ancient author" that we translate into our
own conduct, Bolingbroke writes (194). His critique of antiquarians
who waste their lives among coins and monuments in itself suggests
that however much Bolingbroke valued "original" and "authentic"
relics, fundamentally he thought of genuine history as something
you read. When he speaks of "events that stand recorded in history"
(186), when he describes history as a study "open to every man who
can read" (177), he is not merely guilty of an accidental confusion.
The nondifferentiation of word and thing is essential to the whole
conception of exemplary history.[29] In the phrase "force of example,"
where "force" means power, what is it that has this force, the event
or the narrative of it? Is Scipio Africanus inspired to emulation by
the deeds of Cyrus or by Xenophon's *Cyropaedia*? As judged by the
effect, it really makes no sense to differentiate them. We noted above,
moreover, that when Bolingbroke speaks of "the spirit or force" of
example (178), the word *force* refers not only to power but to meaning. In illustrating this second usage, the *OED* (definition 9) cites

Locke's first *Treatise* ("the force of the text in hand") and Berkeley's *Alciphron* ("I comprehend the force and meaning of the proposition"). What has "spirit and force" is a text or proposition or book, which becomes the paradigm instance of all intelligibility. History that has force and meaning possesses the same intelligibility as a book. The question arises, then, what it means to understand the book of history.

As we have come to expect, Bolingbroke has at least two answers, perhaps complementary but not entirely compatible. First, understanding the book of history entails a kind of decoding.[30] Like finding the moral in a fable, understanding history consists in deducing the precept from the example, the general from the particular. Critical and exemplary history agree in making lawlike generality their aim. Critique insists on establishing accurate facts, but particular facts are valuable only as means toward a general end. For exemplary history too, as we have seen, the philosophical import of examples consists in their generality, though in this case the truth of historical precepts is verified less by certification than by tradition itself. Both visions of history are present when Bolingbroke writes, "[There] are certain general principles and rules of life and conduct which always must be true, because they are conformable to the invariable nature of things. He who studies history as he would study philosophy will soon distinguish and collect them, and by doing so will soon form to himself a general system of ethics and politics on the surest foundations, on the trial of these principles and rules in all ages, and on the confirmation of them by universal experience" (193).

Here Bolingbroke envisions history as nature and nature as the sphere of general principles and rules. Critical history inductively gathers particulars into generals; exemplary history philosophically abstracts generals from particulars. In reaching toward the universal, the invariable, the uniform—that is, the nonhistorical—the variable particulars of history are accidents that must be transcended. Decoding always generates a pile of semiotic waste, as it were; and on this view of what it means to understand history, the decoded particulars are meaningless shells that must be winnowed away if useful historical generalities are to be gleaned. "Particular examples may be of use sometimes in particular cases; but the application of them is dangerous," Bolingbroke warns (191). "Codrus and the Decii devoted themselves to death: one because an oracle had foretold that the army whose general was killed would be victorious, the others in compliance with a superstition. . . . These are examples of great magnanimity, to be sure. . . . But if a general should act the same part now and, in order to secure his victory, get killed as fast as he could, he might pass for a hero, but, I am sure, he would pass for a madman" (193). This is the stuff of comedy, but the point is clear enough. "Guicciardin observes how dangerous it is to govern ourselves by particular examples; since to have the same success . . . the example must not only answer the case before us in general, but in every minute circumstance" (192).

It never does, however, and there—in the irreducibility of historical difference—is the rub. Bolingbroke intimates that insofar as the historical example is particular, no example from the past can apply to the circumstances of the present case (he does not acknowledge that insofar as the example is universal, every example applies to the present case). If history is to be applicable at all, the particulars must first be left behind before it can be reclaimed. As decoding, understanding history means that "we must rise from the particular to the general" (191); as application, it means descending from the general to the particular. This conception of historical interpretation, however, does scant justice to the nature of history and of understanding it. The notion of history is inalienable from particularity, variety, and temporal difference. For that reason, reducing the particular to the general—that is, reducing history to nature, the different to the same, and change to permanence—constitutes not understanding history but ignoring it.

This Bolingbroke also knew. In his view, as we saw at the outset, examples have a dialectical structure, in that they are not only general but also particular. Moreover, their special explanatory advantage, the superior intelligibility of examples over abstract philosophical propositions, results directly from their particularity and concreteness. What makes the historian as such is that he never loses sight of the historical particular, since it is precisely there—in the grit of the circumstantial—that historical meaning is located. In genuine history, Bolingbroke asserts, events are "related in their full extent, and accompanied with such a detail of circumstances, and characters, as may transport the attentive reader back to the very time. . . . Such draughts as these, . . . and such alone are truly useful" (223). "History cannot be said even to relate faithfully and inform us truly that does not relate fully. . . . Naked facts, without the causes that produced them and the circumstances that accompanied them, are not sufficient to characterise actions or counsels. The nice degrees of wisdom and of folly, of virtue and of vice, will not only be undiscoverable in them; but we must be very often unable to determine under which of these characters they fall" (228). Decoding that seeks general meaning above and beyond (or inside and beneath) particular circumstances not only fails in understanding, but distorts the nature of the historical and risks obscuring its meaning.

The hermeneutical problem seems to be, then, that even if history is a book, the model of literary decoding—of abstracting a moral from a fable—does not pertain very well to it. If meaning takes the form of abstractable generality, then history has no meaning, for the universals of history are inalienably concrete. In other words, if understanding is really generalizing, it follows that the ungeneralizable particulars of history cannot be understood; they must be distorted in the very process of understanding them. If, on the other hand, the notion of intelligible historical meaning is to be preserved, the model of understanding as abstracting must be replaced. This does not necessarily mean that the conception of history as book is faulty, however, for if the analogy of abstracting a moral from a fable does not work very well for the book of history, this may be because it does not work very well for other books either.

Bolingbroke's first alternative to decoding is the paradigmatic response to the exemplary: imitation. Referring to both word and deed, imitation has the advantage of signifying both a certain kind of action—"to improve by examples is to improve by imitation" (193)—and a certain kind of translation; so it comprehends not only what is meant by *imitatio Christi* but also (since history is a book) the literary analogue of it. In Pope's imitations of Horace, for example, the British poet substituted George I where the Roman poet praised Augustus.[31] Bolingbroke seems to be thinking of something like his friend Pope's practice when he writes, "History is the ancient author; experience is the modern language. We form our taste on the first, we translate the sense and reason, we transfuse the spirit and force, but we only imitate the particular graces of the original; we imitate them according to the idiom of our own tongue; that is, we substitute often equivalents in the lieu of them, and are far from affecting to copy them servilely" (194). Bolingbroke's model of understanding as imitative translation is designed to solve the same problem as the model of decoding: how is it possible to understand historical difference? Unlike decoding, however, it does not suggest that understanding means subsuming difference into identity or rising above particulars to universality. Rather, imitation consists in "substituting equivalents."[32] In speaking of substitution, Bolingbroke acknowledges the inalienability of difference; while in speaking of equivalents, he nevertheless affirms the possibility of understanding.

The difficulties of this conception of understanding are patent. If our object is to learn something about Augustus Caesar, George I serves no better than George Bush. Pope's *Odyssey* was, by common consent, a very pretty poem—but it wasn't Homer. Pope's master, Dryden, states the charge bluntly: "Imitation of an author is the most advantageous way for a translator to show himself, but the greatest wrong which can be done to the memory and reputation of the dead."[33] Imitation is not translation, Dryden contends; in altering the original, it is parody or traduction. Defending imitation against this charge, Bolingbroke cites Boileau: "'To translate servilely into modern language an ancient author phrase by phrase and word by word is preposterous; nothing can be more unlike the original than such a copy. It is not to show, it is to disguise the author. . . . A good writer, instead . . . will *jouster contre l'original,* rather imitate than translate, and rather emulate than imitate; he will transfuse the sense and spirit of the original into his own work, and will endeavor to write as the ancient author would have written, had he written in the same language'" (193).

A copy is unlike its original: this is the paradox that legitimates the practice of imitation and the model of understanding based on it. For most of us, if we want to understand Homer, Homer alone won't do. We can look at the Greek and understand nothing; we can have the Greek transliterated and still understand nothing; we can have the Greek translated verbatim and even then understand nothing. We have the copy, as it were, but a copy remains unlike the original so long as it is unintelligible. What we need is a translation; we need not a copy but something different from the original; and insofar as a translation differs from the original (while still being similar), it can be called an imitation.

Even Dryden ultimately agrees with this conclusion. He quarrels with Denham's statement that "'Poetry is of so subtle a spirit that, in pouring out of one language into another, it will all evaporate; and if a new spirit be not added in the transfusion, there will remain nothing but a *caput mortuum,*'" but then goes on to say, "I confess this argument holds good against a literal translation; but who defends it? Imitation and verbal version [that is, literal translation] are, in my opinion, the two extremes which ought to be avoided."[34] Ultimately, there is not much disagreement between Denham, Dryden, Boileau, and Bolingbroke. None thinks of copying as the ideal; all conceive of imitative translation (by whatever name) as the key to understanding history. That is to say, the only possible way to be faithful to the past is to differ from it. With respect to the dialectic that we have been following in Bolingbroke's thought, such translation serves as the locus of a synthesis between the same and the different. Whereas critical history conceives of difference as an obstacle to understanding, imitation reconceives difference as a condition of understanding. Given the reality of historical difference, exemplary history finds it no paradox to say that only a historical picture that differs from the historical original can be similar to it. We understand differently if we understand at all.

The model of interpretation as imitative translation shifts understanding out of the vertical or metaphysical plane, which works with "higher" universals and "lower" particulars, onto the horizontal or historical plane, where understanding is not figured as ascending or application as descending. Moreover, on this new model, understanding is not conceived of as the province of the same and application as that of the different, for translation embodies a synthesis in which understanding of the same itself consists in application to the different—a process essentially interminable. Decoding, by contrast, anticipates a definitive interpretation: the moral ends the fable; finding the precept ends the process of interpretation. From the perspective of decoding, the question is always why "the most opposite, the most extravagant, . . . and the most contradictory faiths may be founded on the same text" (232). To this question there are at least two responses. The critical historian answers: "History has been purposely and systematically falsified in all ages" (213). That is to say, meaning is fixed; and difference, plurality, and all the changes that constitute history are remediable accidents to which essentially stable, nonhistorical meaning is regrettably subject. Translation, on the other hand, offers the opposite response to interpretive plurality. Insofar as understanding exemplary history involves something like imitatively translating it, historical change belongs to historical meaning. Such meaning is not historical in the sense of being over and done with; it is historical in that it belongs to an ongoing story. Interpretation of historical meaning, then, is not a teleological process that terminates in something nonhistorical: namely, its meaning. Historical study on the horizontal plane—understood as application, imitation, and translation, rather than decoding—anticipates no terminal revelation, no definitive interpretation, but rather an ongoing process of recoding that is the process of history itself.

By contrast with the model of uncovering and decoding, translation foresees only the irreducible plurality of the same. Like Swift before him, Bolingbroke has fun with the myth of the Septuagint. He laughs "at [Jerome's] story of the seventy-two elders, whose translations were found to be, upon comparison, word for word the same, though made separately, and by men who had no communication with one another" (201). As a model of understanding, translation makes a virtue of plurality and a mockery of the notion of a uniquely correct interpretation. What is funny about the story of the seventy translators is not just their miraculous concurrence but the fact that they work on their versions simultaneously, when it is precisely the fact of temporal succession and change that necessitates the multiplicity of translations and vindicates the variety they represent. "Truth is always and everywhere the same," Toland had written in *Christianity Not Mysterious* (xx), and Bolingbroke too speaks of "general principles and rules of life and conduct which always must be true, because they are conformable to the invariable nature of things" (193). Yet because Bolingbroke is here explaining historical understanding, he moves from interpretation as decoding to interpretation as translation, from the metaphysical to the historical plane, where truth is less a self-identical thing than a process, because it belongs to the ongoing process of history and is inseparable from it.

What, then, prevents the determination of meaning from becoming continuous and indefinitely prolonged? In the case of a book we can say: "The scope and design of the author" (207) prevents it, for to exceed the *skopos* is to cease interpreting. If history is a book, however, it does not have an author but is one, as Bolingbroke says (194). He thinks of history as a kind of ongoing story in which the imperfections of human justice are corrected at last by divine—or poetic—justice. In history, "the villain who has imposed on mankind by his power of cunning and whom experience could not unmask for a time is unmasked at length, and the honest man who has been misunderstood or defamed is justified before his story ends" (185).

It may be true, as Sophocles reminds us, that no man can be called happy before his death. Bolingbroke, however, adds that death does not settle the question either; no man can be called honest or villainous before the whole story is told. Death stops the agent's intentions and desires, but the ongoing process of historical meaning extends beyond death. Historical meaning, in sum, is not determined by the agent's intention, and understanding it therefore does not terminate upon achieving a sympathetic communion of minds.

If historical meaning is not a function of intention, it becomes all the more critical to know when a story—whether of an individual or a nation—is in fact whole, and this raises the issue of periodization. On the one hand, exemplary history denies the very gap between past and present that makes historicism possible; every application of the past to the present not only presupposes but creates the continuity of history. On the other hand, exemplary history is episodic, replete with innumerable exempla and no overall unity. The notion that historical stories do end, which makes periodization possible, is based on the idea that history is not a seamless web of continuity.

> However closely affairs are linked together in the progression of governments and how much soever events that follow are dependent on those that precede, [there always are points where the chain] seems to be broken, and the links that are continued from that point bear no proportion nor any similitude to the former. I would not be understood to speak only of those great changes that are wrought by a concurrence of extraordinary events . . . but even of those that are wrought . . . slowly and imperceptibly, by the necessary effects of time and flux condition of human affairs. When such changes as these happen, . . . then is one of those periods formed at which the chain spoken of is so broken as to have little or no real or visible connection with that which we see continue. . . . Such a period therefore is, in the true sense of the words, an epocha or an era, a point of time at which you stop or from which you reckon forward. (239)

Note that Bolingbroke uses the word *period* in the now archaic sense of point of time. Periods serve history in the same manner as "pointing" serves a text. They interrupt the ongoing process of meaning and round it off, as it were, into an intelligible whole. A period marks the end of an old story, makes it a whole, and separates it from the new. A whole, then, is defined by its external articulation, in that each story has a certain autonomy that must be respected if it is to be understood.

According to the *OED,* Bolingbroke was the first to use *period* in the alternative sense of a duration when he suggests subdividing history in order to understand it: "Divide the entire period into such particular periods as the general course of affairs will make out to you sufficiently, by the rise of new conjunctures, of different schemes of conduct, and of different theatres of action. Examine this period of history as you would examine a tragedy or a comedy; that is, take first the idea or a general notion of the whole, and after that examine every act and every scene apart. Consider them in themselves, and consider them relatively to one another" (249). As in a drama, the wholeness of a period consists in its comprehending all the parts of a complete plot.[35] "The beginning, the progression, and the end appear, not [just] of particular reigns, must less of particular enterprises or systems of policy alone, but of governments, of nations, of empires" (186).

Bolingbroke remains committed here to the notion of history as a book, in this case a play; but in these passages we see how even an authorless book can serve as a paradigm instance of intelligibility insofar as it is a whole. A whole book needs no extrinsic explanation; it is self-explanatory because is understood not by accommodating it to a prior text (that is, the author's intention or some other norm text) or a posterior text (that is, a translation) but rather to itself. It has individual acts and scenes, or beginnings, middles, and ends, which, though separate, are mutually interpretive. Each of the parts has a relative autonomy such that they must be interpreted "in themselves," as Bolingbroke says; yet, because each is only part of a whole, they must also be interpreted "relatively to one other." Intrinsic and extrinsic are complementary.

The two senses of *period* that Bolingbroke employs correspond to these two movements of interpretation. As point, a period articulates and divides and so registers our sense of change and difference; as duration, a period gathers discrete moments into a whole and so expresses our sense that things always stay pretty much the same. The notion of parts, partition, and division bespeaks the discontinuity of history, just as the notion of wholes bespeaks its continuity. Neither can be reduced to the other. Historical periods are always parts of some larger whole—namely, universal history; so also, the wholes that are individual historical periods are susceptible of being subdivided into their constituent parts. Two dialectically related hermeneutic principles are implied by wholes and parts. Given continuity, everything in history is part of something else and is to be explained by reference to its context. Given discontinuity, everything historical is autonomous, a whole that is to be explained only by reference to itself.

Given unperiodized continuity, moreover, nothing in history can be denied relevance to the task of human self-understanding. "Man is the subject of every history; and to know him well, we must see him and consider him, as history alone can present him to us, in every age, in every country, in every state, in life and in death. History, therefore, of all kinds, of civilised and uncivilised, of ancient and modern nations . . . is useful to bring us acquainted with out species, nay, with ourselves. . . . When [a writer] gives us a good history of Peruvians or Mexicans, of Chinese or Tartars, of Muscovites or Negroes, we may blame him, but we must blame ourselves much more, if we do not make it a good lesson of philosophy" (229). Given discontinuity, on the other hand, we need concern ourselves only with one history: namely, our own. "Some [histories] are to be read, some to be studied; and some may be neglected entirely, not only without detriment, with advantage. Some are the proper object of one man's curiosity, some of another's, and some of all men's; but all history is not an object of curiosity for any man" (219). "The shortness of human life considered," we ought to "confine ourselves almost entirely in our study of history to such histories as have an immediate relation to our professions or to our rank and situation in the society to which we belong" (230). For Bolingbroke, this meant that only European political history after 1600 need be studied.[36]

"Bolingbroke cannot imagine any cultivated man studying the remoter and less sympathetic periods of history," J. G. A. Pocock concludes, and he is half right.[37] The truth is that Bolingbroke wants it both ways: only our own history is worth studying, but a good historian can make any history our own. What I am suggesting is that this is an objective contradiction, endemic to the nature of historical study, not merely a reflection of Bolingbroke's prehistoricist naiveté, temporal provinciality, or personal arrogance and laziness. There are a number of reasons why Bolingbroke confines the student of history to modernity: first, since Temple, antiquarians had been accused of being "so injudicious in the choice of what was fit to be told or to be let alone . . . [that] it is hardly worth the time or pains to be informed."[38] Second, as Bolingbroke writes, only a monk could afford not to be selective in some way. "In [Bodin's] method, we are to take first a general view of universal history . . . and then to study all particular histories and systems" (195).[39] Beginning with universal history seems likely to prevent one from ever getting to the end of it: that is, to the present, to life and action. Further, only in modernity are "the facts . . . sufficiently verified" to be reliable and useful (242); ancient history is mostly a fabric of romance, speculation, and lie. Most important, though, is that former times have arrived at their periods. The times before ours are not worth studying precisely insofar as they are over: "The causes then laid having spent themselves, the series of effects derived from them being over, our concern in both [is] consequently at an end" (239).

With the advent of modernity in 1600, the old story came to an end in Bolingbroke's view, and a new one began.

> The longer this new constitution of affairs continues, the more will this difference [from the old] increase; and although some analogy may remain long between what preceded and what succeeds such a period, yet will this analogy soon become an object of mere curiosity, not of profitable inquiry. . . . Should we persist to carry our researches much higher [into the past] . . . we should misemploy our time. . . . A new system of causes and effects that subsists in our time and whereof our conduct is to be a part, arising at the last period, and all that passes in our time being dependent on what has passed since that period or being immediately relative to it, we are extremely concerned to be well informed about all these passages. (239)

What has already passed concerns us now, because the two are mutually interpretive parts of the whole that is "our time."

Bolingbroke's exclusive concern with the present, however, cannot be combined with the hermeneutic principle that only a whole is intrinsically intelligible. Despite its epistemological authority, experience has no historical authority, because it is finite and therefore does not comprehend most historical wholes. "Experience is doubly defective; we are born too late to see the beginning, and we die too soon to see the end of many things. History supplies both these defects" (186). By contrast with the examples gleaned from one's own experience, "the examples which history presents to us, both of men and of events, are generally complete: the whole example is before us, and consequently the whole lesson" (185). More specifically, "in ancient history . . . the examples are complete. . . . In modern history, the examples may be and sometimes are incomplete" (186). The defect of modern history is that it is partial; it shades off inconclusively into the dark future; and a part is necessarily unintelligible if the whole to which it belongs is unknown. With Bacon, Bolingbroke "affirms divine history to have this prerogative, that the narration may be before the fact" (189). Human history, by contrast, can only be written ex post facto, when the story is over and understanding it becomes possible. Periodization reflects the fact that change is real; histories do end. With stories that have come to an end, however, with the past that is past and bygone, we have no immediate concern. The only stories that concern us are our own, those in which we participate. Stories in which "our conduct is to be a part," however, are necessarily incomplete. For Bolingbroke's philosophy of history, then, the quandary is this: only history that is over is understandable, but only history that is not over is worth understanding.

One hesitates to conclude that this represents the fundamental form of Bolingbroke's unresolved dialectic, but it is certainly a far-reaching expression of it. The *Letters* manifest the dual needs of a philosophy of history: the need, first, for a notion of periods, of history as completable and completed, understandable because whole, and whole because over. A past period corresponds, moreover, to history as an object of consciousness, subject to the tests of critical self-consciousness. The very fact that critique is applicable only to a history that is over bespeaks the ideal autonomy of self-consciousness from historical forces. Yet, no less emphatically, the *Letters* affirm the inescapable presence of the past. Nothing is ever completely over. And so Bolingbroke affirms a notion of history—even past history—as irremediably incomplete, ongoing, and belonging to a perpetually unfinished story. Incomplete history is not an object of consciousness. Rather, consciousness is part of it. Being a participant, consciousness registers history less as an intelligible meaning than as a senseless force which reduces its own autonomy and encroaches on its own power.

This duality in all its various forms rends and splits Bolingbroke's *Letters on the Study and Use of History* so thoroughly as to be one of its distinctive characteristics. Undoubtedly Bolingbroke fails to resolve these implicit contradictions. What may be more important than this failure, however, is that he at least exhibits the real, important problems in philosophy of history that he cannot resolve—cannot, in part, because he does not see that they are problems. Yet, even this very obliviousness to contradictions that now seem so patent holds out some hope. Without grasping it, Bolingbroke's *Letters* anticipate a synthesis which, without paradox or simplification, could reconcile the meaning with the force, the factuality with the efficacy, the study with the use of history.

4

Hume on Others

In distinguishing his *Treatise of Human Nature* from the efforts of his predecessors, David Hume described it as being placed on "a foundation almost entirely new," one that comprehended their narrower horizons within "a complete system of the sciences" (*T* xx).[1] More than just an inquiry into the limits of human knowledge like Locke's *Essay,* more than just an investigation of our sense of value like Hutcheson's *Inquiry into the Original of Our Ideas of Beauty and Virtue,* Hume's *Treatise* offers an anatomy of the whole, the heart as well as head. It seeks to include both realms within the comprehensive science that is their common ground. With others in the modern subjectivist tradition, Hume posits that common ground—where reason and passion are one—as human nature; for him the universal science is the science of man.

Bold in its breadth and sweep, the *Treatise of Human Nature* is not only ambitious, but militantly humanistic. However divergent from Toland on the primacy of reason,[2] however dubious about reading nature like a book,[3] Hume takes up a position like Toland's in one important respect. If the science of human nature includes everything that can claim to be called science or knowledge, then two consequences for religion immediately follow. Hume's monism—his premise that all knowledge is unified and integral, such that is forms a "complete system"—implies, first, that the body of knowledge constituting "natural religion" depends on human comprehension no less than any other; second, it implies that supernatural or revealed religion conceived as independent of the science of man is disqualified as knowledge. All understanding is human understanding.

But "human understanding," as we saw in chapter one, is an ambiguous phrase. Locke (I there argued) concentrated so exclusively on understanding *by* human beings that he undervalued and some-times disparaged the understanding *of* human beings, the interpre-tation of what they say and write. Now, in considering Hume's thought on hermeneutic questions, we need to return to this ambi-guity and focus on the relation between its two poles. Hume differs from Locke (inter alia) precisely by explicitly positing a global, in-tegral science in which humankind is both knower and known. Moral science thus comprehends human understanding in both the subjec-tive and objective senses: understanding by man and of man. The *Treatise* suggests by both its theses and its arrangement that knowl-edge—human understanding in Locke's epistemological sense—can be adequately conceived only if joined—human understanding in a hermeneutic sense—to human feeling, and specifically fellow feeling, or sympathy. Hume's science of man is inalienably tied to under-standing others—to being understanding, humane, and kind and manifesting one's inalienable commonality with humankind.

It would be mistaken to posit an absolute break between Hume and Locke, even with respect to the comprehensiveness of their ambitions. One of the major conclusions of Locke's *Essay*, after all, was that "morality is the proper science and business of mankind in general" (4. 12. 1), and Pope apparently understood this to mean that "the proper study of mankind is man." The idea of a global human science that would include ethics had already been conceived, at least in embyro, by Locke. Despite his friends' urgings, of course, Locke did not write a second essay to make good on his claim that "morality is capable of demonstration, as well as mathematics" (3. 9. 16). The essay that he did write, however, must certainly be considered a preliminary contribution to moral science in a certain sense, the empirical sense to which Hume too is committed and which he intends to extend. If Locke concluded that "this way of getting and improving our knowledge in substances only by expe-rience and history . . . is all that the weakness of our faculties . . . can attain to" (4. 12. 10), Hume's efforts in the *Treatise,* from this perspective, are to expand the province of "experience and history" to include human nature as well.

Yet, although Hume "attempt[s] to introduce the experimental method of reasoning into moral subjects," as he puts it in his subtitle, he knew as well as the modern reader that, for not just contingent but essential reasons, transposing the method of the physical sciences to the moral world is hardly unproblematical, for nothing like what is now called the experimental method, he asserts, is possible in the investigation of moral subjects:

> When I am at a loss to know the effects of one [physical] body upon another in any situation, I need only put them in that situation, and observe what results from it. But should I endeavour to clear up after the same manner any doubt in moral philosophy, by placing myself in the same case with that which I consider, 'tis evident this reflection and premeditation would so disturb the operation of my natural principles as must render it impossible to form any just conclusion from the phenomenon. We must therefore glean up our experiments in this science from a cautious observation of human life, and take them as they appear in the common course of the world, by men's behaviour. (*T* xxiii)

Although the synonymity of "experimental" and "experiential" allowed Hume to think of the moral sciences as "experimental," nevertheless, as James Noxon rightly observes, "what [Hume] knew about human nature he had learned from his own observation and the records of history and not from experimental psychology."[4]

Even if he thought of his work as "experimental," we need to give Hume credit for acknowledging that in the science of man one kind of experiment, at least, is impossible: self-experiment. For Locke the case was quite the contrary. "The understanding, like the eye, . . . takes no notice of itself," Locke had written in the introduction to the *Essay;* but he immediately qualifies and retracts the statement, since it implies that the only medium available for investigating one's own understanding is *other people's* experience—and that, for the Lockean empiricist, is an epistemological absurdity: "We may as rationally hope to see with other men's eyes," Locke scoffed, "as to know by other men's understandings" (1. 3. 24).

Hume, by contrast, refuses to back away from the implications of this insight: the human scientist cannot take himself—his own thoughts, words, or practices—as evidence of human nature, for nature is "disturbed" by the very consciousness of it. Since human nature (no less than physical nature) is hidden from mere self-consciousness, what Locke called "reflection" cannot be the foundation of human science; therefore the putatively infallible intuition of self must give way to interpretation. Like his fellow historian Bolingbroke, Hume considers introspection insufficient, even deceptive, for the purposes of human understanding. The solitary individual is unequal to the task of the comprehensive human science envisioned by Hume's *Treatise*. Understanding others, in brief, is the condition of the possibility of the science of man.

This is to state with exaggerated simplicity one strand of Hume's thought, the one I find most prominent in the *Treatise,* viewed from a hermeneutic angle. The fact remains, however, that Hume is very divided on a number of issues bearing on this topic. He is no more favorably disposed toward interpreters and commentators than is Locke—perhaps less so, given his distrust of revealed religion and the interpretation of Scripture. In the *Natural History of Religion* he sounds more like Toland when he calls exegesis "the practice of warping the tenets of religion in order to serve temporal interests."[5] Legal interpretation in the second *Enquiry* fares little better: "In general, it may safely be affirmed that jurisprudence is . . . different from all the sciences, and that in many of its nicer questions, there cannot properly be said to be truth or falsehood on either side. If one pleader bring the case under any former law or precedent, . . . the opposite pleader is not at a loss to find an opposite analogy or comparison; and the preference given by the judge is often founded more on taste and imagination than on any solid argument" (*ECPM* 308–09).

Moreover, even when Hume most closely approaches a full-blown hermeneutics, he does not follow his argument to the end. For instance, it is apparent that self-reflection would be displaced and understanding others would become the exclusive method of human science if it could be shown that, even were self-intuition possible, there exists no self to intuit. Hume's arguments toward that end are among his best known: "There are some philosophers who imagine we are every moment intimately conscious of what we call our SELF" begins the famous section on personal identity. "Unluckily all these positive assertions are contrary to that very experience which is pleaded for them; nor have we any idea of *self* after the manner it is here explained" (*T* 251). Yet, despite this emphatic assertion, the second volume of the *Treatise* flatly ignores it and assumes a consciousness of self, quite oblivious to previous arguments against it: "'Tis evident that the idea or rather impression of ourselves is always intimately present with us, and that our consciousness gives us . . . [a] lively conception of our own person" (*T* 317). Plausible explanations can be offered for this apparent contradiction,[6] and Hume's appendix to the first volume tempers considerably the confidence of his earlier attack on the idea of self. Nevertheless, the fact that in the second and third volumes of the *Treatise* Hume assumes the immediacy and adequacy of self-consciousness illustrates in a striking way his ambivalence on hermeneutic issues. Many elements of his thought (as in the social sciences today) are patently not hermeneutic, and in certain respects are antipathetic to it—so much so that Hume is considered the father not only of the human sciences but also of positivism.[7]

Most of the nonhermeneutic aspects of Hume's thought, as of Locke's, can be grouped under the rubric of "individualism," though perhaps the larger rubric is what we would now call "foundationalism." In the sense employed here, foundationalism is logically antithetical to hermeneutics, in that a foundation is defined as something that grounds interpretation but is not itself an interpretation. On this definition, foundational visions posit some ultimate given, some bedrock of solidity where muddiness comes to an end, some hard knowledge that marks the limit—hence the secondariness—of interpretation.

Hume's *Treatise* is foundational in both purpose and method, as we see from the parallelism in this crucial sentence from the introduction: "As the science of man is the only solid foundation for the other sciences, so the only solid foundation we can give to this science itself must be laid on experience and observation" (*T* xx). To take experience as foundational is, of course, the hallmark of empiricism. But it can be taken as such only because empiricism conceives of experience in a special way: namely, as sensation, perception, or impression. For the foundationalist, something must be first, original, not derivative, not the result of interpretation; and for Hume, impressions constitute that epistemological ultimate. "'Tis certain, that the mind in its perceptions must begin somewhere," Hume writes; "since the impressions precede their correspondent ideas, there must be some impressions which, without any introduction, make their appearance in the soul" (*T* 275). Perhaps experiences conceived as other than impressions are not private mental events; perhaps knowledge (and not just the communication of it) is essentially public, in which case there would not need to be any first knower or first knowledge. Even if we can in some sense know by other men's understandings, however, it is beyond doubt impossible to see with other men's eyes. Humean impressions are private, one's very own, and Hume's empiricism (like that of his forebears) is an individualist epistemology insofar as it makes logically private impressions foundational.[8]

This individualism belongs to a broader foundationalist impulse of empiricism, the nominalist tendency to conceive of the particular as more real than the general, the individual as more real than the communal. "Everything that exists, is particular," Hume asserts in the *Abstract*.[9] The same tendency emerges in Hume's atomism, as when he says: "All beings in the universe, considered in themselves, appear entirely loose and independent of each other" (*T* 466).[10] Beings, including ideas, are associated not in themselves but only by reason of the human mind. Relations are human artifacts. For cognitive atomism, the part is prior to the whole; and insofar as the part is at bottom autonomous and independent of every other part, wholes as such are ontologically suspect. Not relations but only the relata are real, as is evident in Hume's conclusion regarding the ultimate relation, identity. "All the disputes concerning the identity of connected objects are merely verbal, except so far as the relation of parts gives rise to some fiction or imaginary principle of union" (*T* 262).

The phrase "merely verbal" in this sentence exemplifies another nominalist, nonhermeneutic element in Hume's foundationalism: his distrust of language and rhetoric. "Merely verbal" is for Hume and innumerable others equivalent to fictive. Unreal questions occasion merely verbal disputes, words summon more words; and just that interminable flow of language is the evidence of unreality. No profound knowledge is required "to discover the present imperfect condition of the sciences," Hume complains. "There is nothing which is not the subject of debate and which men of learning are not of contrary opinions. The most trivial question escapes not our controversy. . . . Amidst all this bustle 'tis not reason which carries the prize, but eloquence" (*T* xxiii). Individualist foundationalism takes controversy and dispute to be abnormal; language is the symptom of epistemological pathology. The mark of philosophical health is silence; for the solitary individual who has penetrated to the foundations has no need for talk.

"I am first affrighted and confounded with that forlorn solitude in which I am placed in my philosophy, and fancy myself some strange uncouth monster, who not being able to mingle and unite in society, has been expelled from all human commerce" (*T* 264). Whether or not Hume here attests, or merely affects, a desire to escape loneliness and embrace human society, it remains the case that his individualism works in theory against it. Society is doubly suspect, both by reason of the language that is the cause and effect of sociality and because if society is something like a polis, not just an aggregate of individuals, it must constitute a real relation, a genuine whole that cannot be reduced to its parts.

Hume's political theory, according to John Stewart, "includes no real body politic. . . . On the contrary, he begins with individuals—men who perceive—set in a world inhabited by individuals. For him the individual is the original or genuine unit."[11] Hume sometimes refers to a pre-social state of nature in which man lives in a "savage and solitary condition" in which "every individual labors apart" (*T* 485). On this common view, society as such is a post-natural, artificial condition. Justice, an "artificial" virtue, is what makes civil life possible in Hume's view, and the basis of justice is property. "Where there is no property," Hume writes, "there can be no injustice" (*ECHU* 163). "What is a man's property? Anything which it is lawful for him, and for him alone, to use" (*ECPM* 197). Property is the unsharable, what is proper to the proprietor and to "him alone." The civil life erected on this basis is not necessarily social or political life, for property-based justice is merely the legal recognition of inalienable loneliness.

It would seem that Hume's insistence on solitude would be mitigated by his interest in common life, which, as David Fate Norton and David Livingston have convincingly shown,[12] is decisively privileged in Hume's philosophy. "Philosophical decisions," Hume asserts in a paradigmatic sentence, "are nothing but the reflections of common life, methodized and corrected" (*ECHU* 162). Indeed, a treatise on human nature might be said to have the humanly common as its focal subject. When Hume speaks of the "common," however, it is less often with respect to social and public life than with respect to the mean—in both senses. Defined in terms of class, on the one hand, the common is low: "True philosophy approaches nearer to the sentiments of the vulgar, . . . in their common and careless way of thinking" (*T* 222–23). Defined in terms of frequency of occurrence, on the other hand, it indicates the typical, the common being something like the average or the statistical mean. This probabilistic usage points toward what in our century is called the covering-law model of social science, the model underlying positivist conceptions of social science.[13] But in whichever sense we take it, the point here is that, under the individualist impulse, Hume hardly ever associates "common" life with communal life, the life of mutual understanding. When he considers homogenizing influences which unite people in communities, influences such as social tradition and education, he frequently stigmatizes them as either merely seconding the primary capacities of nature—cultivating, though not producing, natural resources—or simply perverting them. If people are naturally individuals, then what is shared and common among them must be in some sense the effect of unnatural forces.

Finally among the nonhermeneutic elements of Hume's thought are the dualisms that pervade his work, especially the *Treatise*. Insofar as ethics is founded on passion not reason, insofar as to call something good or beautiful is never to say something true, insofar as *ought* can never be derived from *is,* there can be no unified human science—only at best the bifurcation of the positive from the interpretive sciences or at worst one real science plus something else that merely pretends to be. Hume's tendency to a scientistic monism, which promises to overcome this schism, only makes matters worse. "The moral philosopher," he writes, "fixes the principles of his science in the same manner as the physician or natural philosopher becomes acquainted with the nature of plants, minerals, and other external objects" (*ECHU* 84). If so, then for the purposes of a science of man it is no more necessary to "understand" other people than to "understand" plants, minerals, and other external objects. Hermeneutics thus gets short shrift or no shrift at all.

Yet it cannot ultimately be right to say that Hume creates a unified science of man by subsuming human science under the science of physical nature, for that is not to create human science, but rather to obviate it. Though the foundationalist elements and their several ramifications, which we have just sketchily reviewed, are entirely characteristic of Hume's major philosophical work, a summary of his thought that stopped here would be drastically truncated, even as an outline. Missing is the entire panoply of implicitly hermeneutic tendencies that make Hume's overall project not reductive but inclusive—"complete." His comprehensive science of man envisions a way of thinking in which understanding others is the condition, as well as the result, of science.

Nothing does more to counterbalance the individualist tendencies in Hume's thought than his emphasis on human nature per se. "It is universally acknowledged that there is a great uniformity among the actions of men in all nations and ages, and that human nature remains still the same in its principles and operations. The same motives always produce the same actions. The same events follow from the same causes" (*ECHU* 83). And again, "nature is more uniform in the sentiments of the mind than in most feelings of the body, and produces a nearer resemblance in the inward than in the outward part of human kind" (*Essays,* 163). What is common among human beings is uniform to the kind, and in that sense natural. Hume here takes not difference but uniformity as given, and so it is not sociality and community but rather individuality that needs to be explained: "We must not . . . expect that this uniformity of human action should be carried to such a length as that all men, in the same circumstances, will always act precisely in the same manner. . . . We learn from thence the great force of custom and education" (*ECHU* 85–86). Custom and education here serve the function of denaturalizing, not by creating conformities but by creating differences among people. From the perspective of human nature, individuality appears derivative and aberrant; difference is the artificial effect of extrinsic influences.

More essential and humanly natural than individuality is sociality, and Hume's emphasis on the fact of communal interdependence as intrinsic to human beings far exceeds what is typical of most empiricists and rationalists both. "Men cannot live without society," he exclaims (*T* 402). "Every man has a strong connexion with society, and perceives the impossibility of his solitary subsistence" (*ECPM* 215). Solitariness is not just inconvenient or unpleasant; it is ultimately impossible. Some of the reasons for this impossibility are biological: because human reproduction is bisexual, "men are necessarily born in a family-society" (*ECPM* 190). After birth, moreover, "the long and helpless infancy of man" insures continuing dependence on the family at least until the age of maturity (*ECPM* 206), and even adulthood does not confer self-sufficiency. "The mutual dependence of men is so great in all societies that scarce any action is entirely complete in itself or is performed without some reference to the actions of others" (*ECHU* 89). Again and again, Hume minimizes, if not denies, individual autonomy.

One consequence of this denial is that, like Shaftesbury,[14] he typically rejects both the Hobbist strong version and the Lockean weak version of the "state of nature": human beings are neither at war with each other nor even essentially estranged from each other. "'Tis utterly impossible for men to remain any considerable time in that savage condition which precedes society; but . . . [man's] very first state and situation may justly be esteem'd social. . . . The supposed *state of nature* . . . [is] a mere philosophical fiction, which never had and never could have any reality" (*T* 493). This bears repeating: the very first state is social. The pre-social condition of man Hume considers not just savage, but unreal. It is not valid, then, to ask what humans were like before they were combined in communal groups; there were none, for there is nothing human that is not social.[15] This is to say, a human society does not consist in an aggregate of atomic individuals; it is itself individual, indivisible, and indecomposable into more fundamental units. When the whole is not derivative from, but coincident with, the parts that comprise it— that is, when part and whole are fundamental to each other—then there is no first, no origin, no absolute foundation. Given the idea of a society which is neither original nor derived, individualist foundationalism becomes impossible.

If Hume rejects the state of nature because man's very first state is social, no more does he have any need of its corollary, contract theory. Like "creationist" accounts of the origin of the universe, contract theory is an account of beginnings, for it purports to explain the origin of society. It is unlike creationism, of course, in requiring no divine agency; but it does require a miracle of sorts—namely, the genesis of social order out of individualist chaos. Hume departs from conventional contract theory in a number of respects, but central to all such respects is the absence of miracles, of the need to postulate a "Suddenly one day . . . ." In Hume's stories, as Jerome Christensen observes, "we can detect no origin that categorically separates the way things are going on now from some past when things were completely different."[16] Instead of a creation story, we find gradual evolution and development—specifically the development of self-interest—which obviates the need to posit a radical break or beginning. In this case, as in others, Hume adopts what he calls "that impious maxim of the ancient philosophy, *Ex nihilo, nihil fit*" (*ECHU*

164n.).[17] When Hume writes that man's "very first" state was social, he evidently means not that man was created social, but that there was no miracle, no creation, no Adamic first man at all. What is does not come from nothing, but always from a prior existent, something that was. In history, all genesis is by unfolding, explication, interpretation.

Just as human society does not begin *ex nihilo,* neither do the social creatures that constitute it. Hume's skepticism about the self or soul, we noted above, has hermeneutic implications in that it points away from introspective self-consciousness toward understanding others as the method of the human sciences. But these two are not antithetical in Hume. Strictly speaking, Hume does not deny the self in the first volume of the *Treatise;* he concludes, more precisely, that "there is no such idea" as the self—that is, the self is not an idea but rather the association of a plurality of ideas. In explicating this associative concept of personhood, Hume employs a telling analogy, one that portrays the self as itself social: "I cannot compare the soul more properly to any thing than to a republic or commonwealth in which the several members are united by the reciprocal ties of government and subordination and give rise to other persons, who propagate the same republic in the incessant changes of its parts" (*T* 261). The primary function of this metaphor is to illustrate the possibility of a nonhomogeneous unity, an identity without underlying permanent substance but possessing a continuity over time. In such an identity no part, but only the whole, stays the same. If commonwealths are real identities, he suggests (and what could be more real than the British Commonwealth?), so are selves. Like England itself, selves are not "self-identical" but exist only hermeneutically, in unity-in-diversity and permanence-in-change. The second implication of the metaphor is no less far-reaching than the first: it is not just that atomic selves unite with others, but that others unite in them. The self is not a self-identity but a relation, something like a social relation, a polis, a republic, a commonwealth. In the one is the many. I look into myself and find others; and when that is the case, introspection of self and interpretation of others meet and merge.

Locke defines reflection as "that notice which the mind takes of its own operations" (*Essay,* 2. 1. 4). In his initial definition (*T* 7–8), Hume concurs; yet, as he proceeds, the difference from Locke becomes palpable. For when Hume thinks of the mind, he thinks not just of a tabula rasa that receives impressions but of a mirror. In it one sees not the world (as in classical representationalism) or even oneself and one's ideas (as in Locke). "The minds of men are mirrors to one another," Hume writes, "because they reflect each other" (*T* 365). When we review our words and deeds, he explains, "we consider how they appear in the eyes of those who approach and regard us"; thus we develop the "constant habit of surveying our-selves, as it were, in reflection" (*ECPM* 276). So conceived, reflective self-knowledge is not intuitive and private, but mediated and social. It is incorrect, then, simply to say that Hume displaces reflection and substitutes interpretation of others as the basis of the human sciences; for, given his concept of reflection as mediated self-knowledge, self-reflection consists in understanding others.[18]

On this view, not only is Cartesian doubt impossible, as Hume argues elsewhere; so too is Cartesian certainty. The cogito loses its foundational function—even though it cannot be replaced by any-thing more primary or original. There is no "original principle, which cannot possibly be fallacious or deceitful," Hume declares (*ECHU* 150). There is no pope within, no bedrock of certainty, no basis of interpretation that is not itself an interpretation, only inter-pretation all the way down. The self—the firmest foundation dis-covered by modern philosophy—turns out to be a reflection, an interpretation, primordially derivative, originally imitative.

Given Hume's notion of the socially constituted self, reason be-comes reasoning-with; thought is no longer just the silent *logos,* but social intercourse, dialogue, talk. Thus language acquires a certain authority. When Hume considers the language of ethics, to take a prominent example, gone is the knee-jerk contempt for the "merely verbal": "The very nature of language guides us almost infallibly in forming a judgment [concerning ethical qualities]; and as every tongue possesses one set of words which are taken in a good sense and another in the opposite, the least acquaintance with the idiom suffices to direct us in collecting and arranging the estimable or blameable qualities of men" (*ECPM* 174). Considered in the context of empiricist distrust of language, Hume's claim of linguistic reli-ability represents an almost complete volte-face. However much moral value is based on sentiment, in Hume's view, it cannot be explained as private sentiment. The good is what people term good, not what any individual person does. There must therefore be such things as public sentiments, common feelings, and these are ex-pressed in common language. "Every man's interest is peculiar to himself, and the aversions and desires which result from it cannot be supposed to affect others in a like degree. General language, therefore, being formed for general use, must be moulded on some more general views . . . in conformity to sentiments, which arise from the general interests of the community" (*ECPM* 228–29). Communally acceptable moral judgments are to be discerned in the communal language that reflects not private feelings, interests, or judgments but the general interests of the community. It is almost as if Hume views language, which cannot be private (if Wittgenstein is right), as the objectivization of the disinterestedness and commonality crucial to moral judgment. For all his denigration of "verbal disputes" elsewhere, then, Hume is relatively trusting of moral language because relatively dubious about solitary experience as the basis of ethics.

That knowledge is social, hence tied to language, is most strikingly apparent in Hume's contention that knowledge is intrinsically public, not just with regard to moral matters but all kinds of opinions. "I am persuaded that upon examination we shall find more than one half of those opinions that prevail among mankind to be owing to education, and that the principles which are thus implicitly embraced overbalance those which are owing either to abstract reasoning or experience" (*T* 117). This should be contrasted with the skeptical critique of "implicit faith" in the Locke–Toland tradition. For the hyperskeptical Hume, not only Catholics' beliefs about transubstantiation, for example, nor, more generally, religionists' beliefs about God, but most people's beliefs about most things derive not from their own but from others' understandings, and theirs from still others'. What Bolingbroke called "the force of example" operates everywhere.

It is understandable, perhaps, that in matters of opinion "we find it necessary to prop our tottering judgement on the correspondent approbation of mankind" (*ECPM* 276). Yet Hume does not limit cognitive interdependence to *doxa* but extends it to *epistēmē* as well. He rather boldly contends that "even mathematics" is "in some measure dependent on the science of man" (*T* xix). In mathematics—in which solitary inquiry would seem sufficient to offer decisive, a priori proof and so determine truth without consultation—"there is no algebraist nor mathematician so expert in his science as to place entire confidence in any truth immediately upon his discovery of it. . . . Every time he runs over his proofs, his confidence increases, but still more by the approbation of his friends, and is raised to its utmost perfection by the universal assent and applauses of the learned world" (*T* 180). Is this increased confidence just a fact of the psychology or sociology of belief? Or, as confidence "raised to its utmost perfection," does it belong to epistemology as well? If publicity makes knowledge certain as well as credible, then indubitable truth (as well as undoubted belief) is never explicable by reference to private thought alone. Even of his own skepticism, Hume wrote at the conclusion of the *Treatise,* "I feel all my opinions loosen and fall of themselves when unsupported by the approbation of others" (*T* 264).

To contend with Hume that all sciences are dependent on the science of man is thus to imply that all science is at least in part hermeneutic. Every realm of knowledge, from self-knowledge to mathematics, to some degree involves understanding others. A critical question for Hume, then, is how understanding others is possible. His best-known answer, in a word, is sympathy. He has a second answer, as we will see, but sympathy is the more fully developed— and several scholars before me have pointed out the specifically hermeneutical significance of Hume's account of it.[19] Admittedly, Hume seems to limit the significance of sympathy to ethics (moral science in the narrow sense), for his primary discussions of sympathy are located in the parts of the *Treatise* and *Enquiries* devoted to feeling and value. But, as I have already begun to suggest, there is good evidence for Hume's having extended the provenance of human understanding—and thus of sympathy—well beyond the social virtues, where the subject is first broached. Nevertheless, it is with ethics that we must begin.

For Hume, it is not too much to say, sympathy is the moral sense. He calls it the "chief source of moral distinctions" (*T* 618) and follows Hutcheson both in postulating a moral sense to combat the moral rationalists and in equating the morally good with the "public good"[20] to combat the Hobbist party of self-love. Hume differs from Hutcheson, however, in discerning no innate human disposition toward the good in the abstract, the public good, or in fact any good other than that of the self. Thus he writes of justice, the fundamental civic value, that it "is certainly approved of for no other reason than because it has tendency to the public good. And the public good is indifferent to us except in so far as sympathy interests us in it" (*T* 618). The morally good consists in good will toward others; but we have no interest in others apart from sympathy, and so moral conduct in this as in all instances depends on the operation of sympathy.

Not just moral but other kinds of value too have a social and hence sympathetic element. Rather than mentioning all the other areas in which sympathy plays a part, I will give just one, particularly striking example, apparently far removed from the social virtues. "No enjoyment is sincere," Hume asserts, "without some reference to company and society" (*ECPM* 280). Even sensual enjoyment is not purely sensory; sexual pleasure is mostly determined by sympathy. In his essay "The Stoic" Hume writes that "neither true wisdom nor true happiness can be found [in *apatheia*]. . . . With whatever ingredient you mix [the social pleasures], they are still predominant. As sorrow cannot overcome them, so neither can sensual pleasure obscure them. The joys of love, however tumultuous, banish not the tender sentiments of sympathy and affection. They even derive their chief influence from that generous passion" (*Essays*, 151). Shaftesbury, from whom Hume is borrowing here, is at once clearer and less sentimental: "The courtesans, and even the commonest of women, who live by prostitution, know very well how necessary it is that every one whom they entertain with their beauty should believe there are satisfactions reciprocal, and that pleasures are no less given than received. And were this imagination to be wholly taken away, there would be hardly any of the grosser sort of mankind who would not perceive their remaining pleasure to be of slender estimation."[21] One's own pleasure in sex is mostly the other's.

This what Hume finds so astonishing about sympathy: it amounts to affirming the empiricist's absurdity. One can in fact be pleased by others' pleasures, feel others' feelings, have their experiences, share their ideas. "No quality of human nature is more remarkable, both in itself and in its consequences, than that propensity we have to sympathize with others and to receive by communication their inclinations and sentiments, however different from or even contrary to our own" (*T* 316). We should be careful here not to equate Hume's usage of the word *sympathy* with our own. For him it does not designate a feeling, and specifically not pity.[22] Hume often writes of sympathy with happiness (for example, *ECPM* 220, 260). Congratulation is no less a function of sympathy than commiseration. Sympathy is not a feeling, then, but rather a sense, a faculty of feeling, specifically of feeling-with.

By *feeling,* moreover, Hume means more than "inclinations and sentiments." Beyond the passions, sympathy comprehends and explains the communication of all manner of opinion, belief, and knowledge. "This is not only conspicuous in children, who implicitly embrace every opinion proposed to them; but also in men of the greatest judgement and understanding, who find it very difficult to follow their own reason or inclination in opposition to that of their friends and daily companions" (*T* 316). As James Farr has rightly noted, "The cognitive implications of sympathy need to be underscored," for although Hume introduces this faculty in book 2 ("Of the Passions"), it involves not just passional but "both cognitive and affective elements."[23] Bridging the two spheres, sympathy grounds the possibility of a unified, "complete" science—a science of the whole man.

Just as important in relation to hermeneutical issues, sympathy unites not only two objects—thought and feeling—but also two subjects. Sympathy receives its first exposition in the section on "the love of fame," where it is summoned to explain how the passions which have ourselves as their object—pride and humility—are excited not only by virtue, beauty, and riches but also by an unexpected source—namely, others' views of us. Beside the "original causes of pride and humility," Hume writes, "there is a secondary one in the opinions of others, which has an equal influence on the affections. Our reputation, our character, our name are considerations of vast weight and importance; and even the other causes of pride—virtue, beauty and riches—have little influence when not seconded by the opinions and sentiments of others" (*T* 316). One might call sympathy a faculty of the secondhand—if there were a first in the matter. But first and second, as we see in Hume's phrasing above, are just the distinctions that sympathy blurs. When the "secondary" causes of pride and humility have "an equal influence" to the "original"—indeed, when the original "has little influence" until it is "seconded"—then the distinctions between primary and secondary, original and interpreted, self and other, lose their hard edges.

More specifically, the point Hume is making is this. Quite aside from the things on which we value ourselves, pride is caused by our being envied, just as humility is caused by our being despised—and what accounts for both is sympathy with others. We adopt their opinions, values, feelings, even and especially when their opinions are about ourselves, the very subject about which (on a Lockean account) it would seem that we are most infallible. In fact, however, about ourselves we are most liable to uncertainty and mistake. Others' judgments and our sympathy with them, Hume insists, "influence almost all our opinions, but must have a peculiar influence when we judge of our own worth and character" (*T* 321).

Hume explains the inner workings of sympathetic influence as follows: "The idea, or rather impression, of ourselves is always intimately present with us. . . . Whatever object, therefore, is related to ourselves must be conceived with a like vivacity of conception. . . . Nature has preserved a great resemblance among all human creatures, and . . . we never remark any passion or principle in others, of which, in some degree or other, we may not find a parallel in ourselves. . . . This resemblance must very much contribute to make us enter into the sentiments of others and embrace them with facility and pleasure" (*T* 317–18). Several features of this account need to be emphasized. First, we understand what is like ourselves, and best understand what is most like ourselves—because we best understand ourselves. The self-presence of consciousness enables sympathy with others. "Our consciousness gives us so lively a conception of our own person, that 'tis not possible to imagine that any thing can in this particular go beyond it" (*T* 317). For Hume, then, the possibility of understanding others is based in part on self-understanding.

Yet he does not conceive this basis of sympathy in the self as an obstacle or limit that circumscribes the possibility of understanding others. "We enter, to be sure, more readily into sentiments which resemble those we feel every day. But no passion . . . can be entirely indifferent to us, because there is none of which every man has not within him at least the seeds and first principles" (*ECPM* 222). Adapting Terence's principle to his own hermeneutic purposes, Hume implies, I am a man, and nothing human can be unintelligible to me. Although sympathy extends only as far as resemblance, then, this implies no restriction of its scope, for the fact of common nature guarantees that "every human creature resembles ourselves" (*T* 359). "The humanity of one man is the humanity of everyone" (*ECPM* 273). Embracing all human beings, the scope of sympathetic understanding is coextensive with human nature.[24]

Insofar as sympathy is Hume's answer to the question of how it is possible to know other people, we can agree with Farr's conclusion that "sympathy is preeminently a category of Hume's epistemology."[25] But more than knowing is involved here. Hume subscribes to a similarity theory of understanding, and because his hermeneutics of sympathy is based on resemblance, what is involved is not just knowing but being, for what one can understand depends on what one is. For this reason, sympathetic understanding exceeds epistemology and approaches ontogeny or philogeny. Sympathy not only derives from the similarity among human beings that makes mutual understanding possible; it also produces it.[26] Hume writes, for example, that "the human mind is of a very imitative nature; nor is it possible for any set of men to converse often together without acquiring a similitude of manners and communicating to each other their vices as well as virtues" (*Essays*, 202). Sympathy communicates and assimilates: it generates the very similarities and resemblances upon which it is based. Such communication operates on the private and domestic level: "A good-natured man finds himself in an instant of the same humour with his company. . . . A cheerful countenance infuses a sensible complacency and serenity into my mind, as an angry or sorrowful one throws a sudden damp upon me. Hatred, resentment, esteem, love, courage, mirth, and melancholy; all these passions I feel more from communication than from my own natural temper and disposition" (*T* 317). The same homogenization through sympathy occurs on a national level: "To this principle we ought to ascribe the great uniformity we may observe in the humours and turn of thinking of those of the same nation; and 'tis much more probable that this resemblance arises from sympathy than from any influence of the soil and climate" (*T* 316–17). It is but one step further (though a step that Hume does not take) to extend the effect of sympathy beyond homes and nations to the species and the genesis of human nature.

The process of sympathetic assimilation goes a good way toward explaining why "there is a great uniformity among the actions of men in all nations and ages and that human nature remains still the same in its principles and operations" (*ECHU* 83). Sympathy is not just the effect of enduring similarities; it is their cause. It communicates, in the Latin sense: produces uniformities among men over differences of time and space. Concerning "tender sympathy with others and a generous concern for our kind and species," Hume writes, "These, wherever they appear, seem to transfuse themselves, in a manner, into each beholder and to call forth, in their own behalf, the same favourable and affectionate sentiments which they exert"

(*ECPM* 178). Humanity recreates itself, calls itself forth. Sympathy, Hume is on the verge of suggesting, produces human nature.

There is another reason why Hume's account of sympathy cannot be confined to epistemology. The communication that he is speaking of, as we have seen, is more unification than transmission of information or transfer of knowledge. It is less cognitive unity—as in consensus, say—than the kind of "communication" referred to in the phrase "communicable diseases." The connotations are often those of contamination and infection: "Who would live amidst perpetual wrangling and scolding and mutual reproaches? The roughness and harshness of these emotions disturb and displease us: we suffer by contagion and sympathy; nor can we remain indifferent spectators" (*ECPM* 257–58). The metaphor of contagion need not imply anything negative about such communication: "Cheerfulness carries great merit with it, and naturally conciliates the good will of mankind. No quality, indeed, more readily communicates itself to all around. . . . Others enter into the same humour, and catch the sentiment, by a contagion or natural sympathy" (*ECPM* 250–51). In such instances of infection, whether of humor or contempt, sympathy is quasi-biological; in other cases, Hume's metaphors of communication are mechanical.[27] "The minds of all men are similar in their feelings and operations; nor can any one be actuated by any affection of which all others are not, in some degree, susceptible. As in strings equally wound up, the motion of one communicates itself to the rest; so all the affections readily pass from one person to another, and beget correspondent movements in every human creature" (*T* 575–76). Sympathy is equivalent in the moral world to gravity in the physical, an action at a distance, a centripetal force that brings people together.

Whether the unity resembles that of epidemic disease or musical harmony, however, Hume's point is that the uniformity effected by sympathy occurs by involuntary, unconscious means. Like Bolingbroke and Reid, Hume does not make the mistake of overintellectualizing the process of understanding. Sympathy is a sense. Like other senses, its operation is more autonomic than conscious; so, too, the community it effects is less like rational consensus than like yawning in unison. Thus conceived, sympathetic communication not only exceeds epistemology—which is exclusively an affair of consciousness, conscious methods, conscious results—it perhaps exceeds hermeneutics as well. It may be that the social virtues are not absolutely different from social diseases. To catch a disease from someone is not necessarily to know anything; nor is it necessarily to understand the carrier either.

Similar questions arise when we consider the more concrete consequences of sympathy as a hermeneutic postulate. Whether conceived as depending on the uniformities of human nature or creating them, the operation of sympathy revolves around resemblance.[28] And insofar as similarity is Hume's primary explanation of how human understanding is possible, the hermeneutics of sympathy essentially reduces to the view that "like understands like." It is a version of the venerable copy model of knowledge, as old as Plato's theory of Ideas and as new as Locke's.

The specific kind of interpretive practice which this hermeneutics authorizes Hume calls "transferring": "Would you know the sentiments, inclinations, and course of life of the Greeks and Romans? Study well the temper and actions of the French and English. You cannot be much mistaken in transferring to the former *most* of the observations which you have made with regard to the latter. Mankind are so much the same, in all times and places, that history informs us of nothing new or strange in this particular" (*ECHU* 83). Just as Toland justifies interpretive accommodation by appeal to the principle that all truth is one, so Hume justifies transfer by appeal to the principle that all humanity is one. With only a few exceptions, in the moral sphere there is "nothing new or strange" under the sun, hence nothing unintelligible.

Given the universal resemblance guaranteed by the uniformity of human nature, the hermeneutics of similarity declares that there is basically no problem in understanding others. We "cannot be much mistaken" in transferring proximate to remote, self to others, for there is nothing radically alien, nothing genuinely other. There is really no gulf to be bridged. "Transfer," in Hume's usage, requires no "transport": "It is but a weak subterfuge . . . to say that we transport ourselves, by the force of imagination, into distant ages and countries" (*ECPM* 217). Involving neither transport nor (in terms of language) translation, transfer indeed eliminates the *inter* of interpretation. In this sense, at least, the postulate of human nature obviates the need for hermeneutics.

In explaining what it means to understand others, it seems, something more is needed than a state of being-in-common. If it is Hume's intent to explain how we can understand others' sentiments, however different from our own, then sympathy is insufficient. Employed as a hermeneutic principle, being-in-common implies, first, that "no one can understand x who is not x," but this does not explain how understanding the different is possible; it merely implies that the different as such is unintelligible. This conclusion is mitigated somewhat by the uniformity of human nature. Hume, we saw, bases understanding in the self; but he does not consider this fact as restricting the horizon of understanding because, given human nature, the self is in principle universal: "We never remark any passion or principle in others, of which, in some degree or other, we may not find a parallel in ourselves" (T 318). I am (like) all men, and ultimately no one can be different from me. Just as the postulate of human nature fails to explain how understanding the different is possible, so it affirms that nothing is ultimately different. In both respects, Hume's account of sympathy as a hermeneutics of similarity begs the question.

That sympathy obscures the difference it is meant to explain becomes even clearer when Hume raises universal resemblance from a positive to a critical function and suggests that we employ it to distinguish probable from improbable stories. "Should a traveller, returning from a far country, bring us an account of men wholly different from any with whom we were ever acquainted . . . we should immediately, from these circumstances, detect the falsehood, and prove him a liar" (ECHU 84). This is a familiar argument to readers of Hume, for it is a version of the better-known argument against crediting miracles. But the argument from the regularity of physical nature is misapplied to moral nature if the latter is not equally regular. It seems evident that it would require no more of a miracle for others to be "wholly different" from us than for them to be wholly the same.

Raised to the status of a critical principle, the thesis of human uniformity not only aggrandizes the self by universalizing it but also conceals a temporal provinciality, a dogmatism that erects the present and familiar as criteria of the real and true. Hume's hermeneutics is open to the same charges as Toland's, because both are hermeneutics of similarity and both are therefore tempted to discount what cannot be assimilated. If what happens in our days, our sense of the common and the usual, is enforced as the critical standard for judging the credibility of historical accounts, then their value has by that fact been much reduced. For if probable histories always conform to present commonplaces, if "history informs us of nothing new or strange" about human beings as such (*ECHU* 83), if human nature is essentially unhistorical, then the study of history can have no use other than to confirm what the reader already knows without it. Resemblance thus discounts a priori everything aberrant and unexpected. The postulate of fixed, immutable human nature eliminates not only the differentness of others; in principle, it eliminates history, which is the advent of the different.[29]

Even without recourse to Hume's own histories, however, we can see that he cannot be accused of wholly ignoring the reality of history and difference. "Those who consider the periods and revolutions of human kind, as represented in history," he writes, "are entertained with a spectacle full of pleasure and variety, and see, with surprise, the manners, customs, and opinions of the same species susceptible of such prodigious changes in different periods of time" (*Essays*, 96). This is but one of many passages emphasizing historical change; the thesis of uniformity was never so rigid as to preclude all variety whatever. At a certain point, however, when the variations that occur in the course of human events are viewed as sufficiently basic and fundamental to alter not only accidentals but essentials in humankind, then the very notion of "kind," becomes suspect. It becomes doubtful that any transhistorical human nature actually exists, and still more doubtful whether anything transhistorical can plausibly explain how historical understanding is possible.

Hume never disavows the existence of human nature, but he does attempt—rarely, though occasionally—to explain how it is possible for like to understand unlike. Yet in each case, he reverts from a hermeneutic model of understanding to a scientific model of knowledge in which unlikeness is conceived as alienness.

One explanation seems at first glance compatible with a hermeneutic view. Hume explains understanding others' emotions by appeal to the interpretation of signs: "When any affection is infused [into us] by sympathy, it is at first known only by its effects and by those external signs in the [other's] countenance and conversation which convey an idea of it" (*T* 317). Later in the *Treatise* he explains why we have no alternative to knowledge through signs: "No passion of another discovers itself immediately to the mind. We are only sensible of its causes or effects. From *these* we infer the passion; and consequently *these* give rise to our sympathy" (*T* 576). Prior to sympathy, and giving rise to it, is semiosis. This priority is significant, in that it manifests the individualist assumptions underlying Hume's account of sympathy, despite its evident tendency to communalize. As the answer to the question of how it is possible for monadic egos to com-unicate, sympathy posits an essential condition of human discreteness and solitude (a state of nature) which must somehow be overcome. "No man can have any other experience but his own," Hume wrote to Blair.[30] "We have no immediate experience of what other men feel,"[31] as Adam Smith wrote. So these private experiences are discernible only mediately, on the basis of something external and public. Hume's model of understanding as semiotic inference that operates prior to sympathy is necessary insofar as one begins with lies and silence as normative—that is, with the imperceptibility of feeling and the privacy of mind.

On this view, the particular feelings that others have, or even that they have feelings at all, can be known only by inference from what are not the feelings themselves but only their manifestations—their signs (if arbitrary) or symptoms (if not). It is not just others' feelings, however, which are only mediately intelligible. Insofar as having feelings defines what it is to be an other, it would seem that the real problem for Hume is that not only emotions but, more important, other human beings as such are not immediately accessible to experience—that is to say, their existence cannot be perceived but only inferred on the basis of what can be perceived. For the empiricist, the mind perceives inanimate things—objects, bodies—and then, on the basis of semiotic inference, endows them with feelings, consciousness, and mind.[32]

Another passage provides a second nonhermeneutical model for understanding otherness. Here Hume specifically uses the word "interpretation": "We mount up to the knowledge of men's inclinations and motives from their actions, expressions, and even gestures, and again descend to the interpretation of their actions from our knowledge of their motives and inclinations. The general observations treasured up by a course of experience give us the clue of human nature" (*ECHU* 84–85). "Interpretation" again means discovering the covert from the overt, inferring the hidden motive from the manifest action. Further, it makes this discovery by learning through experience that such and such actions generally have such and such motives and determining the motive by placing the action to be understood in the appropriate category of actions. Second, then, interpretation means subsumption. As subsumptive discovery, interpreting motives is like finding causes, and interpreting particular acts is like discovering the general laws that cover them.

The interpretation of humankind so conceived is not essentially different from the interpretation of nature, for neither involves understanding. In human science, as in natural, interpretation follows the covering-law model, here generalized from the physical to the moral sciences. This extrapolation accords with Hume's tendency to scientistic monism—his ambition to conduct moral inquiry "in the same manner as the physician or natural philosopher" (*ECHU* 84). The connection between this concept of interpretation as subsumption under empirically derived natural laws and the concept of interpretation as inference about minds not directly experienceable is that neither assumes the a priori intelligibility of the interpreted implicit in the postulate of human nature and the hermeneutics of sympathy that is its corollary.[33] Quite the contrary, both subsumption and semiotic inference assume an initial condition of estrangement and alienation of subject from object which must be overcome. On this view, reminiscent of Spinoza's, other minds are as alien to us as everything in nature, and interpretation conceived on the model of natural science is employed to explain what it cannot understand.

Historical difference offers a challenge distinct from the difference between human and inhuman, mind and body. If we want to look in Hume for a hermeneutic model which shows how it is possible to understand otherness, rather than explain it, it might be profitable to return to the notion of transport that the hermeneutics of sympathy based on similarity obviated. In his essay "Of the Standard of Taste," Hume most fully elaborates the notion of historical transport:

> To enable a critic the more fully [to rank works of art], he must preserve his mind free from all *prejudice,* and allow nothing to enter into his consideration but the very object which is submitted to his examination. We may observe that every work of art, in order to produce its due effect on the mind, must be surveyed in a certain point of view, and cannot be fully relished by persons whose situation, real or imaginary, is not conformable to that which is required by the performance. An orator addresses himself to a particular audience, and must have a regard to their particular genius, interests, opinions, passions, and prejudices; otherwise he hopes in vain to govern their resolutions and inflame their affections. . . . A critic of a different age or nation who

should peruse this discourse must place himself in the same situation as the audience, in order to form a true judgement of the oration. In like manner, when any work is addressed to the public, though I should have a friendship or enmity with the author, I must depart from this situation and, considering myself as a man in general, forget, if possible, my individual being and my peculiar circumstances. A person influenced by prejudice complies not with this condition, but obstinately maintains his natural position, without placing himself in that point of view which the performance supposes. If the work be addressed to persons of a different age or nation, he makes no allowance for their peculiar views and prejudices, but, full of the manners of his own age and country, rashly condemns what seemed admirable in the eyes of those for whom alone the discourse was calculated. If the work be executed for the public, he never sufficiently enlarges his comprehension or forgets his interest as a friend or enemy, as a rival or commentator. By this means, his sentiments are perverted; nor have the same beauties and blemishes the same influence upon him as if he had imposed a proper violence on his imagination and had forgotten himself for a moment. (*Essays,* 239–40)

Here we find Hume's fullest acknowledgment of the reality of historical difference and his most concentrated attempt to confront it head on. Does Hume here develop a genuinely hermeneutic account, one that explains, as sympathy could not, how it is possible for like to understand unlike?

Elsewhere, this essay recalls the hermeneutics of sympathy: "Mirth or passion, sentiment or reflection; whichever of these most predominates in our temper, it gives us a peculiar sympathy with the writer who resembles us" (244). In the passage above, however, it is the opposite case that most interests Hume: namely, when alien customs, beliefs, and practices are to be understood. "A man of learning and reflection can make allowance for [unfamiliar] peculiarities of manners; but a common audience can never divest themselves so far of their usual ideas and sentiment as to relish pictures which no wise resemble them" (245). 'Divestment' and 'making allowance' are not unrelated to sympathy; but what is here described as making them possible is not a sense. It is not common to all but a capacity of the learned few; it is not instinctive, moreover, but a function of reflection that excludes everything from consideration but "the very object." In these respects at least, objectivity is significantly different from sympathy.

In others it is not. Someone who wants to judge a work objectively, Hume says, must endeavor to place himself in the "same position" as its original audience,[34] because the "same beauties and blemishes" have "the same influence" only for someone in the "same position." Like sympathy, transport is still very much a similarity theory, we see. It remains the case that like understands like, but what is new here is that Hume has dispensed with the postulate of human and historical uniformity that guarantees likeness a priori. What is guaranteed, rather, is alienation; and what takes the place of human nature in enabling understanding is historical consciousness. It is an act of "forgetting" oneself, a self-conscious "reflection" that transports the critic in imagination to the other's position.

Hume's argument has precisely reversed itself relative to what it was in the *Treatise*. There he wrote: "Should I endeavour to clear up any doubt . . . in moral philosophy, by placing myself in the same case with that which I consider, 'tis evident this reflection and premeditation would so disturb the operation of my natural principles as must render it impossible to form any just conclusion from the phenomenon" (I xxiii). Now, in the essay on taste, the "learning and reflection" necessary to place myself in the same case do not "disturb" understanding but promote it. They purportedly enable the critic to assume others' points of view as others' and divested of one's own— that is, to understand difference as such. Yet what becomes of the notion of difference if I am eliminated?

Because Hume is still proposing a similarity theory of understanding, he conceives of difference as an obstacle to be overcome. Misunderstanding results either from the critic's failing to rise to generality when the work's own generality requires it or, when the work is particular, from interpreting it from the viewpoint of a different, hence impertinent, particularity, the critic's own. Since Hume views difference as an obstacle to understanding, he associates particularity with partiality and prejudice. In addressing a particular audience, an orator addresses people with "a particular genius, interests, opinions, passions, and *prejudices*," and a critic of such a work who cannot forget his "individual being and peculiar circumstances fails" to "preserve his mind free from all *prejudice*." A critic "influenced by *prejudice*" makes "no allowance for the [original audience's] peculiar views and *prejudices*."

Notice that prejudice pertains both to the object of understanding (the work) and the subject (the historian). The implication is that to understand is to overcome particularity and difference and that to understand others' prejudices is to overcome one's own. Yet there is something troubling about this explanation. First, the overcoming of prejudice occurs on only one side of the equation, that of the historian. While the object of historical understanding is conceived as other people's prejudices, not their knowledge or insights or truths, the historian manages to escape his own. The question raised by this asymmetry is whether the putatively prejudiced past might be a mirage generated by the putatively unprejudiced present. Is it possible for objective interpretation to construct its object as other than prejudiced? If not, this would mean that historical objectivity is itself inevitably prejudiced, since the very process of objectifying the historically different necessarily robs it of its truth claim. "A man of learning and reflection can make allowance for peculiarities of manners," Hume asserts; but the very idea of "making allowances," however apparently generous and broad-minded, is itself an expression of the temporal provinciality and prejudice it is meant to overcome.

Moreover, what is troubling is not just that Hume conceives the past as prejudiced but that he conceives the historian's ideal as overcoming his own prejudice. Hume equates historical particularity with prejudice, which is to say that prejudices are no more or less than manifestations of historicity. This obtains for the historian's prejudices no less than for those of the people he studies. If the historian's overcoming of his prejudices means overcoming his particularities, then it is history itself that he is escaping. If, in order to understand, the historian must rise through reflective self-purgation to the position of a "man in general" and thereby escape the limitations of "his own age and country," then what Hume's notion of transport explains is not just how history (the object) is to be understood but why it must be overcome (by the subject).

Insofar as history is the advent of the different and insofar as Hume considers difference as an obstacle to understanding, history is not just the object of understanding but the very thing that impedes it. History is the domain of particularity, partiality, and prejudice—the domain of the false. Hume's implicit dichotomy of the true and the historical necessarily implies that truth—even the true interpretation of history—is essentially unhistorical. In the process of ex-

plaining how historical understanding is possible, Hume has ironically shown why it is unnecessary.

We saw above that Hume's account of sympathy tends to eliminate
otherness, for sympathy either depends on a preexisting resemblance
or itself homogenizes and produces the very same-kindedness on
which it depends. Hume's hermeneutics of historical difference is
also a similarity theory, in that it requires the critic to assume the
same stance as the original audience. But more important, perhaps,
is that transport—this act of historical imagination—tends to efface
either history itself or the historicity of the "I" that understands.
History is merely an obstacle to understanding which can be removed
by reflective imagination. Correlatively, the self-conscious "I" up-
roots itself and transports itself anywhere or—what amounts to the
same thing—expands itself (not by the commonality of human nature
but by self-consciousness) to godlike universality from which nothing can be different. Through reflection, the "I" rises above the
determinacy that makes it something in particular, something historical, thereby reflecting itself out of existence. But this means that
ultimately Hume leaves unexplained how one finite human being
can understand another, how a particular "I" can understand someone
else who is historically different.

To have explained this would have necessitated developing a way
of reconciling the dichotomies of sameness and difference, generality
and particularity, in which belonging to history (rather than tran-
scending it) would be the condition of understanding history. Bolingbroke took steps in this direction when he conceived of applying
historical examples as making not copies but imitative translations;
Blackstone, we will see, moves toward reconciling reason and history
as well. For Hume, however, such a reconciliation would have required an almost unthinkable revision of some basic postulates: of
prejudice as blindness and history as falsehood. We can see why this
is so by considering Hume's best-known dictum, "Reason is, and
ought only to be the slave of the passions" (*T* 415). This audacious
inversion signifies (inter alia) that reason is and ought to be instrumental reason, reason that concerns itself with maximizing efficiency
in serving ends not its own. On this interpretation, Hume's dictum
specifically excludes the possibility of practical reason, a kind of
reason in which truth is not something general and eternal, first
discovered and then applied to historical particulars. For practical
reason, particular historical circumstances are not subsumed under

covering laws but are themselves the very occasion of knowledge and truth. Practical truth is discovered in practice—not beforehand, but in the very conjunction of the general and particular that constitutes practice.

The lack of a conception of practical reason prevents Hume from envisioning a reconciliation of reason and history. It underlies his statement, already cited, that in jurisprudence "there cannot properly be said to be truth or falsehood on either side. . . . The preference given by the judge is often founded more on taste and imagination than on any solid argument" (*ECPM* 308–09). Either the inflexible universality of law or the vagaries of private feeling, either truth or taste, either general or particular, either same or different, either reason or history—these dichotomies are produced by the absence of any option that could mediate between them. Without such an option, jurisprudence is deprived of its truth claim and so equated with aesthetics. What permits the transition from law to art is that both involve judgment. Hume acknowledged that what is involved in legal judgments is not logical subsumption; but, lacking any other conception of reason than subsumption, lacking a conception of practical or interpretive reason, he then reduced legal judgment to what he thought was not reason at all: aesthetic taste. He then reduced taste to personal preference, and so, having equated justice with arbitrary preference, failed to account not only for a standard of taste but for justice itself.

Consider another passage in the *Enquiry Concerning the Principles of Morals,* however, where we find a similar argument: "Truth is disputable, not taste: what exists in the nature of things is the standard of judgement; what each man feels within himself is the standard of sentiment" (*ECPM* 171). This passage presents the same dichotomy as that on jurisprudence—one or the other, either taste or truth. Yet here Hume immediately calls such dichotomizing "a specious argument." "I am apt to suspect," he concludes, "that *reason* and *sentiment* concur in almost all moral determination and conclusions" (*ECPM* 172).[35] Not dualism and hierarchy, not mastery and slavery, but precisely a concurrence of faculties is what Hume depicts in the second *Enquiry*. Here he disavows the worst consequence of the dichotomy between moral sentiment and reason: the implication that the virtuous man who feels deeply may well be lacking in intelligence or even common sense, that virtue is so far from cunning that a good man, like a Don Quixote or a Parson Adams, must be something of a fool. This implication of his dichotomy between reason and virtue Hume is in fact at pains to deny: "It is always allowed that there are virtues of many different kinds; yet, when a man is called *virtuous* or is denominated a man of virtue, we chiefly regard his social qualities. . . . It is, at the same time, certain that any remarkable defect in [understanding] . . . would bereave even a very good-natured, honest man of this honourable appellation. Who did ever say, except by way of irony, that such a one was a man of great virtue but an egregious blockhead?" (*ECPM* 314).

Such an integration of intelligence and humanity, I think, best represents Hume's fullest intentions, however incompletely realized, since it postulates an integral human being—one that is not just mind and body but whole and one—a complete human being that would be the object and subject of a complete science. Neither juxtaposing two half-sciences, one of fact, the other of value, nor subjugating one to the other suffices to make the comprehensive, integral whole that Hume envisioned at his boldest. Making reason the slave of passion doesn't finally get us any further than the converse, for what is really needed for a complete science is a nondualistic notion of reason that feels, passion that knows, and taste that discovers what is the case.

Hume prefigures this unity in the *Treatise* when he writes: "'Tis not solely in poetry and music we must follow our taste and sentiment, but likewise in philosophy" (*T* 110). But it sometimes seems as if Hume means to draw skeptical conclusions from this observation: not that taste is a mode of real knowledge but rather that philosophy has about as much cognitive value as poetry. He comes closer to formulating a nonskeptical aesthetic epistemology, however, in the *Enquiry Concerning the Principles of Morals,* which he judged "incomparably the best" of all his works in "My Own Life" (*Essays,* xxxvi). Not the moderns, who segregate knowledge from feeling, but the ancients guide Hume here. "Upon the whole," he wrote to Hutcheson, "I desire to take my catalogue of virtues from *Cicero's Offices,* not from the *Whole Duty of Man.*"[36] In making morality (which at first seemed so special and narrow) the prototype of the unified moral sciences, Hume follows "the ancient moralists, the best models, [who] make no material distinction among the different species of mental endowments and defects, but treated all alike under the appellation of virtues and vices, and made them indiscriminately the object of their moral reasonings" (*ECPM* 318). Clearly Hume is not indiscriminate in unifying the entire moral spectrum—more like dialectical. The point is rather that if we usually think of Carnap or the Vienna Circle when "unified science" is mentioned, the ancients to whom Hume appeals here provide an alternative, nonpositivist model of unification. Its cornerstone, the first example of moral virtue that Hume cites from his favorite ancient, is particularly relevant here: "The *prudence* explained in Cicero's *Offices* is that sagacity which leads to the discovery of truth and preserves us from error and mistake" (*ECPM* 318). The prudence that discovers truth—if Hume had allowed Cicero's conception of prudence to inform his own conception of jurisprudence, he would not have concluded against the truth claim of judicial interpretation.[37]

But there are moments when Hume does think like Cicero. He asserts, for instance, that "the quality the most necessary for the execution of any useful enterprise is discretion, by which we carry on a safe intercourse with others, give due attention to our own and to their character, weigh each circumstance of the business we undertake, and employ the surest and safest means for the attainment of any end or purpose" (*ECPM* 236). Insofar as Hume equates discretion with safe means to safe ends, he succeeds only in obscuring what was once meant by this "most necessary" quality of mind. What I want to underscore in concluding, however, are the vestiges of the earlier meaning of the word *discretion* still manifest in Hume's words, since they point toward an implicit hermeneutics of the whole that is more satisfactory than the hermeneutics of similarity and difference that Hume elaborates most explicitly.

For the Ciceronian Hume, *discretion* means, first, not only knowing what is needed in general but also "weighing each circumstance" involved in putting it into practice. Like taste and prudence, *discretion* is a term for practical reason, what Aristotle called *phronēsis*. It is not intelligence or learning that is the "most necessary" quality of mind, for abstract knowledge (*epistēmē*), however necessary, is insufficient in real life. More important are discretion, good judgment, understanding how to apply what one knows in the concrete world of practice. Second, in one's intercourse with others, Hume writes, discretion means giving "due attention to our own and to their character"; this too means balancing, weighing, deliberating among the competing claims of what is "due" to self and to others. Prudence is not limited to jurisprudence or discretion to judicial discretion, though they are most manifest in interpreting law, just as taste is most evident in judging art and tact in understanding others. "Any useful enterprise," Hume insists, requires the hermeneutic *virtù* (by whatever name) of understanding—the practical sagacity, irreducible to abstract reason, that balances the claims of general and particular, self and other, same and different.

5

Reid on
Common Sense

"There is something immediately evident about grounding
. . . the human sciences on the concept of the sensus
communis," writes Hans-Georg Gadamer in *Truth and
Method*. By *sensus communis* he is referring not only to the
ancient Greek and Roman tradition but to Vico, Shaftesbury, and
Thomas Reid as well. Gadamer cites only one line from Reid, but it
is decisive: "'[Commonsense principles] serve to direct us in the
common affairs of life, where our reasoning faculty would leave us
in the dark.'"[1] These few words of Reid's encapsulate Gadamer's
single main underlying thesis: namely, that the human sciences are
based on a commonsense faculty of knowledge which undergirds
reason but also continues on where reason leaves off. Truth, Gadamer
contends in *Truth and Method,* cannot be confined to method—to
methodically certified natural science—but belongs to the unmeth-
odizable interpretive sciences as well. This is not an entirely novel
conclusion, Gadamer readily concedes: "Ultimately, it has always
been known that the possibilities of rational proof and instruction do
not fully exhaust the sphere of knowledge."[2] Before Gadamer, Reid
too explored the limits of rational proof and suggested that knowledge cannot be restricted to the conclusions of discursive reason
conceived on a mathematical model. His *Inquiry into the Human Mind*
(1764) and *Essays on the Intellectual Powers of Man* (1785) elaborate a
philosophy of common sense that takes as one of its main topics the
truth that exceeds provability, that is more at home in words than

numbers and more in metaphorical than literal words, but that never-theless grounds the claims of interpretive knowledge.

"Men rarely ask what common sense is," Reid remarks (423),[3] which is probably just as well, because those who do ask for a definition are unlikely to get a satisfactory answer. The reason is not simply that the principles of common sense are irremediably vague, though that is true;[4] or that the term "common sense" (which includes *koinē aisthēsis* and *sensus communis*) has become a semantic miasma over the centuries, though that is also true.[5] Rather, definitions are rarely requested or offered because, as Reid says, the very claim of common sense to be common suggests that everyone already knows what it is. "Every man believes himself possessed of it, and would take it for an imputation upon his understanding to be thought unacquainted with it" (423). Perhaps, paradoxically, this is itself one of the defining characteristics of common sense: that people do not ask for definitions of it. They do not need any, because they are already acquainted with it through a lived familiarity with communal norms of thought and judgment, not through lexicographical, still less philosophical, definitions.

Reid thought of himself as a "philosopher of mind." The broad questions that aroused his curiosity were very much those which had interested Descartes, Locke, Berkeley, and Hume before him. In Hume particularly, Reid thought, the laidley worm of skepticism immanent in rational and empirical epistemology had finally exposed itself. It was as a counterattack on this element of the epistemological tradition that Reid conceived his defense of common sense, for skepticism had called the basic principles of knowledge into question. Common sense, it seemed, was no longer common—or at least not universal, if Descartes had felt the need to prove his own existence, if Berkeley had dissolved the physical world, and if Hume had denied the existence of the self. But what could philosophy do to restore the lost sense of shared foundations?

Hermeneutically conceived, common sense comprehends all those things that are "understood" in the sense of what goes without saying. Reid describes such beliefs as "taken for granted" (230). They are the givens underlying any thought whatever, tacit rather than explicit, used rather than mentioned. Thus when in the *Intellectual Powers,* for example, Reid explicitly states the seven principles that he will take for granted (that he exists, the world exists, other people exist, and so on), the list per se indicates precisely that they are not taken for granted, not "understood." Philosophical assertion and argument cannot replace the tacit commonalities of lived familiarity. The very existence of common sense philosophy with its explicit definitions and explanations is a symptom of what it exists to cure. Reid's philosophy is not itself commonsensical, and there is therefore a certain unintended pathos in Harry Bracken's description of Reid as "a philosopher of un-common sense,"[6] for Reid's philosophy expresses the loss of common sense as much as the impossibility of getting along without it.

In large part, this quandary results from Reid's having conceived of common sense specifically as a defense against post-Cartesian philosophy of mind. The context of rational and empirical epistemology explains the distinctive flavor of Reid's account, since common sense—though conceived as a counter-epistemology—is for that very reason primarily epistemological. This explains a certain thinness discernible in Reid's conception when compared with the rich tangle of denotations that the term had acquired since Aristotle. Most clearly in Reid's discussion of Shaftesbury, we see how common sense is being pruned down to questions of cognitive understanding. In the "Cura Prima" (1768?) Reid cites the famous passage of Shaftesbury's *Sensus Communis* that deals with the difficulty of defining common sense.[7] Reid then goes on to say: "It were to be wished that [Shaftesbury] had entered more fully into this inquiry than he has done. He has indeed given some reasons and collected authorities of able critics to show that *sensus communis* in Juvenal and Horace signifies humanity, natural affection, or a just sense of the common rights of men. But if these poets made their *sensus communis* relate only to the qualities of the heart, it is most certain *common sense* in English writers is rather applied to the understanding."[8] Though Reid's own interests lie mainly with understanding, Shaftesbury allies himself with the older, broader Roman tradition that did not limit common sense to its cognitive function.

For Shaftesbury, common sense constitutes a "sense of public weal and of the common interest, love of the community or society, natural affection, humanity, obligingness, or that sort of civility which rises from a just sense of the common rights of mankind and the natural equality there is among those of the same species."[9] The province of common sense for Shaftesbury comprehends not just "qualities of the heart," as Reid insisted, but those of the head too: political, moral, social, and aesthetic, as well as cognitive values. In the *Intellectual Powers,* written some twenty years after the "Cura," Reid finally dismisses the broad claims of the older common sense tradition as a jest when he says: "[Shaftesbury shows] in a facetious way throughout the treatise that the fundamental principles of morals, of politics, of criticism, and of every branch of knowledge are the dictates of common sense" (424). In making common sense the universal ground, common to all inquiries, Shaftesbury must have been joking.

By limiting himself to its epistemic function, Reid's humbler claims for common sense are less pretentious and more credible, to be sure, but also noticeably thinner in their range of implication. This is hardly to say that Reid's employment of the term is alien to Shaftesbury and the Roman tradition. Cicero, for example, writes that the whole art of oratory "is concerned in some measure with the common practice, custom and speech of mankind, . . . and the usage approved by the sense of the community."[10] When Reid identifies common sense with the "common opinions of mankind" (229), he sounds much like the Cicero of such passages. Both are anti-individualist in tendency insofar as their understanding of common sense begins with the common, not the individual, as fundamental.

"Mankind," however, had become a good deal larger and more diverse and its recorded lifetime a good deal longer by the eighteenth century. So a new note, absent from Cicero, is to be heard when Reid identifies common sense with "things wherein we find an universal agreement, among the learned and unlearned, in the different nations and ages of the world" (233). The reference to time and national difference indicates that what Reid calls the "common opinions of mankind" could no longer be equated with what Cicero called "the sense of the community." Insofar as common sense refers to an abstract and more or less quantitative generality, it is distinct from *sensus communis.* For Reid, appeals to common sense were not appeals to the cognitive and valuative practice of a concrete community.

Common sense, in short, had become an epistemological ground as opposed to a historical product. Since, Reid admits, it is "impossible to collect the opinions of all men upon any point whatsoever," the putative "consent of ages and of nations, of the learned and the vulgar" (233) can appeal to no actual assent at all. In this respect, Reid's view is like Kant's. Common sense, Kant writes, is "the idea of a sense *shared* [by all of us], i.e., a power to judge that in reflecting takes account (a priori), in our thought, of everyone else's way of presenting [something], in order *as it were* to compare our own judgment with human reason in general. . . . Now we do this as follows: we compare our judgment not so much with the actual as rather with the merely possible judgments of others, and [thus] put ourselves in the position of everyone else, merely by abstracting from the limitations that [may] happen to attach to our own judging."[11] Like sympathy or transport, common sense enables us to put ourselves in others' places. For both Kant and Reid, however, common sense involves not so much sharing with actual others as abstracting from ourselves—becoming "A man in general," as Hume puts it—which is not all the same thing.

Where Reid and Kant differ is in respect to the province of this self-abstraction. "All beauty is truth," Shaftesbury writes in *Sensus Communis*.[12] By contrast with this disarmingly straightforward equation of aesthetic and epistemic value, Reid and Kant both strictly divide the two. The difference between them is that they place common sense on opposite sides of that divide. Whereas Kant maintains "that the aesthetic power of judgement deserves to be called a shared sense more than does the intellectual one,"[13] Reid maintains just the opposite: sound understanding can be called common sense more legitimately than judgments of taste, which are notoriously various. This is a dispute we need not follow any further, except to note that by comparison with the breadth and richness of Shaftesbury's conception, Reid and Kant reduce the claims of common sense and restrict its jurisdiction: Kant to taste, Reid to knowledge.

Reid, then, limits his attention largely to the epistemic implications of common sense, those most relevant to the rational-empirical tradition of epistemology that he wants to correct. Like Descartes— and indeed, virtually every philosopher since Plato—Reid takes mathematics (usually Euclidean geometry[14]) as the paradigm of epistēmē, whether it is called science, knowledge, or demonstration. From an epistemic point of view, then, the first question about common sense concerns the role it plays in the mathematical model of knowledge. "Sophistry has been more effectually excluded from mathematics and natural philosophy than from other sciences," Reid asserts in the opening lines of *Intellectual Powers*. "In mathematics it had no place from the beginning, mathematicians having had the wisdom to define accurately the terms they use and to lay down, as axioms, the first principles on which their reasoning is grounded.

. . . About a century and a half ago, [natural philosophy too] began to be built upon the foundation of clear definitions and self-evident maxims. . . . It were to be wished that this method, which has been so successful in those branches of science, were attempted in others; for definitions and axioms are the foundations of all science" (219).

In taking the maxims of common sense as foundational axioms, Reid situates common sense within the realm of explicit or explicatable knowledge, even though, in suggesting (as we saw above) that common sense cannot be defined, he situates it in the realm of implicit, unaxiomatizable knowledge that cannot even in principle be demonstrated *more geometrico*. The mathematical model of truth offers Reid a paradigm for understanding the specifically epistemological function of common sense. Just as necessary truths have the axioms of mathematics as their first principles, so contingent truths, those of natural science, have their first principles in the axioms of common sense. "All mathematical truths are immutably true. Like the ideas about which they are conversant, they have no relation to time or place, no dependence upon existence or change" (429). Commonsense axioms too are immutable and eternal, unrelated to time and place, in that they enjoy "universal agreement, among the learned and unlearned, in the different nations and ages of the world" (233). The first principles of contingent truths are "common to all men, being evident in themselves. . . . All men that have common understanding agree in such principles, and consider a man as lunatic or destitute of common sense who denies or calls them in question." Having surveyed both analytic and synthetic reason, both mathematical and natural knowledge, Reid concludes that "there are, therefore, common principles which are the foundation of all reasoning and of all science" (230). These are the principles of common sense.

If mathematics, as the paradigm of all reasoning, is grounded upon "clear definitions and self-evident maxims," and if "there is no greater impediment to the advancement of knowledge than the ambiguity of words" (219), then it follows that "a clear explication and enumeration of the principles of common sense, is one of the chief *desiderata* in logic" (209). This citation is from the end of the *Inquiry,* and Reid repeats his call for codification years later at the end of the *Intellectual Powers.* He there expresses the hope that "the decisions of common sense can be brought into a code in which all reasonable men shall acquiesce. This, indeed, if it be possible, would be very desirable, . . . and why should it be thought impossible that reasonable men should agree in things that are self-evident?" (422).

Why indeed? This question not entirely rhetorical, even for Reid, and certainly not for us. Are commonsense maxims really self-evident? If so, what accounts for people like Hume and Berkeley who seem to doubt them? If so, why haven't they been codified so as to function like Euclidean axioms? Or, are codifiable axioms not the only kind of self-evident propositions? And if there are other kinds, can mathematics be the sole avenue to truth? James Beattie, Reid's strident popularizer, puts his finger precisely on the question: "Is truth to be found in mathematics only? Is the geometrician the only person who exerts a rational belief? Do we never find conviction arise in our minds except when we contemplate an intuitive axiom or run over a mathematical demonstration?"[15] Beattie is rehearsing conclusions learned from Reid: "Except we believe many things without proof, we never can believe any thing at all; for all sound reasoning must ultimately rest on the principles of common sense."[16] Hume, we recall, had agreed that people believe many things that haven't been proved: "I am persuaded that upon examination we shall find more than one half of those opinions that prevail among mankind to be owing . . . [neither] to abstract reasoning or experience" (*T* 117). The issue Reid raises is whether such opinions have any reliability and validity or, conversely, whether epistēmē has a monopoly on truth.

As a churchman and sometime holder of the living at New Machar, Reid was certainly acquainted with an avenue of truth that falls outside the mathematical model. "The blind man forms the notion of visible figure to himself, by thought and by mathematical reasoning from principles, whereas the man that sees has it presented to his eye at once, without any labour, without any reasoning, by a kind of inspiration" (144). Perceptual "inspiration" is no casual metaphor. It is announced in the verse from Job that stands as an epigraph to the *Inquiry:* "The inspiration of the Almighty giveth them understanding." Whereas Berkeley (appealing to common sense) had turned ideas into things and situated humankind in a world of spirit, Reid (appealing to common sense) leaves it a physical world but suggests that we are apprized of it by spirit. "Perception, whether original or acquired, implies no exercise of reason" (185). "We are inspired with the sensation, and we are inspired with the corresponding perception, by means unknown" (188).

This religious language goes a good way toward explaining the charges of dogmatism and mysticism that, not very paradoxically, hound common sense philosophy. With regard to the first charge,

Reid wants to claim that the principles of common sense enable dialogue, communication, or what he calls "reasoning together." "Before men can reason together, they must agree in first principles; and it is impossible to reason with a man who has no principles in common with you" (230). The more assumptions you share with someone, the more you have to talk about. Yet common sense also performs somewhat the same dogmatic function as inspiration does for the enthusiast—namely, as the ultimate authority, the conversation-stopper, about which no discussion is possible. "While the parties agree in the first principles on which their arguments are grounded, there is room for reasoning; but when one denies what to the other appears too evident to need or to admit of proof, reasoning seems to be at an end; an appeal is made to common sense, and each part is left to enjoy his own opinion" (422). Rather than an invitation to dialogue, the appeal to common sense indicates irresolvable disagreement and leaves nothing else to say.[17] In response to this charge of dogmatism, however, it should be stressed that, unlike Beattie, Reid considers common sense to be not the standard of truth but the criterion of error. It has largely a critical rather than a positive or dogmatic function. As Reid says, "the province of common sense is more extensive in refutation than in confirmation" (425).

Beyond dogmatism, the suspicion that mysticism, ironically, lies just around the corner from common sense is not alleviated by what Reid says about secondary qualities. The unknown causes of known effects, he writes, might "not improperly be called *occult* qualities" (my emphasis). By this term, however, Reid does not mean to claim knowledge he does not possess; like Toland, he means precisely to affirm his ignorance. "To call a thing occult, if we attend to the meaning of the word, is rather modestly to confess ignorance than to cloak it" (320). The same can be said of his religious language: it is not offhand or casual, but neither is it meant to do any positive explanatory work. For all Reid's opposition to skepticism, there is in his philosophy a refreshing strain of nescience. "Our perception is the result of a train of operations, some of which affect the body only, others affect the mind. We know very little of the nature of some of these operations; we know not at all how they are connected together. . . . We may make a thousand conjectures without coming near the truth. . . . Who knows but their connection may be arbitrary and owing to the will of our Maker?" (186–87). At least Reid knows that he does not know. His claim, moreover, is that nobody knows.[18]

How perception works remains a mystery, and though philosophers sometimes profess to explain it, they are just as ignorant on this subject as anyone else.

Yet, happily, this universal ignorance does not matter in the slightest. "If we understood the structure of our organs of sense so minutely as to discover what effects are produced upon them by external objects, this knowledge would contribute nothing to our perception of the object; for they perceive as distinctly who know least about the manner of perception as the greatest adepts" (187). In a sense we are all adepts, for we all have occult, mysterious, and quite inexplicable knowledge—that the world exists, for example, and that it's pretty much what it seems to be—though we cannot explain how we know such things, so seem vulnerable to skeptical attack. "I am aware that this belief which I have in perception stands exposed to the strongest batteries of scepticism. But they make no great impression upon it. The sceptic asks me, Why do you believe the existence of the external object which you perceive? This belief, sir, is none of my manufacture; it came from the mint of Nature. . . . I even took it upon trust and without suspicion" (183). The existence of the external world—this most commonsensical of beliefs—is quite without foundation, indeed a matter of simple trust. Universal ignorance is counterbalanced by universal faith. "The unjust *live by faith* as well as the *just,*" Reid writes in a rare aphoristic moment (95). Without good reason, and perhaps contrary to it, all human beings have faith in the evidence of their senses. "Shall we say, then, that this belief is the inspiration of the Almighty? I think this may be said in a good sense; for I take it to be the immediate effect of our constitution, which is the work of the Almighty" (329).

This is not to imply that the ultra-skeptical, fideist elements in Reid's philosophy, along with the constant appeal *ad ignorantium,* simply add up to a kind of know-nothingism. On the one hand, he continually asserts that common sense serves as the foundation of all knowledge of the world around us. From the principles according to which we conduct our everyday lives to the axioms of geometry, to Newton's *regulae philosophandi*—all, Reid claims, are maxims of common sense (197).[19] Collectively they are "the foundation upon which the grand superstructure of human knowledge must be raised" (416), the ground upon which all contingent truth is erected. Yet this ultimate bedrock turns out to be occult, a matter of trust, belief, instinct, and faith.

I have said that Reid develops common sense philosophy primarily as a contribution to philosophy of mind and to epistemology in particular. Yet, conceived as inexplicable, common sense is merely a cipher, a placeholder without any positive epistemological function. It explains nothing. Why do we believe the world exists? "We can say no more but that it is the result of our constitution" (341). Common sense does, however, perform a positive nonepistemological function. Like Locke, Reid posits limits to human understanding; but he adds what Lockean epistemology never dreamt of; namely, that understanding itself lies outside those limits. As if our eyesight extended no further than our ankles, the ground that supports us lies beyond our ken. Although the solid rock that epistemology promised has dissolved and turned to water, however, there is this miracle: no one has any trouble walking on it. The practice of understanding does not require the understanding of it. *Pace* Locke, understanding is not improved by understanding it, because it does not depend on theoretical analysis—on philosophy of understanding, if you prefer. Locke thought that he was inquiring into the limits of human understanding, but he was investigating only those of critical self-consciousness; whereas for Reid, to put his anti-epistemology positively, the compass of understanding exceeds the limits of self-consciousness and critique.

"Philosophers, pitying the credulity of the vulgar, resolve to have no faith but what is founded upon reason. They apply to philosophy to furnish them with reasons for the belief of those things which all mankind have believed without being able to give any reason for it" (100–01). In the enterprise of universal proof, however, they fail utterly. This failure occurs in part because they are unsuccessful in finding sufficient reasons for commonsense beliefs and in part because they cannot altogether doubt their own commonsense beliefs and so assume them surreptitiously in the very attempt to prove them. Perhaps, Reid suggests, Descartes in his famous enthymeme meant to assume only "the existence of thought, and to infer from that [thought] the existence of a mind, or subject of thought. But [if he intended to leave nothing without proof] why did he not prove the existence of this thought? Consciousness, it may be said, vouches that. But who is voucher for consciousness? Can any man prove that his consciousness may not deceive him?" (100). Reid's point here is not that consciousness is unreliable but rather that the reliability of consciousness cannot be proved even though it must be assumed. "All reasoning must be from first principles; and for first principles no other reason can be given but this, that, by the constitution of our nature, we are under a necessity of assenting to them. . . . We cannot prove the existence of our minds, nor even of our thoughts and sensations. A historian or a witness can prove nothing unless it is taken for granted that the memory and senses may be trusted" (130).

All knowledge, in sum, rests on premises that cannot be proved. What follows from this? One possibility is that truth rests on non-truth if the latter means simply premises that cannot be proved. It may be that commonsense premises are self-evident and thus do not need proof, but the worry is that self-evident propositions share at least one characteristic with falsehoods: both are unprovable. So, given the possibility that they may be resting their beliefs on false-hoods, "many eminent philosophers [have thought] it unreasonable to believe when they could not shew a reason" (328). Hume admitted that outside his study he couldn't help believing what everyone else does, but he considered such beliefs unfounded and refused to ex-onerate them, even in himself. Reid, by contrast, draws no such inference, since he considers the premises of common sense self-evident. How does he know they are self-evident? The question must be ruled out of order. Self-evident truths are like inspirations or perceptions. There can be no evidence for self-evidence better than itself, and bringing in other evidence in the false hope of proof can have the effect only of raising doubts, not allaying them. If the impossibility of proving our basic, self-evident beliefs does not show *eo ipso* that they are false—if, indeed, they are true—then a rather surprising conclusion follows: truth exceeds what can be proved. With this conclusion, the mathematical model loses its monopoly on knowledge. The polemical point of Reid's common sense philosophy is to expose Hume's mistake and by extension that of all epistemol-ogy: reasonableness cannot be equated with reasoning or truth with provability.

This is not to say that common sense can be opposed to reason; quite the contrary, in the *Intellectual Powers,* at least, Reid considers common sense eminently reasonable.[20] "We ascribe to reason two offices, or two degrees. The first is to judge of things self-evident, the second to draw conclusions that are not self-evident from those that are. The first of these is the province, and the sole province, of common sense" (425). Reid here expands the domain of the reason-able to include nondemonstrable knowledge—that is, the inspirations of common sense. All empiricists argue the insufficiency of reason, of course. In the province of common sense, where truth is not determined by discursive reason, however, it is not determined by sensory experience either. "It is the result of our constitution" (341). This constitutionally determined knowledge Reid sometimes describes as instinctual or innate; at any rate, it is "previous to experience" (195), "a part of that furniture which Nature has given to the human understanding" (209). The tabula rasa .comes with a few characters already inscribed on it.

"Upon the whole, it appears that our philosophers have imposed upon themselves and upon us, in pretending to deduce from sensation the first origin of our notions of external existences, of space, motion, and extension. . . . They have no resemblance to any sensation or to any operation of our minds, and therefore they cannot be ideas either of sensation or reflection" (126). "From whence, then, come those images of body and of its qualities into the mind? Let philosophers resolve this question. All I can say is that they come not by the senses" (140). In expanding the province of reason beyond proof and the province of contingent knowledge beyond experience, Reid puts a good deal of distance between himself and the rational-empirical tradition.

The question is whether this distance leaves him any grounds for truth claims at all. "The sceptic may perhaps persuade himself, in general, that he has no ground to believe his senses or his memory" (416), but that is because he is looking for the wrong kind of ground. In the province of common sense, where truth exceeds rational proof and perceptual experience, Reid contends, the ground of knowing is being. It is for this reason that he has sometimes been charged with confusing logic with psychology, and even physiology.[21] He does indeed align logical necessity with the constitutional necessity of believing what "is not in my power" to deny. In those passages in which he acknowledges "principles which irresistibly govern the belief and the conduct of all mankind in the common concerns of life" (102), Reid makes truth relative to human being and life—that is, to the necessity of believing and the impossibility of doubting some few basic propositions. If commonsense judgments—such as belief in the evidence of the senses and of memory—"may, in the strictest sense, be called *judgements of nature*" (416), then what we know merges with what we are, our nature. At some point, grounds shade into causes, justifications into explanations, propositions into propensities, conscious judgments into unconscious assumptions and natural urges. At this point, mind is continuous with body, philosophy with life.

Reid envisions common sense as the site of this continuity, the missing link between mind and body as it were, so close to sensory perception as to be indistinguishable from it and so close to reason and science as to be continuous with them as well.

> There are some propositions which lie so near to axioms that it is difficult to say whether they ought to be held as axioms or demonstrated as propositions. The same thing holds with regard to perception and the conclusions drawn from it. Some of these conclusions follow our perceptions so easily and are so immediately connected with them that it is difficult to fix the limit which divides the one from the other.
>
> Perception, whether original or acquired, implies no exercise of reason, and is common to men, children, idiots, and brutes. The more obvious conclusions drawn from our perceptions by reason make what we call *common understanding,* by which men conduct themselves in the common affairs of life and by which they are distinguished from idiots. The more remote conclusions which are drawn from our perceptions by reason make what we commonly call *science* in the various parts of nature. . . . [Common sense] dwells so near to perception that it is difficult to trace the line which divides the one from the other. In like manner, the science of nature dwells so near to common understanding that we cannot discern where the latter ends and the former begins. (185–86)

The very word *sense* in "common sense" expresses the continuity fully. "Seeing and hearing, by philosophers, are called senses, because we have ideas by them; by the vulgar they are called senses, because we judge by them. We judge of colours by the eye, of sounds of the ear, of beauty and deformity by taste, of right and wrong in conduct by our moral sense or conscience" (421–22). Both philosophers and the vulgar are right, as common sense makes especially clear. "Seeing what is obvious" can be described as exemplifying either low-level judgment or high-level perception. As sensation, sense is distinguished from reason, but as the capacity to reject nonsense it is a function of reason. Faculty of perception, faculty of judgment, (common) sense constitutes the pivot of the entire gamut of human cognitive activities, from the animal to the divine.

Reid is discussing two senses of the word *sense,* but his point is not merely verbal. And even if it were, he would ask how it happens that *sense* is used so variously, despite philosophical attempts to confine it to the senses and keep it distinct from whatever hermeneutic faculty is involved in making sense of things. This dichotomy Reid is unwilling to concede: "Sense, in its most common and therefore most proper meaning, signifies judgement, though philosophers often use it in another meaning" (423).[22] From the viewpoint of Lockean psychology, the common meaning (sense = judgment) is mere confusion; since it stands to reason that you must have ideas before you can compare them, it follows that sensation (which creates ideas) must precede judgment (which compares ideas), and hence that sense must be independent of it. For Reid this is wrong on both counts. The problem is not just that common sense spans both sense and judgment but that it can do so precisely because sense and judgment are not dichotomous. They are interdependent, just like conception and judgment. "In the mature state of man, distinct conception of a proposition supposes some previous exercise of judgment, and distinct judgment supposes distinct conception. Each may truly be said to come from the other, as the bird from the egg and the egg from the bird" (417). "'Tis certain that the mind, in its perceptions, must begin somewhere," Hume had written (*T* 275). Reid does not consider this certain at all; indeed, he considers postulating such origins and beginnings to be just as wrong and dogmatic as insisting that chickens come from eggs, not eggs from chickens.

Common sense may be the foundation of all contingent truths, then, but that is because in combining sense and judgment it is something paradoxical or monstrous, like an egg-chicken. Common sense is evidently a species of sound judgment insofar as the word *judgment* means "an act of the mind whereby one thing is affirmed or denied of another" (413). Reid, however, claims that such affirmation belongs tacitly not just to common sense but to all sense(s). "Every operation of the senses, in its very nature, implies judgement or belief, as well as simple apprehension. . . . When I perceive a tree before me, my faculty of seeing gives me not only a notion or simple apprehension of the tree, but a belief of its existence and of its figure, distance, and magnitude; and this judgement or belief is not got by comparing ideas, it is included in the very nature of the perception. . . . Such original and natural judgements are, therefore, a part of that furniture which Nature has given to the human understanding" (209). Here as elsewhere, Reid stresses three aspects of the perceptual act. I not only (1) have a conception of a tree but (2) judge that it stands there before me and is of such and such a shape, and (3) I make this judgment commonsensically, without explicitly thinking about it.

In addition to involving tacit beliefs, sense judgments are interpretive—evidently so, because they can be mistaken. Eyes are like camera lenses in that they simply register the light rays that are reflected from things—"visible appearances," Reid calls them, and they are never wrong. "Nature never misleads us in this way: her language is always true; and it is only by misinterpreting it that we fall into error" (199). Although these appearances are all that we see in one sense, in another we almost never see them at all. Paradoxically, visible appearances are typically invisible, and what we usually call "seeing" is not just registering appearances but also processing and reading them. We are "critics in the language of nature" (200), interpreting and judging at every moment. "The visible appearance of things in my room varies almost every hour . . . A book or a chair has a different appearance to the eye in every different distance and position; yet we conceive it to be still the same, and, overlooking the appearance, we immediately conceive the real figure, distance, and position of the body of which its visible or perspective appearance is a sign and indication" (135). All appearances to the contrary notwithstanding, the different is seen as the same, the apparent as the real. The senses not only gather "the facts" but interpret them as well. Prior to consciousness, sense perception is already at work making sense of the world.

Only with intensive training can someone such as a painter learn not to "understand." It takes special effort to see visible appearances: that is, how things "actually" look. Because the primary data of sense are sense judgments, sense data, or pure appearances as such, are in that respect secondary and derivative; and they are to be had, if at all, only by analytically deriving them from sense judgments. That Reid calls these judgments "original and natural" means that what is empirically primordial is not logically simple. "Instead of saying that belief and knowledge is got by putting together and comparing the simple apprehensions, we ought rather to say that the simple apprehension is performed by resolving and analysing a natural and original judgement. . . . Nature does not exhibit these elements [of sensation and belief] separate, to be compounded by us; she exhibits them mixed and compounded in concrete bodies, and it is only by art and chemical analysis that they can be separated" (107). Sense judgments can be analytically decomposed, but only artificially, hence not into more basic or primordial units, such as sensations. Reid's point is that these presumptively atomistic sensations are themselves interpretations. The interpretation is prior to the interpreted.

"Every house must have a foundation," Reid asserts *more geometrico* (435). It turns out, however, that the house of contingent knowledge built on common sense is founded on judgments and interpretations. Seeing is believing—that is, judging that what one sees exists and understanding it. Yet, though the line between sensation and reasoning, fact and inference, axiom and conclusion, is blurred and indistinct, it must be kept in mind that from this blurring Reid draws no skeptical conclusions whatever. Admittedly, what appear to be the raw data of sensation actually come precooked and predigested; but such natural interpretations Reid considers less dubitable and more reliable than the most authoritative experiences or reasonings that contradict them. As an epistemologist, Reid writes a whole chapter on "prejudices, the causes of error." But just two words indicate the real direction of his thought: a judgment of common sense he calls a "natural prejudice" (346),[23] and natural prejudices are distinct from artificial in one important way. All prejudices are tenacious and resistant to doubt; but because natural prejudices derive from our constitution, they are incorrigible. This means that they are fallible but indubitable. However often proved wrong, the prejudices, prejudgments, and fore-interpretations of common sense[24] are always taken to be true.

The primordiality of interpretation does raise doubts about reflection, if not about truth, however. "We take it for granted," Reid avers in his list of commonsense axioms, "that, by attentive reflection, a man may have a clear and certain knowledge of the operations of his own mind" (232). Yet doubts about this supposition arise, as when we are caught off guard with the hermeneutic complexity of sensation. "Under the appearance of the greatest simplicity, there is still in these sensations something of composition" (116). The illusion of elemental simplicity, of uninterpreted sensory data, proves to be a mistake of reflection deriving from the fact that the process of perceptual interpretation goes on *prereflectively.* "Nature carries on this part of the process of perception without our consciousness or concurrence" (187). "We draw the conclusion, without ever perceiving that ever the premises entered into the mind" (135). Inferences are being drawn from unconscious premises; interpretations are being constructed unawares. Such discoveries raise serious doubts about the adequacy of reflection if they are perpetually occurring behind its back, as it were.[25] The unconsciousness of perceptual interpretation raises doubts about the possibility of empirical truth, however, only for those who ground certainty exclusively on the testimony of conscious reflection. "But who is voucher for consciousness?" Reid asks of Descartes. "Can any man prove that his consciousness may not deceive him?" (100). Happily we need not depend on its veracity, Reid suggests, since we have common sense, a constitutional propensity for knowledge, an instinct for truth that serves even when consciousness falls short.

Even unconsciously, we have seen, sense perception and its next of kin, common sense, actively interpret and make sense of the world. This activist conception of the mind (typically associated with the name of Kant) goes to the heart of Reid's contribution to philosophy, as he perceived it. "The merit of what you are pleased to call *my philosophy,*" he wrote to James Gregory, "lies, I think, chiefly in having called in question the common theory of ideas, or images of things in the mind. . . . I think there is hardly anything that can be called mine in the philosophy of mind which does not follow with ease from the detection of this prejudice" (88).

Reid discovered, simply, that ideas, those cornerstones of knowledge, were a figment of epistemology. Those "shadowy kind of beings, intermediate between the thought and the object of thought, sometimes seem to coalesce with the thought, sometimes with the object of thought, and sometimes to have a distinct existence of their own" (279–80). No such entities exist or need be predicated to explain humankind's intellectual powers.[26] Here is how Reid concludes his history of ideal philosophy: "After so long a detail of the sentiments of philosophers, ancient and modern, concerning ideas, it may seem presumptuous to call in question their existence. . . . To prevent mistakes, the reader must again be reminded that if by ideas are meant only the acts or operations of our minds in perceiving, remembering, or imagining objects, I am far from calling in question the existence of those acts. . . . The ideas of whose existence I require the proof are not the operations of any mind, but supposed objects of those operations" (298).

In rejecting the ideal hypothesis, Reid specifically rejected the passivity of mind it implies. When the mind is employed in sensation, imagination, memory, and judgment, he observes, "we say it is very active; whereas if they were impressions only, as the ideal philosophy would lead us to conceive, we ought, in such a case, rather to say that the mind is very passive; for, I suppose, no man would attribute great activity to the paper I write upon because it receives a variety of characters" (115). Rather than passively accepting what it is "given," as on the model of the tabula rasa, "the mind is, from its very nature, a living and active being" (221). Given this activity, to have an idea does not mean to have a certain kind of entity in one's head that is called an idea; it means to perceive or imagine or re-member something. The shift from a passive to an active conception of mind implies that an idea is an act, not a thing; it is something the mind does, not something it receives. Reid's allegedly naive "direct" realism amounts to no more than this: he refuses to equate "stand for" with "stand in for" and refuses to admit that anything interposes between mind and world, because he refuses to reify mental acts into mental things such as ideas. Precisely the active character of mind, the fact that it is hermeneutic through and through, is obscured by the fiction of ideas. To supply the defects of ideal epistemology based on impressions and ideas, therefore, Reid develops an alternative explanation of knowing, which he calls "knowing things by signs."[27]

We, like Locke, ordinarily think of ideas as signs, but Reid evi-dently means to designate by the word *sign* a special kind of repre-sentation distinct from ideas and impressions. To clarify this distinc-tion, it will be convenient to employ C. S. Peirce's familiar classifications. Consider, first, the explanation of perception by ap-peal to impressions, or what Peirce calls "indexes." "This doctrine," Reid states, "appears evidently to be borrowed from the old system, which taught that external things make impressions upon the mind, like the impressions of a seal upon wax" (210). Conceived as indexical signs, signet impressions indicate the pressure of the ring in the same way as a broken twig indicates the passage of an animal or smoke indicates fire. It is a causal relation, and a perceptual impression might well be considered an indexical sign with a causal relation to its object.

Reid does not dispute that "there must be some action or impression upon the organ of sense" (186). Rather, he denies that the action of the thing explains the mind's own activity: "To give the name of an impression to any effect produced in the mind is to suppose that the mind does not act at all in the production of that effect" (228). "In the most extensive sense, an impression is a change produced in some passive subject by the operation of an external cause" (228). If we acknowledge that the mind is active, however, then it follows that perception is not just an effect either; that is, it is not the result of an external cause. The word *impression* implies that perception can be causally explained—indeed, that impressions are the very causes of it—and such for Reid is simply not the case. "That we can assign no adequate cause of our first conceptions of things, I think, is now acknowledged by the most enlightened philosophers. . . . That any kind of impression upon a body should be the efficient cause of a sensation [in the mind], appears very absurd" (326).

What Reid means by *sign,* then, can be negatively defined as not an indexical sign, not the effect of a cause. Our bodies are constantly being affected, our senses constantly bombarded by stimuli, and though some of these "impressions" force themselves on our attention, most are simply ignored—indeed, make no "impression." If a causal explanation of perception were sufficient, however, every effect would result in a percept because, like all indexes, effects indicate their causes whether anyone thinks they do or not. Sensations, therefore, cannot be indexical in any rigorous sense.

Impression refers not only to the causal relation of an indexical sign; it has the character of an iconic sign as well. "As the image of a seal upon wax has the form of the seal but nothing of the matter of it, so [Aristotle] conceived our sensations to be impressions upon the mind, which bear the image, likeness, or form of the external thing perceived, without the matter of it" (131). The similarity of the impression to what makes it—that is, of the iconic sign to its signified—distinguishes the impression of a seal from smoke or a broken twig, which are merely indexical. Hume, we recall, differentiated impressions from ideas on the basis of their vivacity or intensity; Reid typically differentiates them by associating impressions with the indexical relation and ideas with the iconic relation. Ideas considered as icons or images explain perception no better than indexical impressions, however, and perhaps worse.

The paradigmatic metaphor of iconic signification is of course the mirror of nature, and to this metaphor Reid objects even more strongly than to that of impression. "There is no phenomenon in nature more unaccountable than the intercourse that is carried on between the mind and the external world—there is no phenomenon which philosophical spirits have shown greater avidity to pry into and to resolve. . . . [Yet] all the fertility of human invention seems to have produced only one hypothesis for this purpose . . . and that is that the mind, like a mirror, receives the images of things from without by means of the senses" (140). Ideas conceived as images explain understanding by appeal to similarity. On the perceptual level—as, for Hume, on the personal level—like understands like. "The sixteenth century superimposed hermeneutics and semiology in the form of similitude," Foucault explains. "To search for a meaning is to bring to light a resemblance."[28] With this tradition of interpretation Reid broke decisively: "[The] dissimilitude between our sensations and the sensible qualities known to us by their means is the foundation of my system, as their similitude is the foundation of all the systems that went before."[29]

To Locke, who explains the ideas of primary qualities iconically, as "images or resemblances of what is really in the body" (277), Reid responds:

> Nothing can resemble a sensation but a similar sensation in the same or in some other mind. to think any quality in a thing that is inanimate can resemble a sensation is a great absurdity. In all this, I cannot but agree perfectly with Bishop Berkeley; and I think his notions of sensation much more distinct and accurate than Locke's. (290–91) . . .
>
> That external objects make some impression on the organs of sense, and by them on the nerves and brain, is granted; but that those impressions resemble the objects they are made by, so as that they may be called images of the objects, is most improbable. . . . We know that in vision an image of the visible object is formed in the bottom of the eye by the rays of light. But we know also that this image cannot be conveyed to the brain, because the optic nerve and all the parts that surround it are opaque and impervious to the rays

of light, and there is no other organ of sense in which any image of the object is formed. (256–57).

In his thesis that we "know things by signs," then, Reid means by *sign* a representation that is neither an impression nor an idea, neither an effect nor a simulacrum of what it represents.[30] Rather, as Berkeley had argued and Reid asserts, "the signs by which objects are presented to us in perception are the language of Nature to man" (185). Rather than being icons or indexes, sensations are signs in the narrow sense of what Peirce called "symbols," and their paradigm instances are words. Reid conceives signs on the model of language; and this model implies that all signs, whether natural or artificial, are arbitrary. "As in artificial signs there is often neither similitude between the sign and thing signified nor any connection that arises necessarily from the nature of the things, so it is also in natural signs" (121). "Certain impressions upon the body are constantly followed by certain sensations of the mind. . . . We see not the chain that ties these things together. Who knows but their connection may be arbitrary and owing to the will of our Maker?" (187).

Reid intends to draw no skeptical conclusions from the arbitrariness of the sign, as is evident when he refers it to the divine will. That the sign is arbitrary means that it involves no relation of resemblance or causality, not that the relation between signifier and signified is therefore unreal. "Nature has established a real connection between the signs and the things signified; and Nature has also taught us the interpretation of the signs—so that, previous to experience, the sign suggests the thing signified, and creates the belief in it" (195).

In such passages the word *suggests* means "signifies" (what the sign does) or "is interpreted as" (what the mind does).[31] This equation of interpretation with suggestion in the special case of signs proper helps to explain what in particular Reid means by all three. An "effect" indicates its cause; an "image" resembles its object; but an arbitrary "sign," in Reid's usage, "suggests" its signified. If "suggests" connotes something of the occult, the implication is not entirely inappropriate. "Though we never before had any notion or conception of the thing signified, [the signs] do suggest it, or conjure it up, as it were, by a natural kind of magic" (122). We saw above that Reid intends his appeal to the occult as an admission of ignorance, not as an explanation. But is the same true when Reid (or

Saussure, for that matter) asserts that the sign relation is arbitrary? Does this mean simply that we do not understand the relation?[32] To insist on the arbitrariness of the sign as such is to imply that, by definition, a sign is a representation that does not resemble its signified and is not caused by it. Rather, the defining character of a sign as such is that it "suggests" its signified, precisely and only because it is so interpreted.

Now this explanation may be no more satisfying than an appeal to inspiration or the Maker's will, but it seems to be the right one. Effects indicate their causes, and icons resemble their objects, whether anyone thinks they do or not. A (symbolic) sign, by contrast, is not a sign unless it is interpreted as a sign of something. "[What is] requisite to our knowing things by signs is that the appearance of the sign to the mind be followed by the conception and belief of the thing signified. Without this, the sign is not understood or interpreted, and therefore is no sign to us, however fit in its own nature for that purpose" (188).[33] A sign that is not understood is, by definition, not a sign. Interpretation, therefore, is not something accidental that happens to a sign but that which defines what it is. An (arbitrary) sign exists only in being interpreted.

Part of what Reid means by the term "suggestion" is that the interpretation which occurs in perceptual judgments is a matter of nonlogical inference.[34] Interpretive inference is not reasoning, he repeatedly insists.

> Let a man press his hand against the table—*he feels it hard.* But what is the meaning of this? The meaning undoubtedly is that he has a certain feeling of touch, from which he concludes, without any reasoning or comparing ideas, that there is something external really existing, whose parts stick so firmly together that they cannot be displaced without considerable force. There is here a feeling, and a conclusion drawn from it or some way suggested by it. . . . And as the feeling has no similitude to hardness, so neither can our reason perceive the least tie or connection between them; nor will the logician ever be able to show a reason why we should conclude hardness from this feeling, rather than softness or any other quality whatsoever. (125)

The fact is, Reid holds, that perceptual inferences are not primarily epistemic in nature, because they are not logical; nor are they conclusions arrived at through discursive reasoning. In this respect they are more like commonsense judgments, which lie "so near to perception that it is difficult to trace the line which divides the one from the other" (186). Both sense and common sense are inferential. Where they differ is that commonsense judgments are almost always analogical. We need to consider the analogical element in common sense more carefully, not just because it epitomizes the nonepistemic aspect of common sense, but also because Reid never tires of denying any similarity between sensations and the objects perceived. "I am sure," he insists, "that by proper attention and care I may know my sensations, and be able to affirm with certainty what they resemble and what they do not resemble. I have examined them one by one, and compared them with matter and its qualities; and I cannot find one of them that confesses a resembling feature" (141). Sensations do not resemble the qualities of things, just as mind does not resemble matter. The relation between the two is arbitrary and symbolic, not iconic.

Nevertheless, "there is a tendency in men to materialize everything" (470).

> Men whose attention is constantly solicited by external objects . . . [give even to the operations of their own minds] names from things that are familiar and which are conceived to have some similitude to them, and the notions we form of them are no less analogical than the names we have for them. Almost all the words by which we express the operations of the mind, are borrowed from material objects. To understand, to conceive to imagine, to comprehend, to deliberate, to infer, and many others are words of this kind; so that the very language of mankind with regard to the operations of our minds is analogical. (237)

Such analogical language, in fact, is in large part responsible, Reid thinks, for the mistakes of ideal epistemology.

Just as physical objects cannot affect each other at a distance, the old argument went, so two minds can be affected only by immediate objects, called ideas. The epistemology of ideas that postulates these "shadowy kind of beings intermediate between the thought and the object of thought" (279) is based on a physical—that is to say, analogical—conception of the mind's operations. All analogical reasoning is suspect, and such epistemology represents the paradigmatic case of false analogy. "Arguments drawn from analogy are still the weaker, the greater disparity there is between the things compared, and therefore must be weakest of all when we compare body with mind, because there are no two things in nature more unlike" (237). For this reason, the resemblances between body and mind tacitly posited in such key terms as "impression" and "image" have been "the most fruitful source of error with regard to the operations of our minds" (237).

Nevertheless, it is true that "the very language of mankind with regard to the operations of our minds is analogical" (237), and mistakes so widespread cannot be entirely groundless. "Even the prejudices and errors of mankind, when they are general, must have some cause no less general, the discovery of which will throw some light upon the frame of the human understanding" (239). This is not to say that some similarity of mind to body really does exist, but rather that the widely credited analogy between things so unlike indicates the extent to which the frame of human understanding is analogical. "Every man is apt to form his notions of things difficult to be apprehended or less familiar from their analogy to things which are more familiar" (202). Insofar as the human mind (no less than the divine) is itself difficult to apprehend, insofar as it is not open to direct observation and reflection, we have no choice but to understand and explain its functioning by analogy. "It is natural to men to judge of things less known by some similitude they observe, or think they observe, between them and things more familiar or better known. In many cases we have no better way of judging. . . . Analogical reasoning, therefore, is not in all cases to be rejected" (236–37).

In fact, analogy is in all cases accepted until there is reason to doubt it, and sometimes no such reason is found. "All false reasoning in philosophy is . . . drawn from experience and analogy, as well as just reasoning, otherwise it could have no verisimilitude" (199). The difference between true and false analogy is obviously not to be explained by the form of reasoning employed in reaching it: both are analogical. The province of the (veri)similar spans both the true and the false. Reliance on analogy explains our "unaccountable propensity to believe that the connections which we have observed in time past will continue in time to come. Omens, portents, good and bad luck, palmistry, astrology, all the numerous arts of divination and of interpreting dreams, false hypotheses and systems, and true principles in the philosophy of nature are all built upon the same foundation in the human constitution" (113). The perception of similarities is basic to science as well as quackery, to experiments as well as everyday experiences.

From analogy is drawn "the axiom upon which all our knowledge of nature is built: That effects of the same kind must have the same cause." Upon this axiom, which Reid calls "the inductive principle," "all inductive reasoning and all our reasoning from analogy is grounded" (199). He might just as well have called it "the analogical principle," since the question of sameness is always involved. The scientific "anticipation that there is a fixed and steady course of nature" is of a piece with the everyday "prescience that things which [we have] found conjoined in time past will be conjoined in time to come" (199) and with the "foresight . . . of the future and voluntary actions of our fellow-creatures" (196). The general reliability of analogy explains the fact that we are taken by surprise only rarely, rather than by the myriad novelties of every passing moment; it explains the predictability of life that makes us "capable of acting with common prudence in the conduct of life" (422). Such prudence involves simply determining what is appropriate on a given occasion by comparing it with others partly like, partly unlike.[35] Thus Reid concludes in the "Cura," that "the province we assign to common sense is to perceive the obvious agreements and differences and relations of things and to judge in matters of common life."[36] Ordinary good judgment consists in knowing how far two situations are similar and should therefore elicit similar responses. That is to say, common sense is a capacity for drawing apt analogies.[37]

This context makes it less surprising that, for all his caveats, Reid's own thinking is characteristically analogical. Though he cautions us "to be very suspicious of analogical reasoning" (238) in philosophy of mind, he does not try to eliminate it. If the problem is that "no two things in nature are more unlike" than body and mind, the solution is not to desist from analogical thinking but to find something more like mind than matter can be. For Reid the more appropriate analogue, as we have seen, is language.[38] "There is a much greater similitude than is commonly imagined between the testimony of nature given by our senses and the testimony of men given by language. . . . Our original or natural perceptions are analogous to the natural language of man to man" (184–85). Ideas may not exist, but language does; ideas may not explain understanding, but language can. "Language is the express image and picture of human thoughts; and from the picture we may often draw very certain conclusions with regard to the original" (233). Locke's distrust and Hume's reticent trust of language give way to implicit faith in Reid. Conclusions about human understanding drawn from the nature of language he considers certain, because understanding occurs only in the medium of language. More than merely the reflected image of thought, Reid explains, language directs thought.

> No man can pursue a train of thought or reasoning without the use of language. Words are the signs of our thoughts; and the sign is so associated with the thing signified that the last can hardly present itself to the imagination without drawing the other along with it. . . . Our thoughts take their colour in some degree from the language we use; and . . . although language ought always to be subservient to thought, yet thought must be, at some times and in some degree, subservient to language. As a servant that is extremely useful and necessary to his master by degrees acquires an authority over him, so that the master must often yield to the servant, such is the case with regard to language. . . . It is so useful and so necessary that we cannot avoid being sometimes led by it when it ought to follow. We cannot shake off this impediment—we must drag it along with us, and therefore must direct our course and regulate our pace as it permits. (474)

Compared with Locke's description of language as casting a mist of obscurity and disorder on our understandings (*Essay,* 3. 9. 21), the shift in Reid is slight but decisive: there is no longer any possibility of nonverbal thought; and so for better, and worse, the course and pace of thought are directed by language. This does not mean by the content of language; language does not have any content per se. Rather, it means that we discover the ineluctable forms of understanding by "attention to the structure of language" (238). Already in Reid, linguistics is replacing epistemology. We began by observing that Reid's interests are more epistemological than historical; now we must temper that observation by recognizing how strongly Reid affirms "the embeddedness of beliefs, implicit or explicit, in sociolinguistic practice."[39]

"Structure," for Reid, means, first, syntactic structure. Taking "I see the moon" as a typical report of perceptual judgment, Reid finds three elements: an agent, an act, and its object. The structure of language requires all three. Thus, when Hume (according to Reid) denies the existence of the agent and "confounds the operations of the mind and their objects," he must be understood as advocating either the use of bad grammar or the invention of a new one. If Hume assumes without proof that "distinctions found in the structure of all languages have no foundation in nature, this, surely, is too fastidious a way of treating the common sense of mankind" (224). In such passages Reid equates linguistic structure with common sense and employs verbal practice as a criterion for evaluating philosophical theory. "There is reason to distrust any philosophical theory when it leads men to corrupt language and to confound under one name operations of the mind which common sense and common language teach them to distinguish" (362). The fact that Hume must invent a language of ideas that confuses mental acts with extra-mental objects, "a language inconsistent with the principles upon which all language is grounded" (306), which therefore cannot be translated into "plain English" (199), constitutes prima facie evidence against the ideal epistemology on which it is based.[40] "Plain English" is the language of common sense, and making sense (of the mind, or anything else for that matter) involves expressing a content that respects the structures of language. Locke's distinction between acquiring knowledge and communicating it here collapses. Language is not just the instrument or medium or means of understanding but its end as well. Conceived on the model of ideal philosophy, understanding consisted in comparing ideas and accommodating the alien to the familiar; for Reid, by contrast, making sense is more accurately described as making what was silent speak.

The second aspect of linguistic structure that Reid emphasizes may be even more important to common sense. We have seen that Reid explains perception on the analogy of language (rather than of the body), and further that he considers commonsense judgments as themselves analogical. What I want to suggest in conclusion is that the reason why common language offers such an appropriate metaphor for the metaphorical judgments of common sense is because language is itself, in Reid's view, fundamentally metaphorical.

> There is nothing more common in the sentiments of all mankind and in the language of all nations than what may be called a communication of attributes; that is, transferring an attribute from the subject to which it properly belongs to some related or resembling subject. The various objects which nature presents to our view, even those that are most different

in kind, have innumerable similitudes, relations, and analogies, which we contemplate with pleasure and which lead us
naturally to borrow words and attributes from one object to
express what belongs to another. The greatest part of every
language under heaven is made up of words borrowed from
one thing and applied to something supposed to have some
relation or analogy to their first signification. (501)

Hume too had spoken of understanding the Greeks and Romans by
"transferring" to them observations made with regard to the French
and English. Though it might be plausible to say that understanding
so conceived consists of language transfer, Hume does not conceive
of this transference as metaphorical, because no difference is involved. "Mankind are so much the same in all times and places that
history informs us of nothing new or strange" (*ECHU* 83). What I
am suggesting is that Reid's conception of understanding as fundamentally linguistic and of language as fundamentally metaphorical
implicitly addresses a problem Hume left unresolved: namely, how
to understand difference. If common sense consists in finding commonalities between apparently unrelated things, then understanding
difference is like making metaphors. Because of the metaphoricity
of language, Reid is not forced to choose between affirming that (1)
history is essentially unreal because everything is the same as it has
always been, so everything is intelligible, and (2) history really offers
us things "new and strange," but, being genuinely unfamiliar, they
are unintelligible. Metaphor combines the similar and the different
without denying either one. If understanding cannot be separated
from saying what one understands (expressing it in one's own language), that does not mean that it necessarily involves a kind of
repressive assimilation to old forms and ideas, for the metaphorical
nature of language insures that one's own language is always open
to novelty.

Nothing, of course, contributes more to the ambiguity of words
than the ease of slippage from proper to improper usage which
enables language to deal with novelty. "The slightest similitude or
analogy is thought sufficient to justify the extension of a form of
speech beyond its proper meaning whenever the language does not
afford a more proper form" (2:516). This extension explains why all
words in fact have several meanings and can potentially have indefinitely many. To remedy such ambiguity, a terminological ideal of
language was sometimes proposed that would enforce precision by

allowing each word to designate only one thing. The difficulty immanent in this ideal, however, is something like that of Swift's Laputan sages who used things to converse and so carried the means of communication upon their backs; but however great their burdens, it sometimes happened that they found themselves without the very thing they wanted to talk about and so were at a loss. However many words are at one's disposal, one is continually running across something new for which there is no word. No finite pool is sufficient if new things and ideas are always coming up.

One way of attempting to accommodate novelty is represented by John Wilkins's "real character."[41] Recognizing the need to minimize ambiguity and needless confusion, Reid had a great deal of respect for the "grand and noble project of Bishop Wilkins to invent a philosophical language which should be free of the imperfections of vulgar languages" (474). This project accommodated novelty by subsuming it into categories; and being categorial it therefore had the additional advantage over the vulgar languages of logical precision. Everything conceivable was to receive a special kind of sign which itself exhibited the category to which the signified belonged. This necessitated devising categories numerous and capacious enough to cover everything. Wilkins, Reid explains, "founds his philosophical language and real character upon a systematical division and subdivision of all the things which may be expressed by language, and, instead of the ancient division into ten categories, has made forty categories, or *summa genera*" (474).

Accommodating novelty by subsuming it in prearranged categories raises new problems, however. First, there is the general problem that every ideal language calls into question the ideality of common language that Reid considers the very structure and manifestation of common sense. Second, Wilkins's particular ideal language requires that knowledge be complete, that all possible categories be known prior to its construction. It presumes, in sum, that there are no new kinds of things to be discovered, and so fails to accommodate novelty any better than the ideal of one word for one thing. This is the basis of Reid's primary doubt about Wilkins's project: "Whether this division . . . will always suit the various systems that may be introduced and all the real improvements that may be made in human knowledge may be doubted. . . . It is to be feared that this noble attempt of a great genius will prove abortive" (474).

Until knowledge is complete, new discoveries will necessitate the creation of new terms, and genuinely new things will show that not just the old terms but the old categories and, indeed, every finite set of categories are incomplete and need to be supplemented. Every actual language state is impoverished by comparison to what could potentially be thought and said, Reid explains; yet common, unphilosophical language contains within itself the capacity for infinite expansion. "The poverty of language no doubt contributes in part to the use of metaphor; and therefore we find the most barren and uncultivated languages the most metaphorical. But the most copious language may be called barren compared with the fertility of human conceptions, and can never, without the use of figures, keep pace with the variety of their delicate modifications" (496). The fecundity of language made possible by metaphor keeps pace with the fertility of conception and insures that thought is never mute. Precisely defined terms are, by their very nature, of limited application. Categories, whether there are ten or forty or four hundred, can run out, and always do at some point, leaving the logician at a loss for words. But there is nothing that cannot be metaphorically expressed and understood. "There is nothing in the course of nature so singular but we can find some resemblance, or at least some analogy, between it and other things with which we are acquainted" (201). Human understanding has no limits, because human language has none.

At the bottom of Reid's common sense philosophy is the thesis that logical analysis and discursive reasoning stop at some point, but understanding does not. The primordial operations of the mind, Reid admits, "cannot be logically defined" (220); indeed, the very attempt to define the indefinable is misguided. "When men attempt to define things which cannot be defined, their definitions will always be either obscure or false" (220). But the fact that "it is often impossible to define words which we must use" to talk about human understanding (220) does not show that we have no real knowledge of it. We have an acquaintance with it that comes in part from introspective reflection, Reid asserts. But reflection, like all thought, must regulate its course by the language that directs it, and "the very language of mankind with regard to the operation of our minds," Reid insists, "is analogical" (237). What makes "impressions" and "ideas" objectionable in philosophy of mind is not that they are metaphors, but that they are taken for literal descriptions or logical definitions and that philosophers try to reason discursively from them. But that is merely to make reason (or the mathematical model of it) overextend itself and usurp the province of common sense. When we speak of conceiving, imagining, comprehending, inferring, and deliberating, we say as precisely as the nature of the case admits exactly what mental operations are *like;* and though such metaphors are not susceptible of logical definition, there is no language more accurate, more precise, or more intelligible than the commonsense metaphors of common language.

6

Blackstone on Equity

A V. Dicey took the occasion of his retirement from the
Vinerian Professorship of Law in 1909 to pay tribute to
Sir William Blackstone, the first occupant of that chair
and author of the *Commentaries on the Laws of England*
(1765–69). Dicey admitted that Blackstone's great opus was rendered
obsolete by Sergeant Stephen's revision (1841) and, more important,
that its authority was undermined by Jeremy Bentham's *Fragment on
Government* (1776). "The *Fragment,* which was merely a small part
of an intended *Commentary on the Commentaries,* . . . achieved complete success. It proved once and for all that Blackstone . . . was a
lax thinker. . . . Among men of thought Blackstone's reputation as
a profound jurist never recovered."[1] Even readers more generous
than Bentham and less vicious than Austin, his disciple, must acknowledge that "Blackstone was somewhat deficient in keen logical
discernment."[2] "Wherein then," Dicey asks, "are to be found the
permanent merits of the *Commentaries*? They may all be summed up
in a few words. The book is the work of an eminent lawyer who
was also a consummate man of letters; by virtue both of his knowledge of law and of his literary genius he produced the one treatise
on the laws of England which must for all time remain a part of
English literature. The *Commentaries* live by their style."[3]

"This assertion itself needs explanation," Dicey immediately adds;
and so it does, for to celebrate the *Commentaries* as literature is hardly
to pay its author an unambiguous compliment. By style, Dicey says,

he means "power of expression, clearness of aim, [and] literary judgment or tact."⁴ But this does little to avoid the incongruity entailed
by assimilating Blackstone's *Commentaries* to belles lettres. It is not
"literary judgment," primarily, that one expects from a judge or
educator of judges.⁵ Cited some ten thousand times in the decisions
of American courts alone by 1915, the celebrity of the *Commentaries*
would seem to rest on foundations more substantial than literary
merit.⁶ But such an objection to Dicey's apparently faint praise assumes the insubstantiality of literature by contrast with law, and this
is an assumption which Dicey does not make. His respect for literature and the breadth of his conception of it mean that his praise of
Blackstone's literary judgment is neither compensation for some
supposed logical deficiency nor, worse, unwitting insult.

> Of his supreme skill in the use of literary judgement no better
> example can be given than his unrivalled success in blending
> the history with the exposition of English law. How to
> achieve this combination is the problem which drives to
> despair any teacher who undertakes to explain adequately
> and intelligibly the existing law of England. For that law
> itself is the outcome of historical causes often in themselves
> very obscure and recorded, if at all, in judicial decisions and
> a series of statutes extending over many centuries. The per-
> plexed expounder therefore of such a system soon finds that
> if he neglects historical considerations, he falls into the vice
> of logical formalism, whilst, if he pursues the history of any
> law too far, he becomes involved in the mazes of pedantic
> antiquarianism. No formula will tell any man what is the
> method by which to avoid both of these opposite errors. It
> can be discovered only by the use of good sense and tact. It
> is here that Blackstone's sound judgment came to his aid.⁷

Good sense, tact, sound judgment—these are not specially literary
merits. Nor are they merely ancillary qualities contingent to the legal
profession but virtues of mind essential to the just interpretation of
law, whether in the form of commentary or judicial decision.

By Blackstone's "judgment" Dicey refers specifically to the successful blending of historical explanation with systematic exposition
in the *Commentaries*. Neither is dispensable; each counterbalances the
other. Without a sense of history, law is reduced to abstract logic,
as if legal judgments were determined by syllogism; yet without a
sense of its systematic coherence, law is reduced to historical contin-

gency, as if decisions were dictated by chance or power. Not only the commentator but the practitioner needs a sense of both. For just as a sense of history exposes the vacuous coherence of logical system, so a sense of system exposes the insignificance of historical aberrations. "No formula," Dicey emphasizes, can determine the balancing point beyond which the study of law degenerates into "logical formalism" or "pedantic antiquarianism"; and this insufficiency of formulas explains why judgment is necessary. For good sense, tact, and sound judgment are required to determine precisely those questions which cannot be decided epistemically, by formulas, rules, or laws alone.

Under the vast influence of Kant's *Critique of Judgment,* art came to encompass whatever cannot be produced by rule; thus it is not surprising that Dicey should celebrate the *Commentaries* as literature and praise Blackstone's judgment as literary, because more than formulas were involved in his success. But the *Commentaries* has nothing specifically aesthetic about it. That was Kant's aim: to discriminate the specifically aesthetic from other modes of thought; it was not Blackstone's. Blackstone emphasizes not only the integrity of law but its integration with other disciplines. Just as Samuel Johnson can without solecism envision the poet as the "legislator of mankind,"[8] so Blackstone conceives of legal expertise in the context of general literacy. Knowledge of law per se is absolutely necessary, but it is not sufficient to make a good judge. More than the law is requisite to the cultivation of good judgment, legal or otherwise.

A student of the law—whether lawyer or commentator—needs logic, history, literature, and all the diversity of a liberal education to achieve good sense, Blackstone argues, because judgment is not to be acquired through the technicalities of a technical education alone. If the student concentrates solely on the law, he writes, then "ita lex scripta est (so the law is written) is the utmost his knowledge will arrive at" (1:33). "The least variation from established precedents will totally distract and bewilder him" because, lacking a general background, he cannot assimilate novelty and difference, and so must apply the law tactlessly, to every situation identically as if all situations were as immutable as the written law. Such mechanical application of the law in fact proves to be no less capricious and unjust than arbitrary preference operating in disregard of the law. Good judgment is indispensable in achieving the fit between the abstractions of the law and the particulars of the case that justice itself demands; and that judgment is best cultivated through a liberal education.

Among the numerous examples of literary (though not specifically aesthetic) judgment, Dicey mentions Blackstone's "explanation of the growth and nature of equity."[9] This particular blend of narrative and exposition has special significance because equity, in one sense at least, means precisely the common sense, tact, and sound judgment that are needed to interpret the law justly—hence the hermeneutic significance of these qualities. Moreover, the word *equity* refers not only to a juridical ideal but also to a concrete, historical institution: the equity court of Chancery. The Chancery court gradually separated itself from the King's Bench, Common Pleas, and the Exchequer; and the extraordinary court of Chancery was called the "equity court" in distinction from the courts of law.[10] Viewed historically, then, law and equity came to be distinct institutions. Logically considered, however, there could be no difference between the two—as if sound, equitable judgments were the special province of equity courts. It seemed clear to Blackstone that Chancery had no corner on justice. Yet it was no less evident that the courts of law and of equity were in specifiable respects quite different. The problem which this difference presented to Blackstone's judgment, then, was not merely that of balancing logical and historical explanations but of reconciling their contradictions. Either the law and equity courts were essentially one, in which case the history of their division was merely accidental and contingent; or if not contingent, their history had given birth to a logical absurdity: namely, dual systems of justice.

Typically, Blackstone does not and need not confront the possibility that reason and history are other than complementary.[11] These twin grounds of legal authority not only undergird the law but support each other reciprocally, since for Blackstone the real and ideal coincide. This coincidence is reflected in the complementarity of historical narrative and systematic exposition: the two modes of commentary cannot conflict so long as history is itself conceived as rational and ethical.

Blackstone's legal optimism (for which Bentham dubbed him "everything-as-it-should-be Blackstone"[12]) is neither ludicrous nor obsolete. Indeed, many of its fundamental tenets are still very much current. Foremost among them is the premise that "law, in its most general and comprehensive sense, signifies a rule of action" (1:38).[13] More specifically, Blackstone defines municipal law (for example,

British law) as "a rule of civil conduct, prescribed by the supreme power in a state, commanding what is right and prohibiting what is wrong" (1:44). Almost every aspect of this definition could be disputed, and has been; but the premise that a law is a rule has, virtually without exception,[14] seemed indisputable. This premise lies at the root of Blackstone's conception of the law as rational; for rationality is almost synonymous with regularity, the quality of being rule-governed. Laws either describe regularities already existing or create regularities that should exist but would not without them. Either way, what acts according to rule and law is predictable, intelligible, and rational. Moreover, Blackstone continues, a rule is "something permanent, uniform, and universal" (1:44). In these respects, too, the lawful shares essential qualities with the rational. The regular excludes the historical only if history is conceived as the domain of ephemeral, variform particulars, the domain (in short) of the irrational. But like Bolingbroke and Burke, Blackstone hardly ever thinks of history this way; rather, it is a process of regularization, of establishing and preserving fixed regularities.

Repeatedly Blackstone invokes Fortesque's advice that the student should "trace up the principles and grounds of the law, even to their original elements" (1:37). Significantly, he is here advocating both a historical analysis of beginnings and a rational analysis of principles. Blackstone draws no distinction between the two, for in the beginning of history are to be found not only the chronologically initial but also the logically fundamental. In one sense, historical research is the search backward to discover the sacred origin, the first instance, which must be repeated forever after. But from another perspective, one need not undo time to find the original ground, since one of the grounds of law is time itself. Just as Shakespeare's plays, Johnson observed,[15] could claim "prescriptive veneration" by reason of their length of duration and generality of esteem, so also customs long repeated acquire the force of law by their longevity and breadth of usage.

Customs enduring from earliest times have accrued an enormous weight of authority. Often, however, that authority does not derive from some specifiable origin that could be confirmed by historical research, because the oldest, most venerable customs "are of higher antiquity than memory or history can reach, nothing being more difficult than to ascertain the precise beginning and first spring of an ancient and long-established custom. Whence it is that in our law the goodness of a custom depends upon its having been used time out of mind or, in the solemnity of our legal phrase, time whereof the memory of man runneth not to the contrary" (1:67).[16] The authority of common laws is verified not by the success of historical research but by its impossibility. In part, the origin of common laws is obscured by mere lack of data;[17] more radically, however, Blackstone suggests that history cannot retrace customs to their origins not just because they have been forgotten but because, in a sense, the most authoritative customs have no origins. A custom is law if it has "been used so long that the memory of man runneth not to the contrary. So that, if anyone can show the beginning of it, it is no good custom" (1:77). Not the origin but the lack of it confers authority. Like Reid, Blackstone feels no need to bemoan the absence of origins and sure foundations. Customs without a beginning or an enactment, those for which every precedent is precedented, have been "always the custom" (1:68). They are eternal. Permanent, uniform, universal—unoriginated customs are regularities inscribed in the nature of things. As modes of grounding the authority of law, reason and history are complementary.

It cannot legitimately be objected that Blackstone has simply idealized the past and confused history with reason, "was" with "ought to be."[18] If that is a confusion, it is endemic not only to legal conservatism but to justice, for uniformity over time is a characteristic of justice as well as of reason. In the absence of special circumstances, fairness requires that like cases be treated alike. That judicial decisions be in principle predictable is essential to their being just. Therefore "it is an established rule to abide by former precedents where the same points come again in litigation" (1:69). The history of precedent, the heritage of judicial decision, shows what determinations are just and reasonable in a given kind of case. For a judge to decide otherwise, "according to his private sentiments" and not "according to the known customs and laws of the land," makes the law vague and its application tyrannical. Judges are "delegated not to pronounce a new law but to maintain and expound the old one" (1:69).

Though steadfastly conservative, however, Blackstone is in no danger of precluding all innovation or confusing mere inertia with justice and reason. The doctrine of precedents does not imply that established and customary errors should be taken as true or that injustice often enough repeated becomes just.

If it be found that the former decision is manifestly absurd or unjust, it is declared not that such a sentence was *bad law* but that it was *not law;* that is, that it is not the established custom of the realm, as has been erroneously determined. And hence it is that our lawyers are with justice so copious in their encomiums on the reason of the common law, that they tell us that the law is the perfection of reason, that it always intends to conform thereto, and that what is not reason is not law. Not that the particular reason of every rule in the law can at this distance of time be always precisely assigned; but it is sufficient that there be nothing in the rule flatly contradictory to reason, and then the law will presume it to be well founded. (1:70)

Blackstone preserves the perfect rationality of law by distinguishing laws from decisions and confining errors solely to the latter. If only decisions can be mistaken, to say that the law as such represents the perfection of reason is something of a truism. But even if so, it is a salutary truism, for judges should not be asked to choose between making lawful decisions and reasonable ones.

No less than Toland, Blackstone recognizes the slipperiness of the notion of reason. His claim that the law is the perfection of reason relies on at least three senses of the word *reason:* (1) *reason* is synonymous with justice as a general ethical ideal; (2) *reason* means specific practical purposes (or reasons for acting in a particular way); and (3) *reason* refers, minimally, to what is not unreasonable. With respect to the first of these (reason as equivalent to justice), Blackstone cites the *Nichomachean Ethics:* "Aristotle himself has said . . . that jurisprudence is the principal and most perfect branch of ethics" (1:28). To all but legal purists it is evident that law overlaps with ethics; to all but moral purists it is evident that law cannot be reduced to ethical precepts. Blackstone was neither. In his view, the law has not only a historical and rational but also (what was much the same) an ethical ground insofar as justice is a virtue. Insofar as the idea of legality falls within the idea of justice, law belongs to the province of ethics. Thus by the phrase "the law of nature" Blackstone refers not only to physical regularities of animate and inanimate matter but also to moral regularities, rules of conduct or ethical principles—"that we should live honestly," for example, "should hurt nobody, and should render everyone his due" (1:40). These principles (which he cites from Justinian's *Institutes*) are not only moral but rational, because the law of nature is what incontrovertibly makes sense and is discoverable without revelation by "the due exertion of right reason" alone (1:40). "No human laws are of any validity if contrary to this; and such of them as are valid derive all their force and all their authority, mediately or immediately, from this original" (1:41). Ethical principles not only underwrite the human laws binding in courts of law; ethics are binding in the superior court of conscience, which can reverse the decisions of other, lower courts.

Blackstone leaves the door open to principled disobedience of civil law insofar as he assigns moral principles more authority than statutes. Yet he also recognizes that the realm of law exceeds that of ethics, because many laws cover matters that have virtually no moral significance. "Things in themselves indifferent" are subject to legal regulation not for ethical but for practical purposes. "These [morally indifferent things] become either right or wrong, just or unjust, duties or misdemeanors, according as the municipal legislator sees proper for promoting the welfare of the society and more effectually carrying on the purposes of civil life" (1:55). Here "right" and "wrong" do not mean "good" and "evil" but rather "permitted" and "prohibited" by law. Yet such laws too can be called "the perfection of reason" insofar as they do not merely register legislative caprice but discriminate what is socially beneficial from what is harmful. In this context the "reason of the law" becomes the "reasons for the laws," not law as absolute justice based on eternal ethical duty but relativized to the needs of particular social and historical situations as satisfied by particular laws, regulations, and policies.[19] The speed limit is set by the oil supply, not by the principles of natural justice.

This does not mean that the speed limit is unreasonable or unjust, however, and Blackstone is willing to attribute rationality to such regulations so long as "there be nothing in the rule flatly contradictory to reason" (1:70). One must assume that a given regulation was initially made for a good reason, because "we owe such a deference to former times as not to suppose they acted wholly without consideration" (1:70). Yet, more than occasionally, such charity of construal is not forthcoming. In *Tristram Shandy,* for example, Sterne has great fun with the notion (which he found in Swinburne's *Treatise of Testaments and Last Wills*) that in the eyes of the law "the mother was not of kin to her child."[20] We can translate this legal rule (and it really was one) into less ludicrous terms: "The parent, though next of kin, cannot inherit the estate of the child." But even if less inane, this version of the rule seems no more intelligible than Sterne's, and it is particularly instructive to observe how Blackstone saves it from absurdity.

"The first rule" of inheritance, according to Blackstone, is this: "Inheritances shall lineally descend to the issue of the person last actually seized, *in infinitum;* but shall never lineally ascend" (2:208). In Blackstone's brilliantly argued explanation of this rule, we can see how all three senses of reason cooperate to render the law's rationality virtually indubitable.

> This rule, so far as it is affirmative and relates to lineal descents, is almost universally adopted by all nations; and it seems founded on a principle of natural reason, that (whenever a right of property transmissible to representatives is admitted) the possessions of the parents should go, upon their decease, in the first place to their children, as those to whom they have given being and for whom they are therefore bound to provide. But the negative branch, or total exclusion of parents and all lineal ancestors from succeeding to the inheritance of their offspring, is peculiar to our own laws. . . . For, by the Jewish law, on failure of issue, the father succeeded to the son. . . . Hence this rule of our laws has been censured and declaimed against, as absurd and derogating from the maxims of equity and natural justice. Yet that there is nothing unjust or absurd in it, but that, on the contrary, it is founded upon very good reason, may appear from considering as well the nature of the rule itself as the occasion of introducing it into our laws.
>
> We are to reflect, in the first place, that all rules of succession to estates are creatures of the civil polity, and *juris positivi* merely. The right of property, which is gained by occupancy, extends naturally no further than the life of the present possessor, after which the land by the law of nature would again become common and liable to be seized by the next occupant; but society, to prevent the mischiefs that might ensue from a doctrine so productive of contention, has established conveyances, wills, and successions whereby the property originally gained by possession is continued and transmitted from one man to another, according to the rules which each state has respectively thought proper to prescribe. There is certainly, therefore, no injustice done to individuals, whatever be the path of descent marked out by the municipal law.
>
> If we next consider the time and occasion of introducing

this rule into our law, we shall find it to have been grounded upon very substantial reasons. I think there is no doubt to be made but that it was introduced at the same time with and in consequence of the feudal tenures. . . . These circumstances evidently show this rule to be of feudal origin; and, taken in that light, there are some arguments in its favour, besides those which are drawn merely from the reason of the thing. For if the feud, of which the son died seized, was really . . . descended to him from his ancestors, the father could not possibly succeed to it, because it must have passed him in the course of descent. . . . [Moreover, if the feud was] one newly acquired by the son, then only the descendants from the body of the feudatory himself could succeed, by the known maxim of the early feudal constitutions, which was founded as well upon the personal merit of the vassal, which might be transmitted to his children but could not ascend to his progenitors, as also upon this consideration of military policy, that the decrepit grandsire of a vigorous vassal would be but indifferently qualified to succeed him in his feudal services. . . . These reasons, drawn from the history of the rule itself, seem to be more satisfactory than that quaint one of Bracton, adopted by Sir Edward Coke, which regulates the descent of lands according to the laws of gravitation. (2:210–12)

Like Sterne, Blackstone had a sense of humor about his predecessors; but though he denies their explanation, he affirms their conclusion. Once a right to property is admitted, Blackstone argues, the positive rule of *descent* is grounded in natural reason and natural justice— simply, the duty of parents by their children. By contrast, the negative of the rule, precluding *ascent,* appears to be based not on ethical but on historical reasons peculiar to the feudal period, when special conditions necessitated special laws. Insofar as these laws served the practical ends for which they were designed, they were quite rational. The problem arises, however, when precedent requires that laws of policy fitted to particular historical conditions be applied later, when those conditions no longer obtain. Can it be said that history transforms reason into absurdity and injustice?

Blackstone replies that it does not, and here he is at his best. He forestalls the potential conflict between history and natural reason or natural justice by arguing that inheritance is a matter that is ethically indifferent. He does not deny that parents are naturally obligated to care for their children; he denies only that the parents have any natural right to dispose of their property, or indeed any natural right to property at all.[21] Ownership is constituted by occupancy—that is, by power—and is not naturally a right. Once the occupant dies or is otherwise dispossessed, natural reason and natural justice are perfectly silent about who should receive the property. In such matters of indifference, therefore, right and wrong are not determined by natural law. Some statutory law is necessary to prevent everyone from contending for what belongs inherently to no one. Any law prescribing descent of property will suffice as long as it is clear, so the vestigial policies of the feudal period may as well be preserved as not. Applying the feudal rule against ascent to modern inheritance cases is therefore not ipso facto unreasonable or unjust, since reason and justice mandate no particular line of inheritance at all. Blackstone's skepticism is here absolute. History is cleared of the charge of producing unreason, because in this instance only historical reasons are pertinent. Natural reason and justice are mute and irrelevant.

In such matters, where ethical principles do not pertain and there is no overlap between law and morality, legality becomes the criterion of justice and "artificial reason" the ground of legal authority. Somewhat reminiscent of Hume's notion of justice as an "artificial virtue," Blackstone employs this curious phrase "artificial reason" on several occasions. Sometimes it means a particular or historical reason, as above. Concerning the law that half brothers cannot inherit from their half brothers, Blackstone writes, "Herein there is nothing repugnant to natural justice; though the artificial reason of it, drawn from the feudal law may not be quite obvious to everybody" (1:71). As opposed not only to natural but also to absolute reason, the word *artificial* refers to rationality as relative to particular historical circumstances. Artificial reasons, though not obvious to everybody, may be discovered by a legal historian.

Another instance of the phrase, however, makes clear that historical research is not the sole criterion. To be accredited with the force of law, Blackstone asserts, "customs must be *reasonable;* or rather, taken negatively, they must not be unreasonable. Which is not always, as Sir Edward Coke says, to be understood of every unlearned man's reason, but of artificial and legal reason, warranted by authority of law" (1:78). Here the concept of "artificial or legal reason" refers to the autonomy of the legal system, the emancipation of law from religious and political domination. Roscoe Pound, the great

Harvard professor of law, relates particularly well the tale, to which Blackstone alludes, of Coke's role in this liberation.

> On a memorable Sunday morning, the 10th of November, 1612, the judges of England were summoned before King James I upon complaint of the Archbishop of Canterbury. . . . The immediate business of the Sunday morning conference with the judges was to explain this proposition [that the king could try cases himself] and hear what they could say to it. The Archbishop proceeded to expound the alleged royal prerogative, saying that the judges were but the delegates of the king, wherefore the king might do himself, when it seemed best to him, what he left usually to these delegates. He added that this was clear, if not in law yet beyond question in divinity, for it could be shown from the word of God in the Scripture. To this Coke answered on behalf of the judges that by the law of England the king in person could not adjudge any cause; all cases, civil and criminal, were to be determined in some court of justice according to the law and custom of the realm. "But," said the king, "I thought law was founded upon reason, and I and others have reason as well as the judges." "True it was," Coke responded, "that God had endowed his Majesty with excellent science and great endowments of nature; but his Majesty was not learned in the laws of his realm of England, and causes which concern the life or inheritance or goods or fortunes of his subjects are not to be decided by natural reason, but by the artificial reason and judgment of the law, which law is an art which requires long study and experience before that a man can attain to the cognizance of it." At this the king was much offended, saying that in such case he should be under the law, which it was treason to affirm. Coke answered in the words attributed to Bracton, that the king ought not to be under any man but under God and the law.[22]

This anecdote regarding the supremacy of law, to which even the king is subject, describes the independence of the legal system not only from monarchical and ecclesiastical intervention but also its autonomy from common sense. A law, Coke argues, may be good even if it contradicts the king's "natural reason" and "every unlearned man's reason" (1:78), because only the artificial reason of experts within the system is relevant. Even though historically "the particular reason of it cannot be assigned," a law will stand, so long as "no good legal reason can be assigned against it" (1:78). As implied by Coke's notion of artificial reason, rationality consists in the coherence and consistency of laws within a closed system incommensurate with other decision-making procedures and unintelligible to all but those who are "learned in the laws of the land."

But "let the learned say what they will," Uncle Toby obstinately maintained, "there must certainly have been some sort of consanguinity between the duchess of Suffolk and her son." To which Yorick replied, "The vulgar are of the same opinion . . . to this hour."[23] To the learned the notion of artificial reason may be legal sophistication, but to the vulgar it is mere sophistry. If natural justice demands that parents care for their children, as Blackstone admits, it demands by the same argument that children provide for their parents. Inheritance by descendants and inheritance by ancestors rest on one and the same bond. To exclude lineal ascent on the basis of artificial reason is therefore to promote irrationality and injustice not out of conservatism based on fairness and consistency but out of a convenient obliviousness to the reality of historical change motivated by the legal guild's zealous concern to preserve its power.

The rise of equity courts, as Blackstone tells the story, is a response to this obliviousness and the consequent petrification of common law courts (King's Bench and Common Pleas). Unique to British law, "this distinction between law and equity, as administered in different courts, is not at present known, nor seems to have ever been known, in any other country at any time" (3:49). Though the theoretical difference between law and equity was of ancient origin and common to many legal systems, England alone had institutionalized it in separate courts.[24] They were by Blackstone's time not separate and equal: "The extraordinary court [of Chancery], or court of equity, is now become the court of the greatest consequence" (1:49). As such, the equity court was a standing monument to the deficiency and calcification of the law courts, where Coke was Chief Justice.

Blackstone explains the early history of equity as follows: "When the courts of law, proceeding merely upon the ground of the king's original writs and confining themselves strictly to that bottom, gave a harsh or imperfect judgment, the application for redress used to be to the king in person assisted by his privy council . . . and they were wont to refer the matter either to the chancellor and a select committee or, by degrees, to the chancellor only, who mitigated the severity or supplied the defects of the judgments pronounced in the courts of law, upon weighing the circumstances of the case" (3:50). Judgments in law courts were apt to be "harsh and imperfect" on this view, not because of the cruelty of the judges but because law court procedures were few and inflexible. Sometimes it was obvious that a judgment was wrong albeit perfectly legal, and in such cases (prior to the establishment of an equity court) the plaintiff could appeal to the king or chancellor in person. From him the plaintiff sometimes obtained redress, but an offender was punished no further than by forcing him to do his duty.

No equity court would have been necessary at all, however, had not the law clerks been "too much attached to ancient precedent" or had the statute of Westminster II (expanding the power to devise new writs) been interpreted with

> a little liberality in the judges, by extending rather than narrowing the remedial effects of the writ. . . . But when, about the end of the reign of King Edward III [ca. 1350], uses of land were introduced, and, though totally discountenanced by the courts of common law, were considered as fiduciary deposits and binding in conscience by the clergy, the separate jurisdiction of the chancery as a court of equity began to be established; and John Waltham . . . devised the writ of *subpoena,* returnable in the court of chancery only, to make the feoffee to uses accountable to his *cestuy que use* which process was afterwards extended to other matters wholly determinable at the common law. (3:51)

The moral of the story, as Blackstone narrates it, is that the new power of subpoena could easily have been appropriated by common law as well as Chancery but was not; the common law courts were simply too tradition-bound to acknowledge that, with a little adaptability, most of the cases tried in Chancery could just as well be tried in King's Bench or Common Pleas.

Whereas the common law was so regular and predictable as to be rigid and mechanical, however, the equity courts erred in the other direction. Blackstone observes that "no regular system at that time prevailed in the [equity] court" (3:53). This irregularity and unpredictability could be attributed to at least two causes: either equity decisions were adapted to "the circumstances of the case" (3:50) and varied with them, or they were made "according to the private opinion of the chancellor, who was generally an ecclesiastic" (3:53).

William West stresses the first of these causes: namely, that equity accommodates itself to the particulars of the case:

> Strict law and equity differ herein, that strict law sets down in a general sort what it enacts and is severe, and not to be moved one way or other. It takes order for things, once for all; the grounds and principles which it brings forth are universal and full of severity and sharpness, from which rules it will not start aside, no not the breadth of a hair. But equity is fitly compared to a shoemaker's shop, that is well furnished with all sorts and manner of lasts for men's feet, where each man may be sure to find one last or other that shall fit him, be he great or small.[25]

The alternative explanation for the unpredictability of Chancery decisions was that they varied not with the circumstances of the case but with the conscience of the chancellor. Perhaps because acknowledging differences between various situations seemed simply a matter of fairness or perhaps because the chancellor was typically a churchman, not a lawyer, or perhaps because he was titled "keeper of the king's conscience," equity decisions seemed to be determined by the chancellor's conscience; and equity courts under his supervision came to be called "courts of conscience." Yet, however ethically sensitive, conscience is not entirely reliable. In a witty reversal of West's metaphor, John Selden stigmatizes the unreliability of conscience: "For *law,* we have a measure, and know what to trust to; *equity* is according to the conscience of him that is chancellor, and, as that is larger or narrower, so is equity. 'Tis all one, as if they should make the standard for the measure a chancellor's foot. What an uncertain measure would this be! . . . It is the same thing with the chancellor's conscience" (3:432n.).

Blackstone cites this passage, and Sterne no doubt read it too, since he voices the same skepticism as Selden in Yorick's sermon on conscience. Its last paragraph concludes: "And, in your own case, remember this plain distinction, a mistake in which has ruined thousands—that your conscience is not a law. No, God and reason made the law, and have placed conscience within you to determine, not like an Asiatic Cadi, according to the ebbs and flows of his own passions, but like a British judge in this land of liberty and good sense, who makes no new law, but faithfully declares that law which he knows already written."[26] Blackstone notes that Selden's objection to equity courts has "more pleasantry than truth" (3:432n.). Yet whether truly or falsely, laudably or lamentably, conscience could not have become associated solely with courts of equity had not law courts too often handed down decisions that were unconscionable.

One such decision, according to Blackstone's history, occasioned the dispute which raised equity to a position of superiority over law:

> In the time of Lord Ellesmere (A.D. 1616) arose that notable dispute between the courts of law and equity set on foot by Sir Edward Coke, then chief justice of the court of King's Bench: whether a court of equity could give relief after or against a judgment at the common law. This contest was so warmly carried on that indictments were preferred against the suitors, the solicitors, the counsel, and even a master in chancery for . . . questioning in a court of equity a judgment in the court of King's Bench obtained by gross fraud and imposition. This matter, being brought before the king, was by him referred to his learned council for their advice and opinion; who reported so strongly in favour of the courts of equity that his majesty gave judgment on their behalf. (3:53–54)

The decision against the suitor had been legally but fraudulently obtained in King's Bench. Though the witnesses had been tampered with, the evidence of tampering could be not introduced; but when the suitor brought an appeal to Chancery, where such evidence was permitted, he and everyone else concerned were indicted by King's Bench for questioning its judgment. Coke submitted to the king's reversal but was soon thereafter removed from office. This episode marked the fact that the two courts were not only separate but unequal, for the equity court of Chancery now possessed not only moral but political superiority.

What it still did not possess, though, was predictability. It gave full cognizance to unlikeness but had no fixed principles and no rules whereby like cases could be decided alike. This defect was remedied by Chancellor Ellesmere's successors. Blackstone brings the history of equity courts up to the present when he writes that Bacon "reduced the practice of the court into a more regular system" (1:54). That is, through the efforts of Bacon and those who followed him, equity courts began to approximate the regularity of the rule-governed law courts.[27]

Thus the history of equity comes full circle. When in the Saxon period the king's court was divided into separate jurisdictions, "the idea of a court of equity, as distinguished from a court of law, did not subsist in the original plan of partition" (1:50). Over succeeding centuries, a long but temporary schism formed and widened; but in the seventeenth century, after equity had gained the upper hand, the rift closed again, and the equity court was reintegrated into the general "system of jurisprudence" (1:55). There, Blackstone thought, it had remained until his own time.

Fundamentally, then, law and equity courts as judicial institutions display two historical states: union and division. Correlatively, two theoretical relationships—identity and antithesis—obtain between law and equity as abstract, historically disembodied ideas. Viewed historically, however, the schism between law and equity proved to be temporary, for the history of the two courts proceeded from nondifferentiation to reunion. From this perspective, the theoretical antithesis of the two ideas corresponds to a historical abberation: namely, the period of division between the two legal institutions, a period now closed. Thus, though Blackstone fully acknowledges the theoretical dichotomy of equity and law that seemed to be implied by the separation of the two institutions and by classical jurisprudential theory, he ultimately celebrates the union of the two, in principle and in fact.[28] Our question is why the reunion does not imply a logical contradiction. It is the question that Blackstone everywhere raises for us: the relation between history and reason.

Blackstone focuses on the theoretical antithesis between equity and law in the course of concluding his highly interesting discussion of interpretation. Hermeneutically defined, *equity* means generous or liberal or whatever kind of interpretation is the contrary of strict. Although in the sequence of Blackstone's exposition, equity follows his list of the methods of interpretation, in this initial treatment he suggests that equity is not actually one such method.

Blackstone defines interpretation by contrasting "a bad method" (the Roman) with "the fairest and most rational method" (1:59), the British method of interpreting. "When any doubt arose upon the construction of the Roman laws, the usage was to state the case to the emperor in writing and take his opinion upon it. This was certainly a bad method of interpretation. To interrogate the legislature [that is, the emperor] to decide particular disputes is not only endless, but affords great room for partiality and oppression" (1:59). "Authentic" interpretation (interpreting by consulting the author) is a bad method for two reasons. First, authentic interpretation confuses application with enactment, since the emperor's answers to questions of interpretation "had in succeeding cases the force of law." This is a particularly illogical form of enactment, Blackstone argues, because these precedent-setting, law-enacting answers were decisions in particular cases. Thus laws were being generated on the basis of specific cases rather than universal rules. "Contrary to all true forms of reasoning," the emperor was proceeding "from particulars to generals" (1:59). Second, authentic interpretation confuses enactment with application. To change the rule in the very process of applying it is to try the case by a rule hitherto unknown; it is to make a decision by appeal to a law not in existence prior to the decision. That is the recipe for tyranny. Roman, or authentic, interpretation, in sum, contradicts the general principles of the rule of law (not men), the supremacy of law over the monarch, and the separation of powers.

By contrast, "the fairest and most rational method to interpret the will of the legislator is by exploring his intentions at the time when the law was made, by *signs* the most natural and probable. And these signs are either the words, the context, the subject matter, the effects and consequence, or the spirit and reason of the law" (1:59). The difference between this and authentic interpretation does not consist in the ends proposed: both methods aim to recover the legislator's intent. But the better, because fairer, route to this end is the circuitous one—not direct consultation but indirect reconstruction through signs. By "signs" Blackstone refers to any means by which legislative intent is inferred rather than intuited. This distinction is of fundamental importance, for inference or indirection through signs never reaches beyond the "probable" to the certain. That is, the circuitous route which Blackstone advocates introduces the possibility of error into the process of interpretation, a possibility which the authentic method excludes.

The possibility of judicial mistake is not a flaw in Blackstone's theory of interpretation but its cornerstone, because it guarantees the difference between interpretation and enactment. To determine the intent of a law, it would seem obvious that one should consult the legislator who passed it. But, if the legislator is necessarily infallible in declaring its meaning, there is no difference between enacting a law and interpreting it. On the other hand, if the legislator is fallible in interpreting even the laws he enacted, then he is for that reason just like a judge, who has no authority to enact laws at all. "*The law* and the *opinion of the judge* are not always convertible terms or one and the same thing, since it sometimes may happen that the judge may *mistake* the law. Upon the whole, however, we may take it as a general rule 'that the decisions of courts of justice are the evidence of what is common law', in the same manner as, in the civil [that is, Roman] law, what the emperor had once determined was to serve for a guide for the future" (1:71). Rather than a defect in the interpretive process, the possibility of mistake is what defines interpretation per se and prevents the judge from becoming a legislator and hence a tyrant or a pope. Authentic interpretation, if this implies the infallibility of the author, turns out to be not interpretation at all but merely more enactment. Only inauthentic interpretation is genuine.

The distinction between interpretation and legislation forms the context for Blackstone's discussion of the antithesis of equity and law. He lists the several methods of genuine—that is, inferential— interpretation and concludes:

> Lastly, the most universal and effectual way of discovering the true meaning of a law when the words are dubious is by considering the reason and spirit of it. . . .
>
> From this method of interpreting laws, by the reason of them, arises what we call *equity;* which is thus defined by Grotius, "the correction of that, wherein the law (by reason of its universality) is deficient." For since in laws all cases cannot be foreseen or expressed, it is necessary that, when the general decrees of the law come to be applied to particular cases, there should be somewhere a power vested of defining those circumstances which (had they been foreseen) the legislator himself would have expressed. And these are the cases, which according to Grotius, "*lex non exacte definit, sed arbitrio boni viri permittit.*"
>
> Equity thus depending, essentially, upon the particular circumstances of each individual case, there can be no established rules and fixed precepts of equity laid down without destroying its very essence and reducing it to a positive law. And, on the other hand, the liberty of considering all cases in an equitable light must not be indulged too far, lest thereby we destroy all law, and leave the decision of every question entirely in the breast of the judge. And law, without equity,

though hard and disagreeable, is much more desirable for the public good than equity without law, which would make every judge a legislator and introduce most infinite confusion, as there would then be almost as many different rules of action laid down in our courts as there are differences of capacity and sentiment in the human mind. (1:61–62)

Equitable construal is here associated with interpretation, because traditionally it is construal by the spirit rather than the letter of the law; it is also like interpretation insofar as it is concerned with applying the law and with legislative intent. Yet Blackstone makes clear that equity differs strikingly from interpretation narrowly conceived. Rather than inferring meaning through signs, equity does not just interpret the law but "corrects" it. It does not determine what the legislator meant but instead what he would have meant but in fact did not;[29] given that lack, equitable application to unforeseen circumstances is primarily a mode of power left to the "arbitrio boni viri." In theory equity entails all the worst consequences of authentic interpretation (1:62).

Blackstone is here grappling with precisely the same problems as were involved in Bolingbroke's attempt to balance philosophy and history, Hume's attempt to conceive of sympathy in such a way as to make it open to real difference, and Reid's attempt to construe metaphor as a way of accommodating novelty without repressive assimilation. As developed in Blackstone's initial exposition, the theoretical antithesis of equity and law rests on this foundation: equity is the locus of difference, law of what is permanent, uniform, and universal. Though inescapably necessary, equity is to Blackstone a threat to civil order. Equity is called upon to correct the deficiencies of the law, and its use therefore testifies to those deficiencies. If equity is needed to "assist, to moderate, and to explain" law (1:92), law is by that fact shown to be weak, extreme, and obscure. It is a dangerous doctrine that points up defects in the law, the more so because these deficiencies are irremediable. The function of equity is to apply the law to special cases resulting from unforeseen circumstances. But myopia is not a contingent deficiency in politicians that is remediable by finding more far-sighted statesmen; limited foresight is a manifestation of ineluctable human finitude. Some circumstances are always unforeseen, and for them equity is always needed.

Since laws cannot justly be enacted after the fact, they must be future-oriented. Yet legislators, far from being bad prophets, are in fact no prophets at all, for they pretend to foresee no particular circumstances of any kind. Laws must be abstract and general. "A particular act of the legislature to confiscate the goods of Titius . . . has no relation to the community in general; it is rather a sentence than a law. But an act to declare that the crime of which Titus is accused shall be deemed high treason . . . is properly a rule" (1:44). For an act to be a rule, or law, it must be general; it cannot cover only one situation but must cover many, indeed all, instances, without exception. When Blackstone, citing Grotius,[30] says that equity corrects the deficiencies of the law deriving from its universality, these deficiencies include, first, that the universality of the law acknowledges no exceptions, yet exceptions are always forthcoming. Second, the problem is not just that a few cases are exceptional. Because a law must be universal to be a law, it must cover every case in general but can cover no case in particular. If equity is needed to decide particular cases that happen in unforeseen circumstances, then equity is needed not occasionally but in all cases whatsoever, for all cases are demonstrably unique. Though Blackstone warns against "considering all cases in equitable light," his argument shows that nothing less is possible.

"Lex non exacte definit," Grotius writes. A law against stealing bread does not ultimately determine what "bread" or "stealing" means; at some point the explicit shades off into the tacit, and at that point every law will be explicable only by recourse to an entire social context, a form of life.[31] The inexactness of law means, moreover, that law does not of itself determine whether such and such an act by John Smith constitutes stealing bread. That decision is rather a judgment, and a judge (no less than a law) is necessary to make it. In easy cases as well as hard, the law never interprets itself, never determines how its generalities bear on the particulars of the case. General laws decide general cases, but there are no general cases, only particular cases that occur in particular circumstances. The question is whether these circumstances are essential or merely circumstantial, and that question pertains to every case. For this reason, every case is decided by equity, for the law always leaves the decision to the "arbitrio boni viri."

Arbitrium, Blackstone shows, can be conceived of in two ways, corresponding to the two conceptions of equity represented above by West and Selden. First is arbitrament: "Equity thus depending, essentially, upon the circumstances of each individual case, there can be no established rules and fixed precepts of equity laid down without destroying its very essence and reducing it to a positive law" (1:62). Theoretically considered, equity is essentially antithetical to rule and law, because its function is to take cognizance of what is not rule-governed: namely, the concrete particular. Equity is therefore the means by which jurisprudence acknowledges the reality of history as independent of reason. Insofar as history is defined as the flux of unforeseen and unpredictable circumstances and insofar as reason is defined as the system of law-abiding regularity, the antithesis of equity and law is an expression of the greater antithesis of history and reason. The deficiency of law, due to its universality, is the deficiency of abstract reason: its necessary and irremediable blindness to historical uniqueness. In this context, equity is arbitrament—that is, adjudication between the lawful and the lawless, between idea and fact, which are equally relevant and must be reconciled if justice is to be served. Just as common sense cannot be defined, so equity cannot be codified or reduced to law, because its purpose is to prevent unique cases from being reduced to mere instances of laws. It prevents history from being reduced to reason. In every just decision, equity arbitrates between particular cases and general laws.

Yet Blackstone warns against "considering all cases in an equitable light . . . lest thereby we destroy all law" (1:62). Here equity means leaving "the decision of every question entirely in the breast of the judge" (1:62). *Arbitrium* is here defined as arbitrariness, subjectivity, feeling, and conscience. And the problem with courts of conscience, as Samuel Johnson writes, is that "he who is in no danger of hearing remonstrances but from his own conscience will seldom be long without the art of controlling his convictions and modifying justice by his own will."[32] Law is destroyed, Blackstone says, when cases are decided entirely "in the breast of the judge," according to conscience. Moreover, when legal determinations are made by appeal to the feeling of justice, as if moral feelings were infallible, they cannot be mistaken; and "every judge becomes a legislator" (1:62) because the impossibility of judicial error collapses the distinction between interpretation and enactment. Further, feelings as such are peculiar to the individual; so, were judges indistinguishable from legislators, "there would then be as many different rules of action laid down in our courts, as there are differences of capacity and sentiment in the human mind" (1:62). Just as equity in the sense of arbitrament registers differences among particular cases, so equity as arbitrariness registers difference among individual judges. But when the judge's feeling (even the feeling of justice) is made law, the result is anarchy. And, forced to choose, Blackstone is willing in the abstract to ignore differences among cases if that is the price to be paid for controlling judicial arbitrariness. "Law, without equity, though hard and disagreeable, is much more desirable for the public good than equity without law" (1:62).

It seems, then, from Blackstone's theoretical exposition, that one is forced to choose between equity and law and to choose the way Blackstone does. "Equity," he states is "impossible in its very essence to be reduced to stated rules" (1:92). If objective and rational judgments include only those based on laws and rules, equitable judgments must in theory be subjective and irrational. But in fact they are not, Blackstone argues: the present state of the courts of equity, as actual historical institutions, cannot be explained therefore by recourse to the traditional theory of equity. "In short, if a court of equity in England did really act, as many ingenious writers have supposed it (from theory) to do, it would rise above all law, either common or statute, and be a most arbitrary legislator in every particular case" (3:433).

Since equity courts are not arbitrary, however, we can see in retrospect that the history of the equity courts was not theoretically predictable. This unpredictability has at least two possible explanations: first, the theory was mistaken; second, equity courts in 1750 were entirely historical, not rational or theoretically intelligible, institutions. Commenting on Blackstone, F. W. Maitland drew this second conclusion a century and a half later, after the Judicature Acts fusing law and equity courts.

> Suppose that we ask the question, What is Equity? We can only answer it by giving some short account of certain courts of justice which were abolished over thirty years ago. In the year 1875 [just before the fusion of the courts] we might have said "Equity is that body of rules which is administered only by those courts which are known as courts of equity." The definition of course would not have been very satisfactory, but nowadays we are cut off even from this unsatisfactory definition. . . . You will see what this comes to. Equity is now, whatever it may have been in past times, a part of the law of our land. What part? That part [which was once]

administered by certain courts known as courts of equity.
We can give no other general answer. We can give a historical
explanation.[33]

But Blackstone is not such a historical purist as to refuse all but
historical explanations of equity. He argues that the history of equity
courts was not theoretically predictable because classical theory dichotomizing law and equity was itself a historical product, an idea
generated from the particular historical period in which courts of law
and of equity clashed. The classic theory of equity—that of Grotius
and Puffendorf, as well as "Spelman, Coke, Lambard, Selden and
even the great Bacon himself"—arose, Blackstone contends, during
"the infancy of our courts of equity, before their jurisdiction was
settled and when the chancellors themselves, partly from their ignorance of law (being frequently bishops or statesmen), partly from
ambition and lust of power (encouraged by the arbitrary principles
of the age they lived in), . . . had arrogated to themselves such
unlimited authority as has totally been disclaimed by their successors
for now above a century past" (3:433).

An arbitrary age conceived equity as lawless and arbitrary. But
since that time of infantile anarchy, "a set of great and eminent
lawyers, who have successively held the great seal [of the chancel-
lorship], have by degrees erected the system of relief administered
by a court of equity into a regular science, which cannot be attained
without study and experience any more than the science of law, but
from which, when understood, it may be known what remedy a
suitor is entitled to expect . . . with as much precision in a court of
equity as in a court of law" (3:441). Equity judgments, no longer
arbitrary, have become as predictable as judgments of law, because
both are equally regular, equally governed by rule and law. For
Blackstone's time, a more modern theory of equity was needed, one
in which equity per se was not defined as arbitrariness or law as
hidebound regularity.

Thus Blackstone writes:

> Equity, then, in its true and genuine meaning, is the soul
> and spirit of all law; *positive* law is construed, and *rational*
> law is made, by it. In [rational law], equity is synonymous
> with justice, in [positive law], to the true sense and sound
> interpretation of the rule. But the very terms of a court of
> *equity* and a court of *law,* as contrasted to each other, are apt

to confound and mislead us: as if the one judged without equity, and the other was not bound by any law. Whereas every definition or illustration to be met with, which now draws a line between the two jurisdictions, by setting law and equity in opposition to each other, will be found either totally erroneous or erroneous to a certain degree. (3:429–30)

No longer antithetical to law, equity is its soul and spirit. As the foundation of rational or natural law, equity is justice; as the interpretation of positive or human law, equity is truth. Since law cannot be opposed to truth and justice, it cannot be opposed to equity. In other words, equity is in principle indistinguishable from law, and the two-court system of England is legitimate, because the courts are not really but only nominally different.

If, as Blackstone says, "truth and justice are always uniform" (3:429), then "there cannot be a greater solecism than that in two sovereign independent courts established in the same country . . . there should exist two different rules of property, clashing with or contradicting one another" (3:441). "The rules of property, rules of evidence, and rules of interpretation in both courts are, or should be, exactly the same; both ought to adopt the best, or must cease to be courts of justice" (3:434). To say that equity is theoretically indistinguishable from law means that both are reconciled under justice.[34] How is this reconciliation possible?

On the one hand, this reconciliation implies that equity cannot be understood as the abstract opposite of law or as pure irregularity. If "truth and justice are always uniform," then they are regular, for rules are "permanent, uniform, and universal" (1:44). Equity must therefore be governed by rule, and Blackstone shows that in fact it is so governed. According to the standard theory,[35] he writes, "A court of equity is not bound by rules or precedents, but acts from the opinion of the judge, founded on the circumstances of every particular case. Whereas the system of our court of equity is a labored connected system governed by established rules, and bound down by precedents, from which they do not depart" (3:432).

This line of argument leads to the conclusion that equity exists only as an appendage to law. According to its first maxim, "Equity follows law," fact is subordinate to rule and difference to identity. Taken to its extreme, this subordination suggests that equity courts as such do not exist at all, since they must act strictly legally, just like law courts:

> It is said that it is the business of a court of equity in England to abate the rigour of the common law. But no such power is contended for. Hard was the case of bond creditors whose debtor devised away his real estate; rigorous and unjust the rule which put the devisee in a better condition than the heir. Yet a court of equity had no power to interpose. Hard is the common law still subsisting . . . that the father shall never immediately succeed as heir to the real estate of the son; but a court of equity can give no relief, though in both these instances the artificial reason of the law, arising from feudal principles, has long ago entirely ceased. . . . In all such cases of positive law, the court of equity as well as the courts of law, must say with Ulpian, "*Hoc quidem perquam durum est, sed ita lex scripta est.*" (3:430)

On the other hand, although it is true that an equity court must act lawfully, like a court of law, Blackstone argues that the reverse is true as well:

> It is said that a court of equity determines according to the spirit of the rule and not according to the strictness of the letter. But so also does a court of law. Both, for instance, are equally bound, and equally profess, to interpret statutes according to the true intent of the legislature. . . . There is not a single rule of interpreting laws, whether equitably or strictly, that is not equally used by the judges in the courts both of law and equity: the construction must in both be the same. . . . Each endeavours to fix and adopt the true sense of the law in question; neither can enlarge, diminish, or alter that sense in a single title. (3:431–32)

Justice, if uniform, cannot abide the distinction between spirit and letter, assigned to equity and law courts respectively. In either kind of court, a judge must respect the individuality of special cases but cannot enact new laws to cover them; nor if justice is to be served can he alter the rules (like a Roman emperor) in the process of applying them. The law must be always the same; it must exist prior to the sentence and be construed as sufficiently inclusive to cover any and every case. Justice is possible only if it is no contradiction to say genuinely that the same law covers genuinely different cases. The old theory was that laws, as general rules, intend justice for all generally, and that equity intends justice for each person individually. But if equity means "nothing but sound interpretation of the law" and if the sound interpretation of the law is not something other than the true sense of law itself, then the law intends justice not only for all indiscriminately but for each one in their unique circumstances.

It is not merely equity that takes cognizance of particular circumstances but justice itself, in that just decisions are always particular ones. They cannot be automated or mass-produced. The judgment must be in principle predictable but cannot be made in advance of the case. Insofar as the law is intended to serve justice, it is meant to apply not only uniformly to the undifferentiated mass but also to the individual case. If equity is to be considered a mode of interpretation, one that interprets "statutes according to the true intent of the legislature," then that intent must be considered as including application to the special case even if it was quite unforeseen. Special cases are decided according to law (not arbitrarily, outside it) only if *arbitrium* is not merely a power given to judges. If judicial discretion does not operate outside the law and is not merely a name for brute force in polite disguise, then equitability must be not the antithesis of law but immanent in the law itself.

Though, according to classical theory, "equity is . . . impossible in its very essence to be reduced to stated rules" (1:92), Blackstone argues that in point of fact "the system of our courts of equity is a laboured connected system governed by established rules" (3:432). On the other hand, according to classical theory, law is "a rule of action" (1:38) describing what is regular and regulating what is not so. Yet the direction of his argument leads Blackstone to the conclusion that this theory too needs to be corrected. He never draws this conclusion explicitly. Indeed, he tries to avoid drawing it. His primary purpose is to deny that England has two systems of justice and that, since justice is one and uniform, one or the other of the two systems is unjust. In reconciling law and equity, however, he shows not only that equity is more regular but also that law is more irregular than the classic theories had allowed. Blackstone's implicit conclusion is that *law itself,* in its very essence, cannot be reduced to rules.

The essence of law is no less than justice. Justice requires that law be conceived in such a way that accommodation to genuinely different circumstances does not twist the law or displace it but can be faithful to the law itself. To be just, not merely a binding expression of power—that is, to be what it essentially is—a law must be interpreted as if it were intended to be just not only overall and in the main but in every new instance. Of itself, a law whose essence is justice takes cognizance of the uniform and the heterogeneous, the universal and individual. Just as equity (if it is to be just) cannot consist of mere feeling, so just laws cannot be reduced to rules alone.

How, finally, does Blackstone's conception of justice bear on the relation of history to reason? Viewed as the "perfection of reason" in one sense, law is rule: permanent, uniform, and universal. Blackstone shared this view, no doubt, and thus he expounds British law as rational, an autonomous system, invariant in time. For instance, he mentions the need for "reconciling the little contrarieties which the practice of many centuries will necessarily create in any human system" (1:30). Here history is merely a contingent annoyance, easily obviated. Yet it is not the case that Blackstone views the laws only as constituting an integrated coherent system, for he also advocates that "their history should be deduced, their changes and revolutions observed, and it should be shown how far they are connected with, or have at any time been affected by, the civil transactions of the kingdom" (1:36). Blackstone's *Commentaries* embodies this advice. Laws that undergo revolution, laws that are not autonomous and independent of time, laws influenced by political, military, and social events—such laws need to be explained historically, not just systematically by appeal to absolute reason.

A body of law that undergoes historical change approximates equity. Viewed as the pure expression of history, equity is flux: ephemeral, heterogeneous, and infinitely unique. Blackstone shares this view also, as when (following Grotius) he defines equity as the remedy for precisely the deficiencies of the law that derive from its universality, absoluteness, and rationality (1:62). Yet Blackstone does not view equity simply as pure, unregulable contingency, for even that is a definition of equity from the viewpoint of absolute reason: namely, as the abstract antithesis of reason. When he looks not at abstract ideas but at historically embodied institutions, he sees that "the systems of jurisprudence in our courts, both of law and of equity, are now equally artificial systems"—that is, "equally governed by established rules" (3:433–34). Equity that establishes itself in rules and consolidates itself into a coherent system must be explained systematically as an expression of reason and not just relatively by recourse to history.

A. V. Dicey, as we noted at the outset, locates the enduring significance of the *Commentaries* in Blackstone's good sense, tact, and sound judgment—as illustrated by his "blending the history with the exposition of English law." To this insight I have attempted to add that Blackstone's success in achieving this blend was not merely a matter of organizational or stylistic felicity. The *Commentaries on the Laws of England* joins historical narration with systematic exposition, because that its the nature of justice itself. To ask how it was possible, without contradiction, to amalgamate story and system in the *Commentaries* is to ask how equity and law can be reconciled. Blackstone's implicit answer strikes me as profound and far-sighted: equity is of itself lawful; law is of itself equitable—insofar as both aim to promote justice. In that justice itself requires the union of legal predictability with equitable adaptability, the just decision unites idea and fact, reason and history. In a court of equity, Blackstone writes, "sometimes a precedent is so strictly followed that a particular judgment, founded upon special circumstances, gives rise to a general rule" (3:433). An equitable judgment of a particular case, if it is just, necessarily implies that all former cases like it were, if just, decided in the same way, and that such cases ought to be so decided in the future. Regularity is not foisted on equity but derives from it insofar as the equitable decision claims to be just. Conversely, application of the law that disregards circumstances a priori has not only applied the law unjustly but also misinterpreted it. The judgment that intends to be both lawful and just may indeed disregard circumstances but only a posteriori, after taking cognizance of them; thus its very disregard is an equitable decision. Equity does not bend the law but arises from it insofar as the law claims to promote justice. Correlatively, rationality and historicality cannot be opposed in abstract antithesis. Just as "summum jus, summa injuria," so too reason itself becomes unreasonable when it is oblivious to history.

7

Burke on Taste

dmund Burke not only was a politician; he thought and
wrote as one. Excepting his youthful *Philosophical Enquiry
into the Sublime and Beautiful,* he wrote no philosophy, no
abstract treatises; rather, his mature work was specifically
occasional, and its greatness derives in part from its being evoked
by great occasions. Not just a member of an ideal republic of letters,
moreover, Burke served as an actual Member of Parliament for
Bristol, where he spoke for the Rockingham Whigs. What he said
and wrote was motivated not only by times and occasions but by
politics—and explicitly partisan politics at that. For Burke, a word
was a deed, a political act.

The interpreting word had for him the same engaged, political
character. His *Reflections on the Revolution in France,* like the *Appeal
from the New to the Old Whigs,* opens with a hermeneutic debate over
the meaning of the Glorious Revolution and Declaration of Right.
Did the events of 1688 signify that eighteenth-century Englishmen
had the right to frame governments, elect kings, and cashier them
for misconduct? This was not a merely historical question but a
genuinely political one, because more than the interpretation of the
Glorious Revolution was at stake. The meaning of 1688 was inseparable from 1789. For a politician, as for a judge or clergyman,
hermeneutics involves the task of application; that is, it aims not
only to understand a past event in itself—a revolution, a law, a verse
of Scripture—but to discern how the past pertains to the present.

The goal of political interpretation is not just epistemic but normative and practical; more than understanding, it is understanding what to do.

Burke explicitly raises and addresses the questions involved in political—that is, applied—interpretation per se, questions about the relation between the two moments of application: knowing and doing, past and present. As usually conceived, application means applying past knowledge to present action: first the general principles of right action are discovered; then, second, one's conduct is based on them. This might be called the "epistemological model" of application—"epistemological" because it gives priority to knowing over doing. In order to make this ranking, the epistemological model necessarily posits the existence of pure knowledge—for example, passive perception (as Locke conceived it)—which has no element of doing in it. In the *Reflections,* we recall, Burke terms pure knowledge "speculative" and "theoretical."[1] Belonging to what he contemptuously calls the "conquering empire of light," *speculari* and *theorein* figure knowing as seeing; unlike the grasp of "apprehension," say, they privilege the eye over the hand, distance over engagement, metaphysics over politics, contemplation over action.

On the epistemological view, action is itself conceived as a kind of theory: applied theory. For epistemology, political praxis consists in discovering or devising the best form of government, the true nature of the state, or the ideal social structure—in other words, action consists in first having a theory—and then bringing the actual government, state, or social structure into alignment with it. On this view, all political practice worthy of the name is revolutionary, since it consists fundamentally in conforming the concrete to the abstract, the real to the ideal, and hence assumes an intrinsic deficiency in the real. The revolutionary conception of action is by definition epistemological insofar as it makes practice, including political practice, derivative from and secondary to passive, contemplative knowledge.

But if we think of the politician as Burke did—not as a kind of philosopher first and an actor second, but rather as a "philosopher in action" (*T* 2:317)[2]—then political praxis can no longer be conceived as the post facto application of prior theoria.[3] Burke's significance in the history of hermeneutics, I want to argue, is that he overturns this epistemological model of application in favor of what I will call, with reservations to be explained, an "aesthetic model" based on taste. By the term "aesthetic," I do not mean primarily to emphasize the parallel to Reynolds's *Discourses* on the idea of prejudice or Thomas Warton's *History of English Poetry* on the passing of the age of chivalry, though in concluding I will touch on their importance. Rather than any question of influence, I want to focus on Burke as a hermeneutic counterrevolutionary, as it were, someone who opposed the epistemological model of political understanding based on the priority of knowing over doing to an alternative and in my view superior model based on taste, decorum, and artistic judgment. "More than any other single figure," Gerald Chapman has written, Burke typifies the union "of what are perhaps the two greatest achievements of English culture to date—its literary imagination, and its success in practical politics."[4] As in the case of Blackstone, I want to suggest that this conjunction was not entirely fortuitous. Aesthetic taste offered Burke not only certain stylistic ideals but, more important, the model of a genuinely political conception of understanding.

The new aesthetic model Burke develops does not just privilege practice over theory (though he sometimes says or seems to say this). Instead of merely reversing epistemological priorities, Burke attacks the dichotomy itself. Speculative knowledge is not enough to guide action, he repeatedly insists. Having an abstract theory, a moral ideal, a political principle is always necessary but never sufficient to decide what ought to be done in a given situation. Not by contemplative detachment, but only by immersion in the particular situation, by mucking about in the actual, concrete circumstances in all their messiness, can one obtain practical knowledge—the only pertinent knowledge for the politician—which is knowing what to do.

This practical knowledge is acquired by exercising political judgment.[5] Like Bolingbroke, Reid, and Blackstone, but far more explicitly, Burke challenges the epistemological model of application because it ignores the irreducible gap, bridgeable only by judgment, between all general rules and the specific situation at hand. He refuses, in a memorable passage, to praise or blame any political principle in "all the nakedness and solitude of metaphysical abstraction" (*R* 8:58), apart from the circumstances in which it has been and will be embodied. This inevitable gap between abstract principles and concrete circumstances makes every political decision a judgment call. Epistemologists and revolutionaries, Burke says, are always wanting to find absolutes that would render unnecessary any consideration of particular instances and special circumstances. Such absolutes would obviate the need for weighing, deliberating, and judging.

Any number of profoundly important political universals do exist, but none—Burke insists more openly than Blackstone—is ever perfectly suited to the peculiarities of the here and now; and so meeting the exigencies of the specific occasion requires judgment in applying these universals. Thus to do justice to practical, political judgment as a special way of knowing not reducible to speculation and theory, it is necessary to find an alternative to the epistemological model of application, one in which acting judiciously consists not merely in knowing what is right ideally, generally, or in the abstract but in judging what is right here and now. Burke's new model that begins with the ineluctable necessity for practical political judgment can, I think, be usefully described as aesthetic.

Taste, J. G. A. Pocock has observed, occupied a "central place . . . in Whig ideology between the English and the French Revolutions."[6] Whereas Pocock focuses on the important social aspects of taste—tact and manners—I want to draw attention to the aesthetic aspect. The French Revolution, for Burke, constituted an offense against good taste. This was not his only objection, obviously, but with Pocock I want to call it a central one. In our time, of course, it is scarcely central at all, and that is one measure of the difference between Whig ideology and our own. Even those now on the right and the left who are reluctant to celebrate the French Revolution as one of the great victories of Western civilization may well hesitate to characterize it as "tasteless." The aesthetic criterion seems so irrelevant and mindlessly anemic that to employ it constitutes an offense against other, infinitely more important values.

Clearly Burke had a different notion of taste. The place to find it, significantly, is not primarily in his aesthetic treatise. The essay titled "On Taste" prefixed to the second edition of the *Enquiry* mostly reiterates the commonplaces of its time, as Boulton has shown, and fails to offer the "profundity of argument and mature reflection" that readers of the later Burke have come to expect (*E* xxxix). One reason why this early piece seems disappointingly un-Burkean, in fact, is precisely that it is a treatise: it tries to establish universals, as Burke's mature works do not. Like Hume's better-known essay, Burke's "On Taste" posits the existence of "fixed principles," "invariable and certain laws" governing aesthetic ideas which, once discovered, could be employed to explain or even produce the aesthetic.

Burke's stance in this early work is thus epistemological, as that term has been employed above. The positive significance of the epistemological approach to taste so prevalent in the eighteenth century is that it assumes that judgments of taste can be true (or false), an assumption no longer possible after Kant severed the true from the beautiful and good, the scientific from the artistic and ethical. For Burke and many of his contemporaries, by contrast to us post-Kantians, taste was the object of a possible science: aesthetic value could be known, and taste was the way of knowing it.

The question, however, is whether taste constitutes an epistemological way of knowing. That the beautiful and sublime are knowable means in the *Enquiry* that the realm of taste must be governed by laws. Were there no such, Burke contends, "our labour is like to be employed to very little purpose, as it must be judged a useless, if not an absurd undertaking, to lay down rules for caprice, and to set up for a legislator of whims and fancies" (*E* 12). This generally prevalent dichotomy we have previously encountered in Hume. Either laws or fancies, either rules or caprice: for the legislator, whether aesthetic or political, no third alternative is possible. That exclusion suggests the negative significance of the epistemological approach to aesthetics: namely, that it outlaws any knowledge that does not conform to the rule-based, nomological view of knowledge—namely, that of epistemology.

Specifically, the rule–whim dichotomy excludes the possibility that judgment—whether aesthetic or political—might claim any independent (nonepistemological) cognitive value. If knowing consists in subsuming multiform instances under their uniform governing laws, as epistemology would have it, then judgment (whose laws cannot be codified) must be not knowledge but either an ex post facto application of knowledge or else mere whim. Good taste is a kind of knowledge, Burke undoubtedly asserts in this essay; but applying the universal rules which he assumes underlie good taste in fact requires no taste or judgment precisely insofar as these rules are universal—that is, applicable to any and all instances, regardless of particular circumstances. On this view of application, the law subsumes all cases. It always fits and raises no problem of appropriateness or suitability: that is what makes it a law. Epistemology, in sum, tries to obviate the need for taste insofar as its aim is to replace judgment calls with the certainties of logical subsumption.

Burke's essay offers hints pointing in another direction, however. Whereas Reid (unlike Shaftesbury) restricted judgment and common sense to their epistemic role, Burke returns to the older tradition in breaking open any artificial narrowing of aesthetic judgment. "What is called taste," he remarks, refers not only to our evaluation of "works of imitation" but more broadly to "our skill in manners, and in the observances of time and place, and of decency in general" (*E* 23). It is taste's breadth and scope that Burke here stresses. The taste that judges imitations cannot be circumscribed within any narrowly artistic conception of mimesis but comprehends the entirety of social manners and civil life. The same can be said of politics. It too is comprehensive. The point is that, for Burke, the aesthetic, the social, and the political do not occupy distinct and segregated sectors of communal life but rather all share the undivided whole governed by taste. Given the non-autonomy (that is, the comprehensiveness) of the aesthetic in the civil world, Burke cannot be charged with making a category mistake in judging a political act to be in bad taste. Quite the contrary, just as epistemology (one could almost say) exists to provide absolutes and eliminate the need for judgment, so revolution based on absolutes is ipso facto tasteless.

The problem, in Burke's view, is that no such absolutes are available. The politician, no less than the playwright or citizen, needs skill in making decisions of taste, defined as "the observances of time and place." Not all actions are suited to all places or to one place at all times. When actions are to be suited to particular historical circumstances, in other words, absolutes are insufficient; and it is precisely in this case that taste is needed. In Burke's words, taste is required "where disposition, where decorum, where congruity are concerned" (*E* 26). All these terms—tasteful, decorous, congruous, appropriate, fitting, becoming, proper, decent, seemly—that sound to modern ears so stiff and unbending register not the inflexibility of absolute rules but, just the opposite, their absence and indeed impossibility. Decorum, like equity, names the insistent claim of something that is irreducible to rules but may nevertheless be more important than any. General maxims of action are inadequate to the specific demands of specific occasions. For just that reason—because there are no suprahistorical laws applicable in every case—taste is always mandatory. Whether a given action is suitable to a particular time and place requires a judgment, and taste is required to make it.

Since Plato, this notion of the suitable (*to prepon*) has been aligned with—though not limited to—the beautiful (*to kalon*), and I am drawing on that ancient tradition in aligning political and aesthetic judgment. In the *Enquiry into the Sublime and Beautiful,* however, Burke flatly denies that beauty consists in suitability, proportion, or fitness (*E* 91–111). There he reduces proportion to geometrical symmetry, and reduces fitness to utility in serving a given end. It is certainly true that these do not define the beautiful, but then they do not define the pertinent senses of proportion and fitness either. Geometry and utility are strawmen. The relation of *to kalon* and *to prepon* cannot be so easily defined and dismissed; and, as is evident from his discussion of decorum in the prefatory essay, Burke sometimes acknowledged as much. It is not in the *Enquiry,* however, that Burke's most significant meditation on taste is to be found. What he neglects there, he recalls, amplifies, and affirms in the *Reflections* and the *Letters on a Regicide Peace.*

"Good taste, manners, morals, religion, all fly, where the principles of Jacobinism enter" (*L* 5:486). In this sweeping indictment of French revolutionary philosophy, the offense against good taste heads the list. By accusing Jacobinism of bad taste, Burke intends not just a vague, superficial, and rather snooty insult but a fairly specific and substantive charge, one that he elaborates in the classical terms of dramatic decorum. Criticizing the Revolution as a theater critic would be a bad play, Burke writes: "In viewing this monstrous tragicomic scene, the most opposite passions necessarily succeed, and sometimes mix with each other in the mind: alternate contempt and indignation, alternate laughter and tears, alternate scorn and horror" (*R* 8:60). Here, as in his "Hints for an Essay on the Drama," Burke images indecorum as monstrous.[7] In this he follows Horace. "Humano capiti cervicem pictor equinam / iungere si velit, et varias inducere plumas undique collatis membris," begins the *Ars Poetica.*[8] For Horace, as for Burke, tragicomedy becomes the dramatic equivalent of the human feathered horse—risible, contemptible, frightening, stupid. Separately, of course, there is nothing repulsive or even funny about feathers or horses or human heads, but together they make a monster. The question of decorum or monstrosity, we can say initially, arises with reference to some kind of dubious grafting, suturing, or juncture of different things. An indecorous or monstrous juncture ignores the inappropriateness of the one thing to the other.

The scene of the revolutionary tragicomedy that for Burke most explicitly raises the question of appropriateness and decorum is the "triumph"—the procession in which the fallen Louis is paraded off in merry degradation to the Tuileries. Burke describes it in sumptuous detail. The royal family, he writes, were

> forced to abandon the sanctuary of the most splendid palace in the world, which they left swimming in blood, polluted by massacre, and strewed with scattered limbs and mutilated carcasses. Thence they were conducted into the capital of their kingdom. . . . [Two of the king's body guard], with all the parade of an execution of justice, were cruelly and publicly dragged to the block, and beheaded in the great court of the palace. Their heads were stuck on spears, and led the procession; whilst the royal captives who followed in the train were slowly moved along amidst the horrid yells and shrilling screams and frantic dances and infamous contumelies and all the unutterable abominations of the furies of hell. (*R* 8:122)

"No theatric audience in Athens would bear what has been borne in the midst of the real tragedy of this triumphal day" (*R* 8:132). Athenians would hoot such monstrosities off the stage.[9] This is not merely Burke the drama critic speaking, of course, but Burke the political critic, since he steadfastly refuses to differentiate the values of art from those of life. (Precisely this nondifferentiation defines political art criticism.) When an event exhibits "the unstable condition of mortal prosperity," it makes no difference whether the scene occurs on stage or not. The question of appropriate, fitting, decorous reaction remains the same: what kind of response befits the spectacle of the "tremendous uncertainty of human greatness"? "When kings are hurled from their thrones by the supreme director of this great drama" (*R* 8:131), Burke expects the spectators to react "naturally" to this tragedy, and by that he means with Aristotelian "terror and pity." This alone is the decorous response.

Richard Price, Burke reminds us, reacted quite differently in his address to the Revolution Society: "What an eventful period is this! I am *thankful* that I have lived to it. I could almost say, *Lord, now lettest thou thy servant depart in peace, for mine eyes have seen thy salvation.* . . . I have lived to see *Thirty Millions of People,* indignant and

resolute, spurning at slavery and demanding liberty with an irresistible voice. *Their King led in triumph, and an arbitrary monarch surren-
dering himself to his subjects*" (*R* 8:115–16). Of this scene, Burke asserts
that only a political preacher (itself a kind of feathered horse) could
"think it pious and decorous to compare it with the entrance into
the world of the Prince of Peace" (*R* 8:123). What Burke is objecting
to is the analogy, and we need to note that judgments of decorum
concerning dubious junctures always have an aesthetic side in that
they pertain to something like similes or metaphors. Here the analogy—of carnage to peace, of Price himself to Simeon—is simply
forced. Like a bad metaphor, its terms are (in Samuel Johnson's
words) "yoked by violence together." Indecorum is an act of rhetorical violence, as it were, and this violence perverts both things
compared. Price's analogy of the *Nunc dimittis* to revolutionary sav-
agery seems to Burke to compare things entirely different and even
opposite, without regard to what belongs to each. A good metaphor
not only elicits some surprise that a tenor and vehicle so apparently
unrelated should be joined but also convinces us that the two indeed
share something: however different, they really do belong together.
An integration of the many and one, different and same, proper and
improper, is tasteful and decorous only if unforced. Monstrousness,
by contrast, leaves the sutures visible: it manifests the violence, the
disregard for difference, by which incongruities have been stitched
together.

"This 'leading in triumph,'" Burke writes in disgust, "which fills
our preacher with such unhallowed transports, must shock, I believe,
the moral taste of every well-born mind" (*R* 8:117). The notion of
moral taste Burke mentions here is closely tied to that of political
decorum. Implicit in Burke's appeal to moral taste, as in Shaftesbury's almost a century earlier, is the continuity between art and
ethics, aesthetics and politics—a conjunction that may well seem
dubious, if not shocking, now.[10] Readers of the *Enquiry* will recall
that Burke had not always affirmed this continuity. Having there
asked "how far the application of beauty to virtue may be made with
propriety," he replied that the good and the beautiful (not to mention
the good and sublime) belong to distinct and separate realms (*E* 112).
Dividing the beautiful from whatever might be "improperly applied"
to it gives the treatise a determinate object: namely, the aesthetic
proper. Moral taste, by contrast, implies that there is no aesthetic
proper, but rather a shaded continuum between aesthetic and non-

aesthetic. Moral taste does not deny that the beautiful exists, of course—only that it exists autonomously and can be isolated from the gross and messy world of politics. Moral-taste aesthetics is the very reverse of effete.

The author of the *Enquiry,* however, complains that "the application of [beauty] to virtue has . . . left us no standard or rule to judge by that was not even more uncertain and fallacious than our own fancies" (*E* 112). The fear is that moral-taste philosophy, equating moral judgment with aesthetic taste, will reduce ethical principles to caprice. But that fear is justified only if taste is capricious. Forgetting for the moment that an express purpose of the *Enquiry* is precisely to disclose the standards and rules of beauty, Burke here supposes not only that judgments not conforming to laws are arbitrary but also that there are no laws that judgments of taste could conform to.

If so, beauty cannot be defined or codified. Even the *Enquiry* does not so much define beauty as describe its effects; but in the great political writings of two decades later, Burke's views on this matter undergo a major reorientation, for there he no longer assumes that all truth is rule-governed as he did in the *Enquiry*. Truth and taste, therefore, become continuous. In the political realm, the role of taste comes to be played by discretion or, more usually, prudence—which Burke calls the "god of this lower world" (*S* 2:226). He can identify political prudence with aesthetic taste because both operate in the absence of absolute rules. In the mature political work, moreover, Burke no longer tries to discover the absent rules or laments their loss, because he no longer assumes that the absence of rules necessarily implies arbitrariness. In politics, the irregular judgments of taste and prudence come to bespeak not capriciousness about regular, definable things but, quite the opposite, wisdom about irregular, indefinable things.

"No lines can be laid down for civil or political wisdom," Burke wrote in 1770. "They are a matter incapable of exact definition. But though no man can draw a stroke between the confines of day and night, yet light and darkness are upon the whole tolerably distinguishable" (*T* 2:282).[11] The absence of lines and laws and definitions does not preclude the politician's telling night from day, any more than the absence of rules prevents us from distinguishing beauty from ugliness. This same observation pertains to what Burke calls the "medium" or "middle." "The pretended rights of these theorists are all extremes," he complains. "The [real] rights of men are in a sort of middle, incapable of definition, but not impossible to be discerned. . . . [They are found] in balances between differences of good; in compromises sometimes between good and evil and sometimes between evil and evil" (*R* 8:112). The *via media* which Burke describes here has nothing to do with eclecticism, compromise, fence sitting, or timidity. The "mean," rather, is the classical term for an ideal of action that is indefinable but nevertheless quite real and knowable. Extremes are reassuringly clear and distinct; but their clarity is always achieved at the expense of ignoring the advantages of the opposite extreme. If, however, the ideal is to see that "one advantage is as little as possible sacrificed to another" (*R* 8:217), then the politician needs to find the point of balance between them all. But this middle can be decided only ad hoc, by weighing this advantage against that; it cannot be defined or specified in advance of that weighing.

Moreover, in political and moral matters, as in aesthetics, the very attempt to rely on rules is misguided. "Pure metaphysical abstraction does not belong to these matters. The lines of morality are not like the ideal lines of mathematics. . . . They admit of exceptions and modifications. These exceptions and modifications are not made by the process of logic, but by the rules of prudence. Prudence is not only the first in the rank of the virtues, political and moral, but she is the director, the regulator, the standard of them all. Metaphysics cannot live without definition; but prudence is cautious how she defines" (*A* 4:80–81). Burke situates himself a good way off from the epistemological tradition that insists on definition as the first step to rigor. Like common sense, prudence is averse to definition, and for that very reason it regulates all the other virtues. It is not that all virtue is indefinable because irrational, as if it were mere feeling in need of rational control. The reason is rather this: of nothing can it be said that it is always correct, politically or ethically.

"Virtues have their place; and out of their place they hardly deserve the name—they pass into the neighbouring vice" (*L* 5:390). If a virtue out of place is not a virtue, then what makes an action virtuous is not its conforming to a universal moral law per se but its suitability to the particular time and place. "I never was wild enough," Burke asserts, "to conceive that one method [of government] would serve for the whole, that the natives of Hindustan and those of Virginia could be ordered in the same manner" (*S* 2:227). In politics, as in ethics, prudence is the name Burke gives to judgments of suitability and fit—that is, to judgments of decorum. Whether termed "prudence" or "taste," knowing what action is decorous in this or that circumstance constitutes a special, irreducible kind of knowledge: namely, knowing what to do.

Knowing what to do here and now, in this particular instance, cannot be transferred to any and all places and times; this intrinsic non-universalizability indicates no deficiency in practical knowledge but rather belongs to its nature. "Nothing universal can be rationally affirmed on any moral or any political subject" (*A* 4:80). In raising the question of what can be "rationally affirmed" in the political sphere, Burke cannot be justly accused of being an irrationalist; rather, he is formulating a new conception of what will count as reason and knowledge—as political reason, that of the philosopher in action. Neither repeatable nor transferable, prudential or political knowledge is not what epistemology would call rational knowledge at all.

That is because epistēmē is suited to the higher world—typified by mathematics—undeviatingly governed by definition, identity, and universality. The very suitability of epistēmē to the higher world, though, explains its unsuitability to our own—the lower political world. The futile attempt to govern politics by appeal to a mathematical model of genuine knowledge turns statesmen and moralists into "economists and calculators" (*R* 8:127). No one sets out to do politics as a kind of mathematics, to be sure. Nevertheless, this is what happens when politicians "lay down metaphysical propositions which infer universal consequences" (*R* 8:269). Regardless of whether such propositions absolutize divine right or the rights of men, once universalized, such principles are elevated into dogma; and adherents who find no need for taste because they admit no exceptions to the dogma become, thereby, fanatics. "[The] old fanatics of single arbitrary power dogmatized as if hereditary royalty was the only lawful government in the world, just as our new fanatics of popular arbitrary power maintain that a popular election is the sole lawful source of authority. The old prerogative enthusiasts, it is true, did speculate foolishly . . . as if a right to govern by inheritance were in strictness *indefeasible* in every person who should be found in succession to a throne and under every circumstance, which no civil or political right can be" (*R* 8:77).

Applying any absolute—a proposition that is true under every circumstance—obviates consideration of any circumstance. It precludes judgment or taste, since it obviates all questions of appropriateness, fit, and decorum. Absolute rights admit of no gradation, no extenuation, no circumstances in which they might obtain less or more. In particular, the rights of men "admit no temperament and no compromise; anything withheld from their full demand is so much of fraud and injustice. . . . If its forms do not quadrate with their theories, . . . an old and beneficient government [is considered as unjust as] the most violent tyranny or the greenest usurpation" (*R* 8:109). The revolutionaries who in December 1792 declared that "all government not being a democracy is a usurpation" (*L* 5:308) became fanatics—that is, mathematicians out of their sphere—with the utterance of the universal quantifier "all."

In the variform, irreducibly particular world of politics, universality cannot be taken as the exclusive form of the rational. Quite the contrary, forcing together higher and lower worlds that do not belong together, reducing the many to the one and the particular to the universal—that is, the very act that constitutes rational knowing in the epistemic world—constitutes a kind of cognitive violence and irrationality here below. "Circumstances are infinite, are infinitely combined, are variable and transient; he who does not take them into consideration is not erroneous, but stark mad" (*M* 7:41). Universality, the paradigm of epistemic rationality, is also the paradigm of political madness.

"Times and occasions," Burke writes, "will teach their own lessons" (*R* 8:81). This brief, simple statement might well be taken as the foundation of Burke's hermeneutic counterrevolution, since once we accept it, application can no longer be understood in the epistemological way. Practical knowledge—that is, understanding what to do—cannot be conceived as applying the universal to the occasional or the eternal to the temporal, precisely insofar as "times and occasions teach their own lessons" and therefore provide a mode of knowledge not reducible to the universal and atemporal. In the lower world where we live, there is a wisdom higher than epistēmē, a "wisdom without reflection and above it" (*R* 8:83): that is, practical, political, prudential knowledge, which comes not before applying but only in applying itself, in the very juncture of the universal and particular.

It may seem that we have strayed a long way from the subject of taste. However, if political or applied knowledge is considered according to the new model that Burke suggests, not as a subsumption of the particular under the universal but as a juncture of the two, then it is of a piece with the quasi-aesthetic judgments of taste and decorum that assess such junctures. With regard to the prudent and tasteful, with regard to the politic, everything depends on how the particular situations and universal principles are joined. Neither can be ignored. Now if Burke considers practical knowledge as a juncture of universals and particulars, then he cannot simply dismiss universals. If he does not advocate merely reversing the priority of theory to practice typical of epistemology, then we should expect to find not only contempt for theory but, in certain contexts, respect for it as well.

This is just what we do find—in his speech on the reform of parliamentary representation, for instance. "A prescriptive government such as ours never was . . . made upon any foregone theory." This is the familiar anti-theoretical Burke; but then he immediately adds in a much less familiar strain, "I do not vilify theory and speculation; no, because that would be to vilify reason itself. . . . Whenever I speak against theory, I mean always a weak, erroneous, fallacious, unfounded, or imperfect theory" (*C* 7:97). This sounds like concessive hedging to readers primarily acquainted with the *Reflections;* but elsewhere we find the same moderation. "I never govern myself, no rational man ever did govern himself, by abstractions and universals," Burke asserts in the speech on the Middlesex election. He then goes on to say: "I do not put abstract ideas wholly out of any question, because I well know that under that name I should dismiss principles, and that without the guide and light of sound, well-understood principles, all reasonings in politics, as in everything else, would be only a confused jumble of particular facts and details" (*M* 7:41).

For all his memorable pronouncements on the "practical wisdom that supersedes theoretic science" (*R* 8:83), Burke, it seems, does not universalize even his skepticism about universals. He nowhere argues that times and occasions are self-interpreting, that they dictate a proper response to themselves. "Prudence must have rules,"[12] even if by themselves such rules are not enough. In every case, since prudence and decorum are not themselves principles but ideals for applying them, they cannot dispense with principles in the attempt to base themselves on circumstances alone. A political judgment not characterized by a "firm adherence to principle" (*L* 5:414) is merely unprincipled, expedient, convenient—usually to the politician's advantage.

None of this is meant to deny that, in Burke's view, cognizance of circumstances is indispensable to political judgment; it is rather to affirm what also needs to be remembered, that for Burke, theories, abstractions, universals, and rules are just as indispensable, even if he preferred that political principles be of historical rather than spontaneous generation. Just as a microscopic eye is needed to attend to the situation at hand and avoid abstraction, so a telescopic eye is needed to avoid myopia and attend to the needs of the long run. Cognizance of circumstance registers the insistence of present necessities; cognizance of principle addresses the unpredictability of the future and the fact that expediency, even if not venal, may turn out to be short-sighted. The ideal of practical, political judgment is to reconcile the two. This ideal is thus best conceived as a balance or juncture, not as an exclusion or subsumption of one element or the other. Exigency, the demand of immediate circumstances, needs to be balanced by "a standard of virtue and wisdom beyond the vulgar practice of the hour" (*R* 8:86). Equipoise is all.

Whether understood as balance, prudence, or the decorum of good taste on which we have focused, Burke's ideal of political judgments exhibits a certain two-in-oneness, an indissoluble ambiguity between sameness and difference, unity and duality. Beginning with the element of duality, this ambiguity will occupy our attention in the remaining pages.

The standard of decorum, we have seen, always pertains to a joining of two things. This union does not dissolve their difference in homogeneity, however. Though decorum consists precisely in the belonging together of the two, nevertheless the judgment that one thing befits another does not at all imply that they are identical. That the middle point, the site of good taste, is indefinable means not only that it cannot be identified with either this or that among the definable extremes, but also that the both/and of equipoised antitheses do not cohere in undifferentiated unity. Even in good metaphor, the tenor and vehicle are still distinct: they remain two. Though an indecorous juncture exhibits no unity, even in the most decorous there remains an irreducible duality.

This duality inevitably verges on duplicity, as we can see when we recall that the apt, fitting, decorous thing is called a decoration, which can be merely decorative and so too potentially deceptive. In that celebrated, notorious passage describing Marie Antoinette as the morning star "decorating and cheering the elevated sphere she just began to move in," Burke images the queen herself as a kind of decoration (*R* 8:126). By this he means that she not only belongs to her sphere; she also ornaments it with her "life, and splendour, and joy." As a fitting decoration, she is not just more of the same but something distinct that adds by being different, a difference Burke here underlines by saying "she hardly seemed to touch" the earth she walked on. This distance, or difference, is the hinge of the tragic peripateia. The decoration that adds something because it is not more of the same must be, for just that reason, separable from what it decorates. The queen that "decorates" her sphere can, for that very reason, be removed from it. A decoration is always in some sense adventitious and superfluous.

Decoration is also superficial, a phenomenon of the outside and the surface. Being the proprietor of land, Burke writes, "demands at least an exterior decorum and gravity of manners" (*R* 8:212). In this phrase, the exteriority of decorum invites our attention. When Burke asserts in another place that "justice is grave and decorous" (*R* 8:134), we could easily explicate these epithets (recalling Blackstone) in terms of equity and the prudence of jurisprudence. But when, using the same pair, Burke speaks of *exterior* decorum and gravity in the context of property (the putative basis of justice), we can understand why Sterne would say, "The very essence of gravity is design, and consequently deceit."[13] Exteriority and difference are the conditions of deception. The duality of decorum always creates the opportunity for duplicity. It never quite permits decoration and decorated to coalesce and so implies that the decoration as such belongs to the order of the signifier, not the signified; the apparent, not the real. By contrast with what is decorated, the decoration is mere surface appearance, phenomenon as opposed to noumenon.

It follows that decorum potentially constitutes concealment of the true and very thing itself. The work of hermeneutics, conceived epistemologically as dis-covery of the true, is precisely to undo the work of decoration. Understanding consists in disconcealment and exposure. Burke certainly sees his task as exposing the "cheats and deceivers" who speak "in the *patois* of fraud; in the cant and gibberish of hypocrisy" (*R* 8:154). When Jacobin professions of absolute right give way to exertions of force, Burke says, "at length the mask is thrown off" (*R* 8:277). Describing the revolutionaries' desperate attempt to forestall national bankruptcy by reviving one of the king's old ideas, voluntary donations, Burke writes: "They took good an old huge full-bottomed perriwig out of the wardrobe of the anti-quated frippery of Louis XIV to cover the premature baldness of the national assembly" (R 8:277). The very description snatches the tou-pee from their bald pate. An honest man living among "the mas-querades of the grand carnival at our age" (N 5:178) is compelled to unmask illusion and reveal mere appearance as deception.

Burke, then, employs the language and method of exposure when it suits his purpose. This would be unremarkable enough were it not that in the most remarkable passages of the *Reflections,* heading the list of Jacobin offenses against taste and decorum, is precisely the hermeneutics of strip search and exposé. "All the decent drapery of life is to be torn off. All the superadded ideas, furnished from the wardrobe of a moral imagination, which the heart owns and the understanding ratifies as necessary to cover the defects of our naked shivering nature and to raise it to dignity in our own estimation, are to be exploded as a ridiculous, absurd, and antiquated fashion" (R 8:128). Stripping the court of the queen who decorated it or— what amounts to the same thing—stripping the queen of the royal drapery that decorated her constitutes indecorum as such. Removing the decorations exposes the naked queen, the true and real queen, to be no queen but only a woman, an animal, and not of the highest order.

Burke's problem here is not always recognized. So long as the naked is equated with the true, decoration must be equated with the false, and there can be no fundamental objection at all to the para-digmatically indecorous practice of strip search. Far from reprehen-sible, Jacobin indecorum must be applauded as the epistemic act par excellence, the act of knowing the real thing in itself. The problem, then, is that Burke's metaphorics of drapery, dress, and clothing, so justly celebrated, is exactly wrong because it implies precisely what Burke wants to deny: "that government may vary like modes of dress and with as little ill effect" (R 8:139). Everything belonging to the rhetoric of the wardrobe is verbal territory occupied by the enemy. Dress symbolizes all the arbitrary supplements of decorum that can be replaced or, better yet, removed entirely. Exposé is the hermeneutic equivalent of revolution.

Burke is aware of this, of course, and that is why he employs the rhetoric of dress ironically. Even so, it must nonetheless be conceded that Burke has no alternative, equally powerful, positive rhetoric that could replace the ironic rhetoric of the wardrobe. More important, the ironic language is not entirely successful because it is not entirely ironic. The poignancy of this passage is due in part to the fact that the logic of decorum that Burke embraces compels him into complicity with the very metaphor of government as dress that he would deny. Decoration, we have said, is something adventitious. When Burke complains that "all the superadded ideas . . . are to be exploded," he may well lament the explosion, but he does not deny that the wardrobe of a moral imagination is in fact superadded and hence can be torn off without harm—or indeed, that it was a merely imaginary wardrobe in the first place, like the emperor's new clothes. This latter seems to be the implication of Burke's lament that "all the pleasing illusions . . . are to be dissolved." Their dissolution may be unpleasant, yet he does not deny that they are illusions; and dissolution is what one does—and should do—with illusions, however pleasing.

Nostalgic for the lost values of chivalry, yet unable to completely deny that they are illusory and, insofar as they are, well lost, Burke the politician finds himself in very much the same state of ambivalence as the Gothic revivalists in the sphere of aesthetics. Foremost among them, Thomas Warton voices this ambivalence in the climactic closing pages of the second volume of *The History of English Poetry*. There, in a genuinely moving mixture of regret and approval, Warton describes how the close of the chivalric age and the dawn of the renaissance have affected literary history.

> The customs, institutions, traditions, and religion of the Middle Ages were favourable to poetry. . . . Ignorance and superstition, so opposite to the real interests of human society, are the parents of imagination. The very devotion of the Gothic times was romantic. The Catholic worship . . . encouraged or rather authorized every species of credulity. . . . These illusions were heightened by churches of a wonderful mechanism and constructed on such principles of inexplicable architecture as had a tendency to impress the soul with every false sensation of religious fear. The savage pomp and capricious heroism of baronial manners were replete with incident, adventure, and enterprise. . . . [But with the advent of the Renaissance,] literature and a better sense of things not only banished these barbarities, but superseded the mode of

composition which was formed upon them. Romantic poetry gave way to the force of reason and inquiry. . . . Erudition was made to act upon genius. Fancy was weakened by reflection and philosophy. The fashion of treating everything scientifically applied speculation and theory to the arts of writing. Judgement was advanced above imagination, and rules of criticism were established. The brave eccentricities of original genius and the daring hardiness of native thought were intimidated by metaphysical sentiments of perfection and refinement. . . . [Despite all the improvements brought about by the renaissance, however,] we have lost a set of manners and a system of machinery more suitable to the purposes of poetry than those which have been adopted in their place. We have parted with extravagances that are above propriety, with incredibilities that are more acceptable than truth, and with fictions that are more valuable than reality.[14]

Among the several parallels that could be drawn between Warton's and Burke's eulogies for the age of chivalry, I can mention only the most fundamental, and this appears in Warton's last sentence. For both men, the disenchantment that ended the age of chivalry marked the divorce of epistemology and aesthetics, the epochal severance of truth from taste. This division created a special, autonomous domain for pure aesthetics, but the price paid for its autonomy was truth. Extravagances, incredibilities, and fictions, however valuable to poetry, Warton acknowledges, are in fact unreal, false, and illusory.

Burke almost unwillingly expresses a very similar ambivalence. The language of disillusionment in which he describes the "pleasing illusions," the "fictions of a pious imagination," the "rust of superstition," and all the other chivalric "delusions" and "amiable errors"—this self-undercutting, aesthetic language of fiction and illusion itself indicates why the things he so much wants to conserve must and ought to be abandoned. Truth is a formidable opponent, and by employing such language, Burke has ceded it to the opposition. The Jacobins may well be "destitute of all taste and elegance" (*R* 8:128), but if they are nevertheless right, if what they say is true, if any ruler not elected is ipso facto despotic, then the issue is decided, and the fictions of taste and elegance are illusions not just irrelevant but criminal.

This is what makes Burke's aesthetic politics seem so impoverished, inadequate, and indeed deceitful: namely, that when pressed, he sometimes envisions politics on the analogy of Warton's purist aesthetics; that is, Burke occasionally relinquishes the truth claim that was always implicit in the impure aesthetics of taste. "The practical consequences of any political tenet," he writes, for example, "go a great way in deciding upon its value. Political problems do not primarily concern truth or falsehood. They relate to good or evil. What in the result is likely to produce evil is politically false; that which is productive of good, politically true" (*A* 4:169). The politician as "philosopher in action" must be concerned with practice, no doubt, and not just as a secondary matter. Nevertheless, by equating political truth with advantageous consequences, Burke both disallows inconvenient truths and fails to disallow convenient falsehoods. Expediency is a knave's notion of truth—or a politician's. Thus, when Burke denies the truth claim of sound judgment and charges that the Jacobins, though injudicious, "build their politics not on convenience but on truth" (*A* 4:206), his condemnation can easily be mistaken for applause; and when he writes that, in the Declaration of Right following 1688, Lord Somers "threw a politic, well-wrought veil" over everything that might set precedent for future revolutions (*R* 8:69), Burke's praise of Somers's good taste might easily be misunderstood as contempt for artful deceit.

The problem, here and always for Burke, derives from the ambiguity of decorum: how to distinguish the veil of deceit and cover-up from the veil of decency that covers the defects of our naked shivering nature. To prevent all decorum from collapsing into deception and all politics into prevarication, Burke must refuse to forfeit the truth claim of taste, prudence, and political judgment. In order to maintain that claim, he needs above all a non-epistemological way of thinking about truth, one in which the naked thing in itself cannot be identified with the real, in which the veil of decency does not conceal but reveals the true, and in which the Jacobin strip search therefore could not possibly arrive at the truth because it indeed constitutes falsification.

Burke's often cited paragraphs on prejudice seem an unpropitious place to locate this alternative conception of truth. His injunction not "to cast away the coat of prejudice and leave nothing but the naked reason" reiterates the familiar metaphorics of the wardrobe, implying that prescriptive values, however decorous, are also decorative, disposable, deceptive, and finally arbitrary. The term "prejudice," too, has the same ambiguities as the "pleasing illusions" discussed above. On the one hand, for Burke to talk about "cherishing" prejudices amounts to bearding the Enlightenment lion in his den; on the other hand, though "prejudice" may well be employed ironically, Burke is fighting his battles on verbal ground already occupied by an Enlightenment notion of truth. Any talk of preferring prejudice to reason has already accepted the dichotomy between them and so conceded victory to the conquering empire of light.

It is most significant, therefore, that Burke rejects this dichotomy in his conception of "just prejudice." "Many of our men of speculation, instead of exploding general prejudices, employ their sagacity to discover the latent wisdom which prevails in them. If they find what they seek, and they seldom fail, they think it more wise to continue the prejudice, with the reason involved, than to cast away the coat of prejudice and to leave nothing but the naked reason, because prejudice, its reason, has a motive to give action to that reason and an affection which will give it permanence. . . . Through just prejudice, his duty becomes a part of his nature" (*R* 8:138). The question is not just whether some values are prejudices but whether any values are not. Are there any moral and political values at all, including the rights of man, whose claim does not depend on prescriptive traditions, social and civil habits, and enduring prejudices? This is merely the question of whether there are any suprahistorical absolutes, and Burke thought not. If even such values as human rights depend on prejudices, and if we are not willing or even able to call them "pleasing illusions" and "amiable errors," then it cannot be true that all prejudices are by definition false, unjust, and unreasonable, as Enlightenment epistemology would have us believe. There must be such a thing as what Burke calls "just prejudice"—that which has "its reason" and so can be maintained "with the reason involved," a kind of prejudice to which reason and truth cannot be opposed.[15]

What this has to do with aesthetics we can see by glancing at Sir Joshua Reynolds, whom Burke called an "excellent and philosophic artist, a true judge, as well as a perfect follower of Nature" (*A* 4:212). This compliment was probably occasioned by Reynolds's twelfth discourse; but we are more interested in the seventh (1776), since it parallels and elaborates Burke's insight into the nondichotomy of reason and prejudice. Just as Reid's notion of "natural prejudices" (that is, the principles of common sense) suggests that not all prejudices are artificial and dispensable, so Reynolds develops the possibility of what Enlightenment epistemology considered no less impossible: a true prejudice. This insight, I suggest, is specifically aesthetic and is fundamentally accessible through an "impure" aesthetics such as that of the *Discourses*.

In Reynolds, unlike Warton, we find no talk of incredibilities higher than truths or fictions more valuable than realities. The impurity of Reynolds's aesthetics consists in the fact that (like the young Burke) he still thinks of art as a way of knowing truth. Yet, distinguishing him from the Burke of the *Enquiry* and allying him with the Burke of the *Reflections* is that Reynolds does not concede the epistemological premise that all truth is rule-governed. "Could we teach taste or genius by rules, they would be no longer taste and genius. . . . Experience is all in all."[16] Experience, practical knowledge, always contains an element of genius insofar as it always exceeds the rules.

The main point is that Reynolds affirms the truth claim of art. "A picture that is unlike," he states, "is false. Disproportionate ordonnance of parts is not right, because it cannot be true . . . that the parts have no relation to the whole. Colouring is true when it is naturally adapted to the eye, from brightness, from softness, from harmony, from resemblance; because these agree with their object, *nature,* and therefore are true, as true as mathematical demonstration, but known to be true only to those who study these things."[17] The truth of a true painting consists in its agreeing with the object (resemblance) and agreeing with itself (harmony); and these, Reynolds insists, are ways of agreeing with the viewer (adaptation to the eye). It is this last element of truth that is most striking because, unlike the first two, it exceeds the limits of epistemology. Correspondence and coherence can be subsumed under the analytic and synthetic or empirical and mathematical versions of epistemological truth. Adaptation to the eye cannot. Any kind of adaptation to the perceiver is precisely what eighteenth-century epistemology would call "prejudice"—or, alternatively, "beauty," which has reference to the eye of the beholder—but not truth.

Just this epistemological premise is what Reynolds disputes when he claims truth for art. But what kind of truth is this?

> Beside *real,* there is also *apparent* truth, or opinion, or prejudice. With regard to real truth, when it is known, the taste

which conforms to it is, and must be, uniform. With regard
to the second sort of truth . . . it is not fixed, but variable.
However, whilst these opinions and prejudices on which it
is founded continue, they operate as truth. . . . In proportion
as these prejudices are known to be generally diffused or long
received, the taste which conforms to them approaches nearer
to certainty and to a sort of resemblance to real science, even
where opinions are found to be no better than prejudices.
And since they deserve on account of their duration and
extent to be considered as really true, they become capable
of no small degree of stability and determination by their
permanent and uniform nature.[18]

To which of the two kinds of truth should art aspire? Reynolds
unhesitatingly replies: "The art whose office it is to please the mind,
as well as instruct it, must direct itself according to *opinion,* or it will
not attain its end."[19] Being "adapted to the eye" means that art has
reference to the way things look, how they seem to be. It is the art
of appearance, but an appearance which cannot be exploded because
that is the way things truly do look and which must therefore be
called true. Art's truth is apparent truth.

To defend the truth claim of art, while at the same time asserting
that art must be based on opinion and prejudice, Reynolds must
affirm the same nondichotomy of prejudice and truth implicit in
Burke's notion of "just prejudice"—that is, "not a prejudice destitute
of reason, but involving in it profound and extensive wisdom" (*R*
8:142). On this matter Reynolds is perfectly explicit: "We are creatures of prejudice; we neither can nor ought to eradicate it; we must
only regulate it by reason; which kind of regulation is indeed little
more than obliging the lesser, the local and temporary prejudices, to
give way to those which are more durable and lasting."[20] Provincial
or short-term reason Reynolds calls prejudice; general and long-term
prejudice he calls reason. Between the two is only a difference of
degree.

The nondichotomy between truth and taste in art corresponds to
the nondichotomy between reason and prejudice with which Burke
challenges Enlightenment epistemology. What Reynolds helps us see
is that politics does not differ from art: both depend on opinion,
prejudice, and "apparent truth." The innovations of the Jacobins,
Burke asserts, "have not one of the great influencing prejudices of

mankind in their favour. They avow their hostility to opinion. Of course they must expect no support from that influence" (*R* 8:213). They have forgotten that "all government stands upon opinion" (*C* 7:91). In this assertion Burke follows not Reynolds but Hume, who considered opinion to be the basis of government: "Nothing appears more surprising to those who consider human affairs with a philosophical eye that the easiness with which the many are governed by the few. . . . When we enquire by what means this wonder is effected, we shall find that, as *force* is always on the side of the governed, the governors have nothing to support them but opinion. It is, therefore, on opinion only that government is founded; and this maxim extends to the most despotic and most military governments, as well as to the most free and most popular."[21] Burke repeats Hume's maxim often, though without drawing any skeptical conclusions from it. Its consequence, rather, is that, even if it were possible to realize the revolutionary epistemological ideal of avoiding all "apparent truth," prejudice, and opinion in favor or "real truth" alone, the result would not be true government but no government at all.

"Whether a *measure* of government be right or wrong," Burke claims, "is *no matter of fact,* but a mere affair of opinion, on which men may, as they do, dispute and wrangle without end" (*T* 2:319). There is in fact no standard outside the debate by which political rectitude could be tried and the debate ended, no real truth to which the "merely" apparent truths of politics could be opposed. Now the next step, it might seem, would be to take the leap into skepticism by inferring that in political matters there is no truth at all. It is worth underscoring, however, that *no such inference is warranted.*[22] That would be merely to beg the question by denying the existence of apparent truth—which, the argument is, constitutes the truth of art and politics, the domains in which reason cannot be opposed to prejudice or truth to appearance.

This brings us back to the issue of decorum. A decoration, we have seen, is surface appearance, phenomenon as opposed to noumenon; and in considering the irreducible two-in-oneness of decorum, we have perhaps sufficiently emphasized the element of twoness, the duplicity that invites the seeker after truth to strip off the pleasant but deceitful decorations to disclose the real thing in itself. It is now time to turn to the oneness of decorum, this unity which can somehow exist without denying multiplicity.

What makes a decoration decorative or decorous at all—and not merely a tasteless, detractive blot—is that it belongs to what it decorates. This is true of even the most adventitious decoration if it is genuinely decorative: it accentuates and enlivens only if it really does fit in and belong. Though it remains a surface appearance, a decorous decoration is, because of that belonging, not just a mere appearance that could be differentiated absolutely from some alien thing in itself that it decorates; rather, in decorous decorations the thing presents *itself,* the thing in itself appears. Decorum, I want to suggest, is a juncture of the thing and its appearance such that the appearance belongs to and is inseparable from it. To say that art and politics, the domains of apparent truth, are governed by the standards of decorum is to say that in these domains appearance cannot be dichotomized from real truth. Here, all truth is apparent—and this does not mean that there is no truth but, quite the contrary, that truth appears.

In this it is like beauty. On the one hand, beauty is phenomenal, mere appearance, only "skin deep," as the saying goes. On the other hand, what appears beautiful is beautiful in truth. What seems is. With respect to the beautiful there is nothing "mere" about appearance, and correlatively no noumenal beauty in itself, no beauty that does not look beautiful, nothing not "adapted to the eye." In domains of apparent truth, just as prejudice cannot be opposed to reason, so the apparent and the true are indivisible. This indivisibility, I am suggesting, constitutes the aspect of oneness in the two-in-oneness of decorum. In the seemly, being and seeming are one.

The notion of apparent truth provides a bridge between Burke's conceptions of decorum and human nature. It is the prerogative of man, he writes, "to be in a great degree a creature of his own making" (*R* 8:143). By this, Burke scarcely means to applaud the hardy individualism of so-called self-made men. Quite the opposite, he states that "every sort of moral, every sort of civil, every sort of politic institution" is necessary "in order to build up that wonderful structure, man." To be human is to be a creature of human making; and that, in Burke's view, means being a creature of the institutions that humans have created. This circle goes a good way toward explicating the notion of apparent truth, since it explains why it makes no sense to ask what human being truly is, as opposed to the way it manifests itself in its institutions. Humanity is precisely what it appears to be— in its objectifications (as Hegel would call them), its self-interpretations (as Heidegger would say): its clothes. *Homo politicus* displays, expresses, and utters himself in his creations; he appears as he truly is, even when decked out in Parisian fashion. For politics as a realm of apparent truth, the metaphorics of the wardrobe—of the self-created, self-creating surface—is precisely right, since it expresses not just the illusion that is vulnerable to disillusionment but also a kind of self-disclosure that is unfalsifiable.

To be sure, Burke often enough accuses the Jacobins of ignoring basic human nature, as if that referred to some bedrock of naked essence: "This sort of people are so taken up with their theories about the right of man that they have totally forgotten his nature" (*R* 8:115). But when we ask what human nature is, Burke replies, "Art is man's nature" (*A* 4:176). This reply evacuates the state of nature of its political significance, since such an "artless" state would include nothing human.[23] For the same reason, Burke's reply also deprives the notion of "artificial" institutions of its pejorative force. "If civil society be the offspring of convention, that convention must be its law. That convention must limit and modify all the descriptions of the constitution which are formed under it. Every sort of legislative, judicial, or executory power are its creatures. They can have no being in any other state of things" (*R* 8:110). Since no government is nonconventional, conventional governments cannot be opposed to any others supposed to be more natural, genuine, true, or real. Where convention is law, the real is the conventional, and no less real, genuine, and true for that. Indeed, it cannot be untrue. In the realm of apparent truth, artifice and decoration cannot be relegated to the order of the signifier, defined as that which can be used to lie. If art is man's nature, art is no lie per se, and genuine human nature is not concealed but revealed in its artifacts.

Constitutions, Burke says elsewhere, are "a vestment which accommodates itself to the body" (*C* 7:95). If so, that puts the Jacobin Shylocks, who would strip the body politic of its clothes, in a quandary, for divestment cannot avoid lascerating the body itself. If art is man's nature, all attempts at exposé that try to penetrate the surface of artificiality become futile, because fundamentally mistaken. The attempt to discover human nature in itself, apart from artifice and decoration, is already to have missed it. Stripping the court of its ornaments does not expose the court for what it really is, since in that very exposure it vanishes. Disrobing the queen reveals not the real queen but no queen—indeed, nothing human—at all. Perfect decoration, surface through and through, she hides nothing and so eludes exposure. Human nature most reveals itself when it veils itself in the clothes of its own making; unveiling therefore not only fails to disclose the thing itself but in fact conceals the artifice that is most natural.

It may seem somewhat counterintuitive to characterize politics as a domain in which deceit is impossible since things can be none other than what they seem. Needless to say, this characterization is scarcely meant to deny the potential for political corruption, mendacity, and concealed self-interest. These are not peculiar to politics, however. Rather, issues that can be called specifically political, in the sense intended here at least, are among those which must be disputed and wrangled over precisely because there is no fact of the matter that could be appealed to or secret political truth whose discovery could silence debate. "Civil freedom," Burke writes, "is not, as many have endeavoured to persuade you, a thing that lies hid in the depth of abstruse science" (*S* 2:229). Political morality holds no secrets. "We know that *we* have made no discoveries, and we think that no discoveries are to be made, in morality" (*R* 8:137). Moral principles are self-evident, or they are nothing. Of any right that purported to be newly discovered and hitherto unheard of, we could predict with some assurance that it was a sham. In the realm of apparent truths, those we hold to be self-evident, nothing is covered, and so there are no dis-coveries to be made. No hidden truths can be brought to light, not because there is no truth but because truth is apparent.

This notion of decorum as belonging to the order of apparent or self-evident truth, I want to suggest in conclusion, helps to explain why Burke appeals to aesthetic criteria in condemning the Revolution and why in the *Reflections* he asserts with Horace, the great advocate of decorum, that states should be constructed like poems. The Jacobins, Burke claims, hold that

> the murder of a king or a queen or a bishop or a father are only common homicide. . . . On the scheme of this barbarous philosophy, which is the offspring of cold hearts and muddy understandings and which is as void of solid wisdom as it is destitute of all taste and elegance, laws are to be supported only by their own terrors. . . . Our institutions can never be embodied, if I may use the expression, in persons, as to create in us love, veneration, admiration, or attachment. But that sort of reason which banishes the affections is incapable

> of filling their place. These public affections, combined with manners, are required sometimes as supplements, sometimes as correctives, always as aids to law. The precept given by a wise man, as well as a great critic, for the construction of poems, is equally true as to states. *Non satis est pulchra esse poemata, dulcia sunto.* (*R* 8:129)

What does Horace mean? For Burke, this is a political question, a question of application that aims to understand not just a past meaning in itself but how it bears and applies, how the past appears in the present. In 1790, Burke argues, the *Ars Poetica* appears as an *ars politica*. What does Burke mean? In our century, interpreting Burke has always been a political act. Now, in the 1990s, however, Burke can no longer be used to swell the ranks of the cold warriors, as he was even a few years ago.[24] The cold war is over, and even the Vietnam era, which evoked protests against being enlisted in those ranks, is over. Now, at a time when politics dominates intellectual life and "everything is political"; now, when the aesthetic is taken to be a concealment and culpable ignorance of real (that is, political) truths, Burke means in citing Horace that the political can be divorced from the aesthetic only at the cost of their mutual impoverishment. That divorce, he suggests, necessarily makes aesthetics effete and politics violent.

In the above passage Burke terms the point of contact between the political and the aesthetic "embodiment." Although the Jacobins assumed that "institutions can never be embodied in persons," the disembodied, unimpersoned government-in-itself that results from dividing king from country must necessarily be oppressive insofar as it thinks it can base itself on the rule of what is right in itself and so dispense with the "love, veneration, admiration, and attachment" of the governed.[25] The kind of reason that sunders is from ought and ideal from real does not also banish laws but merely leaves them divested of veneration. And laws, stripped of respect and willing compliance, are "supported only by their own terrors." Jacobin political philosophy, the philosophy of exposé and disembodied truth, Burke argues, unwittingly advocates government by terror. "In the groves of *their* academy, at the end of every visto, you see nothing but the gallows." The naked truth, stripped of prejudice and opinion, is the epistemological arm of naked force.

To counter a philosophy "destitute of all taste" because it divides embodiment from embodied and sees only duplicity in decoration,

Burke cites the locus classicus of decorum, Horace's *Ars Poetica:* "Non satis est pulchra esse poemata, dulcia sunto." Here poetry becomes, as it were, the embodiment of embodiment, the symbol par excellence of decorum and apparent truth, which unites is and seems, in itself and for us. It is not enough for a poem to be correctly beautiful, Horace says; it must please. That it follows rules or laws or abstract universals of whatever kind is not enough; it must delight us and attract our desire as well. It is not enough that the poem's content be beautiful in itself; it must be apparent and evidence itself to us in its decoration. This underscores the fundamental two-in-oneness of decorum. In decorous poetry, content (in itself) and form (its appearance to us) are not the same but two different things; yet artistic form is one with content precisely insofar as that form is decorous. The form is the very "embodiment" of the content, the appearance that bodies forth the content itself and so is one with it.

The application to the political sphere follows from this conception of embodiment. It is not enough to envision governments on the basis of ideal principles and then conform the real to those ideals. "I cannot stand forward," Burke writes, "and give praise or blame to any thing . . . on a simple view of the object, as it stands stripped of every relation, in all the nakedness and solitude of metaphysical abstraction. . . . The circumstances are what render every civil and political scheme beneficial or noxious to mankind" (*R* 8:58). Naked, disembodied abstractions have no political significance per se (except as rationalizations for power); only when embodied and circumstanced do principles have political value, either positive or negative. This is neither to recommend mere expedience nor to assert that nothing in the political sphere is either right or wrong; it is to say only that there is nothing right or wrong absolutely, in itself, regardless of circumstances—that is, apart from its tasteful embodiment.

Burke might well have quoted what Hume says about reason: law as such "is perfectly inert, and can never either prevent or produce any action or affection" (*T* 458). "That sort of reason which banishes the affections is incapable of filling their place. These public affections, combined with manners, are required sometimes as supplements, sometimes as correctives, always as aids to law." No one obeys a law, "stripped of every relation," merely because it is right in itself or right in the abstract; so to insure compliance with its abstractions, calculative reason, lacking the supplement of affections and manners, always finds it necessary to replace them with a power of equal force and thereby substitute violence for veneration. A different kind of reason is necessary if a government is to be rational yet motivate action without resorting to force, a kind of reason that is indivisible from historical practice. If "naked reason . . . leaves the man hesitating in the moment of decision, sceptical, puzzled, and unresolved," Burke prefers clothed reason—embodied, practical reason, that is, prejudice—"because prejudice, with its reason, has a motive to give action to that reason and an affection which will give its permanence" (*R* 8:138).

To secure voluntary obedience, a government needs embodied law, law that is inseparable from manners, mores, traditions, and customs. For "custom has two original effects upon the mind," as Hume wrote: "in bestowing a facility in the performance of any action . . . and afterwards a tendency or inclination towards it" (*T* 422). For this reason, "public affections, combined with manners," remain inescapably requisite as supplements, correctives, and aids. Only customary, common laws that people obey because they have always obeyed them, and indeed want to do so, are capable of securing compliance without coercion. When right is abstracted from custom and tradition, the vacuum must be filled by force. However adventitious, embodiment in historical circumstance and historical custom is an essential supplement to the spirit of the laws if they are not to become machines of oppression.

Burke thought all of this had something to do with taste and decorum as exemplified in poetry. A decorous poem, for Burke as for Horace, symbolizes the "supplement" that is nonetheless "required," the two-in-one, the surface that is not the same as the depth but not divisible from it either. The epistemological politicians, he thought, were always wanting to divide the spirit of the laws from their embodiment and to leave the latter, the application, to the technicians, the social engineers. To say with Burke, however, that "the precept given by a wise man, as well as a great critic, for the construction of poems is equally true as to states" is to say that while it is impossible to identify the real with the ideal and so ratify the status quo, neither can they be dissociated. For to presume that political ideals as such are not embodied, that justice per se can be sundered from the reality of history, is, as we have seen, an invitation to injustice. There is in politics, Burke passionately believed, only practical reason, no pure science apart from past and future application. There is no ideal apart from the real, though there is no equating them either. Perhaps that, in brief, encapsulates the meaning of Burke's aesthetic politics: the two-in-one of decorum exemplifies how the ideal of political justice always is, yet is always still to be, realized in history.

Epilogue

If there is one theme fundamental to eighteenth-century hermeneutics, it is the impetus to think reason and history together—to liberate reason from rationalist formalism and history from antiquarianism, the two extremes which are always tending to fly apart into antitheses. Both extremes were perceived to be inadequate, and both equally barren. Though rationality is surely regulated by laws, principles, and rules, laws are not enough in jurisprudence; principles are not enough in politics; and genius cannot be regulated by rules. Yet we have seen that many were unwilling to consign domains such as these to caprice and arbitrariness—that is, to the kind of senseless history compiled by annalists and antiquarian chronologers. This left those who refused to equate the lawless with the irrational with a formidable task: namely, to reconceive reason and history in such a way that reason does not consist merely of clear and distinct but empty forms, nor history of actual but chaotic and opaque contingency. The task of eighteenth-century hermeneutics was to understand historical reason.

With spectacular success, Newton had mathematized nature and thereby shown the rationality and intelligibility of the physical cosmos. The realm of history, however, proved more resistant to understanding—or seemed to, as long as intelligibility and reason were confined to mathematical rationality. Before Dilthey, even before Hegel, history in the form of eighteenth-century politics, aesthetics, and jurisprudence called for a more capacious model of intelligibility than that provided by the mathematization of nature. Post-Newtonian nature could be described (in Pope's words) as "one clear, unchanged, and universal light," and laws could be conceived of as "nature methodized" ("Essay on Criticism," 11.71, 89). If so, it would seem that post-Newtonian history—the realm of changing particulars not governed by laws—should have been just muddy darkness. Yet it was not. As a new generation of British historians from Clarendon to Gibbon had shown, history was intelligible despite the fact that historians' conclusions were not demonstrable. In this and many other ways it became apparent to eighteenth-century thinkers, as it had to Aristotle and Cicero earlier, that the scope of understanding exceeds that of rational demonstration.

Understanding surpasses rationality, narrowly conceived. Though reflective or theoretical rationality is subservient to rules, reason is not, for it also includes what is reasonable. Reason (in Toland's usage) comprehends everything that makes sense, even though sense making is not strictly axiomatizable or regulable. If intelligible reasonableness therefore cannot be limited to codifiable universals, then the remainder whereby reason exceeds them can be acquired only through the irregular, mutable particulars that constitute history. Thus broadly conceived, reason and history are not antithetical, except in their extreme forms. There must be some overlap between them, something historical about reason, something reasonable about history.

This common ground comprehending reason that cannot be reduced to rationality and history that cannot be reduced to irrationality can be termed "sense," "meaning," and in general everything that is understandable. And if so, it becomes clear why hermeneutics, the theory and practice of understanding, is so intimately involved in the project of thinking history and reason together. Where reason and history overlap is in the realm of whatever can be understood. Historical understanding is specifically required to understand the unique, never to be repeated events of history. Hermeneutic understanding in general, moreover, is like historical understanding in being required whenever a special situation governed by no known rules or laws nevertheless calls for a decision. Such judgment calls, though ad hoc and irreducibly historical, can still be reasonable and understandable. Yet their reasonableness cannot be defined in terms of their obeying or breaking some rule, since the absence of a rule is precisely what necessitated the judgment call in the first place.

Understanding is a mode of reason, moreover, precisely insofar as such ad hoc judgments can be mistaken: it is not the case that anything goes if misunderstanding is possible. Since judgments can be found mistaken, they must appeal to standards, the very standards by which they can themselves be judged. The criteria to which such judgments appeal, however, are essentially indefinable, for to define a criterion is to state a rule. If not all ad hoc judgments are false, and indeed some are true, then some truths are not strictly provable. Some truths, that is, depend on indefinable though quite real criteria. Not coincidentally, eighteenth-century hermeneutic philosophers were drawn to just these uncodifiable criteria: sympathy, common sense, taste, prudence, and equity. These are the criteria that govern the truths shared by reason and history—that is, the truths that exceed demonstration but cannot be reduced to whim or preference.

"Equity," Blackstone writes, "thus depending, essentially, upon the particular circumstances of each individual case, there can be no established rules and fixed precepts of equity laid down without destroying its very essence and reducing it to a positive law" (*Commentaries,* 1:61). Although the standard by which judicial interpretation itself is judged is *essentially* indefinable, sometimes, at least, the law is interpreted truly, and justice is served. What, then, is this indefinable standard of truth? Just this: the equitable is what "the particular circumstances of each individual case" call for. The circumstances keep changing; they are historical, unpredictable, contingent. This contingency explains why the standard of legal explication cannot be made explicit a priori, for in the final analysis the circumstances to which the law is to be applied are themselves the standard by which the law is to be interpreted.

The standard of truth, in other words, is fittingness. The true interpretation of the law is the one that fits the case, and since the case cannot be understood in advance, before it arises, neither can the meaning of the law. It must be understood ad hoc. The judge is therefore required to understand not only the law, "the perfection of reason," but also the particular situation. He needs to understand what history too demands, what the circumstances of the case call for, because history no less than reason is productive of truth. In the equitable interpretation, in which the law itself cannot be understood without understanding the circumstances, not only is history made reasonable; the historical occasion brings about "the perfection of reason."

Burke is saying something very similar, I think, when he writes, "No lines can be laid down for civil or political wisdom. They are a matter incapable of exact definition" (*T* 2:282). Or again, "The [real] rights of men are in a sort of middle, incapable of definition, but not impossible to be discerned" (*R* 8:112). "I cannot stand forward, and give praise or blame to any thing . . . on a simple view of the object, as it stands stripped of every relation, in all the nakedness and solitude of metaphysical abstraction. . . . The circumstances are what render every civil and political scheme beneficial or noxious to mankind" (*R* 8:58). Political wisdom does not differ from legal interpretation, in that both are situated in "a sort of middle," as Burke says. Both occupy the common ground uniting principle and circumstance, reason and history. Aesthetic judgment is situated here as well. Just as "nothing universal can be rationally affirmed on any moral or any political subject" (*A* 4:80), so too no universals obtain in aesthetic judgment. Here reason is rational only when it is not abstracted from history—that is, from the particulars of the case being judged. Universal laws and inflexible rules may explain painting by numbers, but they account for nothing worth knowing about art. "Could we teach taste or genius by rules," as Reynolds observed, "they would be no longer taste and genius."[1]

This, we recall, was the great theme of Kant's *Critique of Judgment*. Unquestionably Kant developed the notion of judging without rules far beyond anything Reynolds dreamed of. Yet the interesting thing about the eighteenth-century notion of judgment as found in Reid, Blackstone, and Burke and the respect in which Kant's notion failed to supersede theirs is that they retained the truth claim of judgment, whereas Kant jettisoned it when he reduced the claim of taste to subjective universality. The result is that eighteenth-century British thought is closer in some respects to Hegel than to Kant, since Hegel, like Reynolds and Burke, for example, thought of truth as indissociable from life and history. Consider how Reynolds describes what he calls "sagacity" or "habitual reason":

> There is in the commerce of life, as in art, a sagacity which is far from being contradictory to right reason, and is superior to any occasional exercise of that faculty. . . . [Sagacity] does not wait for the slow progress of deduction, but goes at once, by what appears a kind of intuition, to the conclusion. A man endowed with this faculty, feels and acknowledges the truth, though it is not always in his power, perhaps,

to give a reason for it, because he cannot recollect and bring before him all the materials that gave birth to his opinion; for . . . though these in process of time are forgotten, the right impression still remains fixed in his mind.

This impression is the result of the accumulated experience of our whole life, and has been collected, we do not always know how or when. But this mass of collective observation, however acquired, ought to prevail over that reason, which however powerfully exerted on any particular occasion, will probably comprehend but a partial view of the subject; and our conduct in life as well as in the arts, is, or ought to be, generally governed by this habitual reason. . . . If we were obliged to enter into a theoretical deliberation on every occasion, before we act, life would be at a stand, and art would be impracticable.[2]

Based on what Hegel was to call "objective mind" and what Reynolds elsewhere calls "prejudice," sagacity "appears [to be] a kind of intuition" by reason of its speed and sureness. But it is not intuition—at least not in Locke's sense. For the special kind of self-evidence resulting from sagacious judgment is not the transparency of mathematical axioms or reflective self-consciousness. Hume, as we have seen, did not think these transparent either. But, like intuition, sagacity cannot give its reasons; yet this absence does not condemn it to arbitrariness, since those who employ it "feel and acknowledge the truth." Unlike reflective reason, which tries to claim a monopoly on truth, "habitual reason" is like a sense—common sense, perhaps—because it has no theoretical reasons, whether known or unknown, with which to defend itself. Sagacity has its own reasons, to be sure; but these reasons cannot be formulated theoretically since they derive from "the accumulated experience of our whole life." They derive from history.

Habitual reason, or sagacity, is historical reason. More dependable in unforeseen circumstances—in history—precisely because it is not formulable, historical reason cannot be reduced to philosophical precepts. Its sureness does not depend on its codifiability. When we understand life not merely as a state to be known but as action and conduct to be undertaken, then we find that abstractions prove "impracticable," as Reynolds says, because we are not always sure how they apply. What Reynolds calls "habitual reason," by contrast, has its roots in what Aristotle called "phronēsis," practical or applied reason. Praxis requires that the truths claiming to apply to life must themselves derive from it. This does not mean that philosophical precepts need to be abstracted from life; they are already embodied in it. "History is philosophy teaching by examples," Bolingbroke asserts, like many before him (*Letters*, 1:177). Historical reason is informed by examples—embodied knowledge—for examples themselves exemplify the common ground of history and reason, practice and theory, life and truth.

Applying the exemplary to one's conduct requires not a process of vertical abstraction and subsumption, as in the case of rule-governed reason. Instead, interpreting the past in the present, re-embodying already embodied truth, involves translation—that is, conserving the same in the process of transferring it to the different. In this process, neither may be distorted if understanding is to occur; both past and present must be taken into account. Thus the standard of true translation is not only the text as such, the past *wie es eigentlich gewesen*. Just as the equitable decision takes cognizance not only of the law but also of the circumstances of the particular case, so too historical interpretation must be faithful not only to the past as such but to the present in which it is to be understood. And if understanding through translation is to occur, their relation must be conceived of neither as a changeless continuity between past and present, which would obviate translation, nor as the pure discontinuity and incommensurability that would preclude it. In its dual fidelity to the past and the present, historical reason finds, as Burke puts it, the tasteful conjunction that combines a oneness that cannot be reduced to identity with a duality that cannot be reduced to unrelatedness. More simply, as we saw in Reid, understanding history is like making a good metaphor.

Consideration of eighteenth-century hermeneutics, then, suggests that the nonreductive reconciliation of reason, which is always one and the same, with history, which is always many and different, is embodied in every true interpretation. Perhaps this interpretation of interpretation allows us better to understand Swift's allegory of the self-altering coats. These coats, the dying father explains to his sons, "will grow in the same proportion with your bodies, lengthening and widening of themselves, so as to be always fit." Located at the point of intersection between the fixed will and the growing body, the eternally changeless meaning and the eternally changing situation in which it is understood, the coats represent true interpretation.

They represent the difference that preserves sameness, the faithful alteration, the common ground between reason and history. The true interpretation of the law, we have seen, is the one that fits the case. But interpretations always involve questions of fit, and so Swift equates interpretive truth with the fitting. He reviles tasteless readers who "have neither candour to suppose good meanings nor palate to distinguish true ones" (5), because taste governs questions of congruity and fit. For Swift, as for Burke, the faculty that determines whether an interpretation is true, that determines truth as fitness, is taste.

Taste is an appropriate synonym for historical reason in that it is a way of knowing the truth that consists in the fit between history and reason. What is "always fitting," as Swift writes, must be perpetually "lengthening and widening." But what kind of truth is this that can only remain the same by altering and is not distorted but revealed in history? Such truth cannot be equated with the Platonic Ideas, for the Ideas do not appear here below, in the world of contingency, particularity, actuality: in history. Thus, in search of an alternative model of truth which does not dichotomize the real and the apparent and which can therefore reconcile truth and history, we have turned to the Neoplatonic tradition. It is variously recognizable in Hume and Reid, as well as in Blackstone and Burke; but it is perhaps most simply represented by Shaftesbury's assertion that "All beauty is truth."[3] This Neoplatonic equation of truth and beauty, I want to suggest in conclusion, best elucidates the reasonableness of history and the historicality of reason.

Beauty not only appears beautiful; its reality is to be found nowhere but in appearance. For this reason, we have said, beauty symbolizes what Reynolds called "apparent truth"—that is, the truth which appears, which cannot be contrasted with appearance because its very nature is to make itself visible and evident. History conceived as philosophy teaching by example belongs to this model of truth, too, in that it conceives the true as appearing in the very flesh, as it were. It is revealed not in the abstract but as embodied in history, and only there. "Such is the imperfection of human understanding, such is the frail temper of our minds," Bolingbroke observes, "that abstract or general propositions, though ever so true, appear obscure or doubtful to us very often, till they are explained by examples" (178). History illustrates the true, which would remain in darkness without it.

Consisting of unfalsifiable appearance, moreover, beauty figures the self-evidence of truth. To think of self-evidence, this self-illumination of the true, historically rather than theoretically, however, we need to recall how Burke conceived of the self-evidence of political truth. There is only disputing about politics; thus political truth emerges into the open only through the process of discussion and public debate, though it is no doubt obscured by the same process. We need to think of truth generally in Burke's way: as revealing itself and emerging into the open in a succession of appearances, and not otherwise. Understood historically, the self-evidence of truth is a process, the historical process of truth's evidencing itself in historical appearances, and nowhere else.

No longer equated with plainness and patency, self-evidence conceived of historically cannot be the quality of obviousness which for Locke obviates interpretation. Quite the contrary, the self-evident text, as Locke says, interprets itself, alters in such a way as to preserve itself. Self-evidencing is the self-interpretation of truth, the process whereby the same is continually translated into the different. In history, reason neither becomes self-alienated nor remains self-identical. It grows. In Swift's *Tale,* we recall, Martin refuses to strip away all the accretions that his coat has acquired over the course of time; he declines to reject all its historical appearances; and he thinks this "the best method for serving the true intent and meaning of his father's will" (136–37). This hermeneutic ideal refuses to sever meaning—including true meaning—from history. Reconciling the oneness of the same with the plurality of the different, and thereby satisfying fools and knaves alike, Swift's *Tale* of the self-altering coats suggests that on occasion the father's will reveals itself as it truly is—in different, but fitting, tasteful, and therefore true, interpretations. It suggests that truth itself appears occasionally, in history, and is no less true for that.

Notes

Introduction

1. For readings of the *Tale* that concentrate on its interpretive aspects, see Louis, *Swift's Anatomy of Misunderstanding;* Zimmerman, *Swift's Narrative Satires,* esp. pp. 39–60; and Nash, "Entrapment."

2. Parenthetical citations of *Tale of a Tub* refer to the text edited by Guthkelch and Smith. Citations of Swift's other works are from *Prose Works of Jonathan Swift.*

3. I agree with Paulson that "the choice [between knave and fool] is a false one" (*Theme and Structure,* p. 187. The question is what the alternative is.

4. Nash differentiates two ironic modes in the *Tale* and two kinds of interpretive activity, which he calls "distinguishing" and "recognizing" meaning, without pointing out that these correspond to the hermeneutics of knaves and fools respectively ("Entrapment," p. 416).

5. Compare Clarke: "Allegorizing is a fine double-edged method that permits 'levels' of meaning. In allegory, as in no other literary form, the levels of meaning—surface and depth—are successfully united" (*Form and Frenzy,* p. 63).

6. "The current interest in the art or craft of Swift's works, the anatomy of his masks," Voigt concludes in his final paragraph, has prompted "an engagement not limited to the surface. Analytical criticism has pierced that surface and has discovered a lost, if not a new, world" (*Swift,* p. 164).

7. Compare Newton's contention that the prophets "all write in one and the same mystical language, as well known without doubt to the sons of the prophets as the hieroglyphic language of the Egyptians to their

priests. And this language, so far as I can find, was as certain and
definite in its signification as is the vulgar language of any nation
whatsoever, so that it is only through want of skill therein that interpreters so frequently turn the prophetic types and phrases to signify
whatever their fancies and hypotheses lead them to" (*Theological Manuscripts*, p. 119).

8. See Pinkus, "*Tale of a Tub*," and Andreasen, "Swift's Satire." Korshin
traces the history of the demystification of typology in *Typologies in
England*, pp. 39–74.

9. Swift, "Cassinus and Peter" (1.118), in *Poetical Works*, p. 531.

10. Wittgenstein, *Lectures and Conversations*, pp. 23–34.

11. Nowhere more clearly than in this half-ironic critique of unmasking
does Swift justify Rawson's comment "The rigidities of mask-criticism
(even in its more sophisticated forms) tend to compartmentalize what
needs to remain a more fluid and indistinct interaction" (*Gulliver and the
Gentle Reader*, p. 23).

12. I follow Harth in identifying both the materialists and the tailor-wor-
shipers as monists; I cannot agree, however, that Swift embraces an
"uncompromising epistemological dualism" (*Swift and Anglican Rationalism*, pp. 96 and 143).

13. Coleridge, *Biographia Literaria*, 1:90.

14. Compare Cope: "The 'clothes philosophy' passage is no fluke. . . . Swift
argues, for example, that kings must always be kings de jure and de
facto; one cannot identify someone as a king without consenting to and
experiencing his kingly offices. Whoever looks and acts like a king is a
king, and vice versa; a king *is* a suit of clothes, but that suit presents a
whole political system" (*Criteria of Certainty*, p. 120).

15. Swift counts "on a certain norm of agreement in his audience that will
enable them to recognize the irony," Weathers rightly observes ("Technique of Irony," p. 55). It may also be the case that the very instability
of the *Tale*'s irony reflects fractures in the *consensus gentium*.

16. Reid, *Philosophical Works*, p. 438.

17. See Starkman, *Swift's Satire on Learning*, p. xvi.

18. Burke, *Vindication of Natural Society*, in *Works*, 1:52.

19. Idel, *Kabbalah*, p. 215. See also Bloom, *Kabbalah and Criticism*.

20. Bolingbroke, *Works*, 3:464.

21. Dryden, "Religio Laici" (11.366–69), in *Poems*, 1:320.

22. Bolingbroke, *Works*, 3:464.

23. All quotations from scripture are from the Authorized Version.

24. Locke, *Paraphrase and Notes*, p. 103.

25. Dryden, "The Hind and the Panther" (2.359–60, 379–84), in *Poems*,
2:494.

26. Bolingbroke, *Works*, 4:464–65.

27. Compare Swift's famous letter to Pope (29 Sept. 1725): "Upon this

great foundation of misanthropy (though not in Timon's manner) the whole building of my *Travels* is erected: And I never will have peace of mind till all honest men are of my opinion" (*Correspondence*, 3:103).

28. Dryden, "Religio Laici" (11.309–10), in *Poems*, 1:319.
29. Taylor, *Whole Works*, 7:439.
30. Bolinbroke, *Works*, 3:465.
31. For an alternative reading of this passage, see Rawson, *Order from Confusion*, pp. 253, 326.
32. Compare Rembert: "Swift believed more in dialectic, the reasoning between two people leading, it is hoped, to agreement, than he did in solitary reasoning" (*Swift and the Dialectical Tradition*, p. 103). See also Paulson, *Theme and Structure*, pp. 101 and 112.
33. Sterne, *Tristram Shandy*, p. 108.
34. Hume, *Dialogues Concerning Natural Religion*, p. 26.
35. See also Traugott: "In the great satires he is not only cruelly complex but even mysterious" ("Tale of a Tub," p. 96); and Burrow: "I will argue that Swift counters the freethinkers by a concealed argument that runs throughout the *Tale*. . . . The seriousness of his political purpose is revealed throughout by the lengths he goes to in order to conceal the *Tale*'s depths" ("Credulity and Curiosity," p. 313).
36. Dryden, "Religio Laici" (11.292–94), in *Poems*, 1:318.
37. Taylor, *Whole Works*, 7:511.
38. Pope, "Preface to Shakespeare," p. 164.
39. F the most authoritative treatment of the quarrel between the ancients and the moderns, see Levine, *Battle of the Books*.
40. Bolingbroke, *Works*, 4:98.
41. For an excellent essay explicating the "growing coats" by reference to Hooker, see Chiasson, "Swift's Clothes Philosophy." In addition to law, literature—especially the practice of textual emendation—might be taken to represent the impossibility of stasis. Theobald denies that "we ought to be as cautious of altering [Shakespeare's] text, as we would that of the sacred writings" (*Shakespeare Restored*, p. iv). On the other hand, Edwards sarcastically infers from Warburton's emendations that "a professed critic has a right to declare that his author wrote whatever he thinks he ought to have written" and "he has a right to alter any passage which he does not understand" (*Canons of Criticism*, p. 25).
42. Blackstone, *Commentaries*, 1:62.
43. Hume, *Enquiry Concerning the Human Understanding* and *Concerning the Principles of Morals*, pp. 308–09.
44. Williams at first says that the "ironic method is the result of Swift's reluctance to put forward an unambiguous standard," but later remarks that "we blunder in expecting . . . that he should set us, simply and unequivocally, a standard to follow" (*Jonathan Swift*, pp. 164 and 191).

Chapter 1. Locke on Human Understanding

1. Locke, *Two Tracts,* p. 119, italics omitted.
2. Ibid., p. 118.
3. Abrams makes this point forcefully in his introduction (ibid., p. 63).
4. Ibid., p. 121.
5. Ibid., p. 118.
6. Ibid., p. 210.
7. Locke, *Essay Concerning Human Understanding,* 4. 16. 4. Subsequent quotations from the *Essay* are cited parenthetically by book, chapter, and section number.
8. Locke, *Four Letters,* in *Works,* 6:53.
9. "[Locke excludes] from toleration all who are themselves intolerant, and who will not own and teach the duty of tolerating all other men in matters of religion" (Fraser, *Locke,* p. 96).
10. Quoted in ibid., p. 12.
11. Ibid.
12. Locke, *Conduct of Understanding,* p. 131.
13. Locke, *Law of Nature,* p. 131.
14. Despite the fact that I here emphasize the anti-hermeneutic elements in Locke, I do not mean to deny that insofar as the *Essay Concerning Human Understanding* shows that most of our knowledge consists not of certainties but of judgments, Locke demonstrates that understanding is primarily semiotic, inferential, and therefore interpretive. See Patey, *Probability and Literary Form,* esp. pp. 3–74.
15. Locke, *Two Tracts,* p. 64.
16. Locke, *Correspondence,* 1:124.
17. Quoted in Fraser, *Locke,* p. 47.
18. Locke, *Two Treatises,* p. 282.
19. Locke, *Four Letters,* p. 23.
20. Schouls has shown that Locke arrived at the concept of the individual through the method of logical "resolution," a method which he and Descartes were among the first to extend to all areas of inquiry. See Schouls, *Imposition of Method.*
21. In this and the following two paragraphs I am concurring with MacPherson's *Political Theory* and Strauss's *Natural Right* with respect to the theses that Locke at least tacitly sanctions unlimited accumulation and undermines social obligation. For a very cogent, if not finally convincing, rebuttal of the MacPherson–Strauss position, see Dunn, *Political Thought.*
22. Locke, *Thoughts Concerning Education,* in *Works,* 9:101.
23. If to have made all ideas one's own constitutes rationality, then MacPherson is correct in asserting that for Locke "unlimited accumulation is the essence of rationality" (*Political Theory,* p. 221).
24. Locke, *Paraphrase and Notes,* p. 115.

25. Locke, *Conduct of Understanding*, p. 73.

26. To Locke's contention in *Reasonableness of Christianity* that "I know not but that it may be true that the anti-Trinitarians and Racovians understand [certain texts] as I do: but 'tis more than I know that they do so," Cranston replies, "It was not true that Locke had never read the Racovians. His notebooks contain excerpts from their writings" (*John Locke*, p. 392). In the nineteenth century, according to Aarsleff, Locke's "philosophy was called unoriginal and a mere unacknowledged plagiarism of Gassendi and Hobbes" (*Locke to Saussure*, p. 120). See also Gibson, *Locke's Theory*, p. 182.

27. In *Imitation* I have discussed at length Locke's relation to the rise of originality as a value.

28. Locke, *Two Treatises*, p. 327.

29. Ibid., p. 281.

30. Ibid., pp. 351–52.

31. The absence of the judiciary is particularly glaring to readers in the United States, of course, since the American Constitution specifies three powers. Yet Blackstone shows that the need for an independent judiciary had been perceived in Britain as early as 1640: "[Liberty] cannot subsist long in any state unless the administration of common justice be in some degree separated both from the legislative and also from the executive power. Were it joined with the legislative, the life, liberty, and property of the subject would be in the hands of arbitrary judges, whose decisions would then be regulated only by their own opinions and not by any fundamental principles of law, which though legislators may depart from, yet judges are bound to observe. Were it joined with the executive, this union might soon be an over-balance for the legislative. For which reason, by the statute of 16 Car. I, c. 10 (Star Chamber, 1640), which abolished the Star Chamber, effectual care is taken to remove all judicial power out of the hands of the king's privy council" (*Commentaries*, 1:269).

32. See Laslett's introduction to Locke, *Two Treatises*.

33. Biddle, "Locke's Essay," p. 317.

34. Although he does elsewhere in the treatise.

35. Biddle, "Locke's Essay," p. 317.

36. Locke, *Thoughts Concerning Education*, p. 189.

37. Locke, *Conduct of Understanding*, p. 107.

38. Locke, *Paraphrase*, p. 108.

39. Locke, *Reasonableness of Christianity*, p. xxvii.

40. Evans, *Language and Logic*, p. 32. Commentators have tended to content themselves with noting Locke's insistence on the principle of the coherence of scriptural texts, especially the Pauline epistles. But this coherence, important as it is, is nevertheless not an end but a means enabling the private (i.e., Protestant) understanding of Scripture. For a fine statement of the traditional view, see Pahl, "John Locke."

41. See Hurley, "'Scriptura Sola'." See also Gadamer, *Truth and Method,* pp. 174–75.
42. Biddle, "Locke's Essay," p. 327.
43. Compare the two definitions of interpretation implied by the following: "Anybody may attach a new meaning to the words to suit his own taste, find some remote interpretation, and twist the words to fit the situation and his own taste" (ibid., p. 317); "to interpret is nothing else than to bring out the meaning of obscure words and to express unfamiliar language clearly in words of everyday speech" (ibid., p. 323). The second, clarification which doesn't change the meaning, is—in terms of the first—mere paraphrase, not interpretation at all. So also, judged in terms of clarification, the second—interpretation that changes meaning—is not interpretation but perversion. Not until Heidegger did it become possible to think of these two senses as noncontradictory.
44. Locke, *Two Tracts,* p. 174.
45. Thus I cannot agree with Tuveson that, for Locke, "correction of error in opinion is largely a matter of bringing more light to bear" (*Imagination,* p. 21).
46. Schouls counts some fifty instances of "plain" in the *Reasonableness of Christianity* and over one hundred in the *Paraphrase* (*Imposition of Method,* p. 238n.).
47. Biddle, "Locke's Essay," p. 323.
48. This implies, of course, that the distinction between clear and obscure is itself clear. It never occurs to Locke that it could be otherwise, since that would mean the judgment that a given passage is clear is itself an interpretation.
49. Locke, *Reasonableness of Christianity,* p. 59.
50. *Essay Concerning Human Understanding,* Locke's introduction, p. 10, italics omitted.
51. Locke, *Four Letters,* p. 40.
52. Locke, *Conduct of Understanding,* p. 86.
53. Locke, *Law of Nature,* p. 123.
54. Locke, *Conduct of Understanding,* p. 122.
55. Locke, *Thoughts Concerning Education,* p. 189.
56. Locke, *Law of Nature,* p. 131.
57. Ibid., p. 125.
58. "[Locke] is very elaborate in the proof that there are no innate ideas and, consequently, propositions, which are compounded of ideas. All which I think might have been saved in the strict sense which he puts upon the word innate; for therein surely he has no adversary. For no one does or at least can rationally assert, that the minds of embryos . . . are ready furnished with ideas" (Lee, *Anti-Scepticism,* Sig. Ab.).
59. *Essay Concerning Human Understanding,* Locke's introduction, p. 8.
60. The viability of Locke's epistemology depends on it going unnoticed that this conclusion is either truistic or false. If there is no possible

difference between my ideas and what I think they are, then by the rule of Occam's razor, one of the two (either I or my ideas) must be consigned to nonexistence. As we will see in the chapter on Reid, the obvious candidate for elimination is the idea itself. In thinking, Reid argued, I think about the very things I am thinking about, not my ideas.

61. Locke, *Conduct of Understanding*, p. 36.
62. Ibid., p. 58.
63. M. A. Stewart finds the same circularity in Locke's conception of language as nomenclature: "The annexation of sounds to perceptions, thoughts, images, etc. *of the right things* must presuppose the linguistic understanding it is supposed to illumine" ("Locke, Steiner and Understanding," p. 22).
64. I do not mean to deny the validity of Tooke's insight that not just the third book but "the greatest part of Mr. Locke's Essay . . . does indeed merely concern language" (*Diversions of Purley*, 1:39). But Locke didn't think so.
65. In a brilliant article, Zuckert shows that even while Locke, as a linguistic therapist, is prescribing rules for clarifying language, he also explains why they cannot be kept, and thus why he himself consistently violates his own prescriptions ("Fools and Knaves").
66. As Aarsleff remarks, "To Locke, unlike Descartes, the obstacle to good sense and knowledge was not merely a verbose enemy, not just some men's words, but words" (*Locke to Saussure*, p. 44).
67. Locke, *Conduct of Understanding*, p. 98.
68. See Aarsleff's observations concerning Condillac: "Language is not merely, as Locke has been content to maintain, the necessary means of communication and an aid to memory. It is more than that, for thinking could neither begin nor continue without it" (*Study of Language*, p. 19).
69. I have shown elsewhere that the conception of words as signs, which for the most part we share with Locke, is not neutral but belongs to precisely the instrumentalist conception of language so evident in the *Essay*. See my "Word is Not a Sign" and "Hermeneutic Semiotics."

Chapter 2. Toland on Reason

1. See Willis: "This author does not in his book expressly deny the Trinity, though we have reason to fear that his book was chiefly designed against it" (*Reflections*, here cited from 2d ed. of 1701, p. 20).
2. Johnson, "*Rasselas*," chap. 48.
3. I state my thesis this bluntly because addressing the issue of whether Toland was right will help guard, I hope, against the sarcasm and paternalistic arrogance that characterize such accounts of Deism generally and Toland in particular as that of Stephen.
4. Toland's *Letters to Serena* contains an explicit refutation of Spinoza, on

the relation of matter and motion. Moreover, in "Spinoza and the Early English Deists," p. 37, Colie notes that Toland's political tracts were un-Spinozan. She does not consider whether the same is true of *Christianity Not Mysterious,* however.

5. See Sullivan, *Toland and the Deist Controversy,* p. 51. Reedy develops the full intellectual context of *Christianity Not Mysterious* in "Socinians."

6. From another perspective, rationalist theologians such as Barrow, South, Tillotson, and Stillingfleet might well be called liberal. But I concur with Reedy that "their insistence on the reasonableness of Christianity was an iron grip not on a deistic future but on the traditional past" (*Bible and Reason,* p. 12). In this respect, Toland's position does not differ from theirs; he merely radicalizes it.

7. Parenthetical references to *Christianity Not Mysterious* are to the reprint of the 1st, 1969 edition.

8. Parenthetical references to the *Theologico-Political Treatise* refer to vol. 1 of *Chief Works.*

9. Todorov, *Symbolism and Interpretation,* p. 136.

10. Stillingfleet, *Sermons,* 3:212.

11. In this regard Toland was anticipated by Spanheim and LeClerc. See Daniel, *John Toland,* p. 124. I have found this chapter of Daniel's book, "Historical and Literary Exegesis," especially helpful and informative.

12. Contrast Toland: "What is revealed in religion . . . may be easily comprehended, and found as consistent with our common notions, as what we know of wood or stone, of air, of water, or the like" (80).

13. Strauss, "Spinoza's *Theologic-Political Treatise,*" pp. 148ff.

14. When Spinoza says that the "cardinal precept is: To love God above all things, and one's neighbours as one's self" (172), his conclusion may well be based on the following key passage: "For now we see through a glass, darkly; but then face to face. . . . And now abideth faith, hope, and charity, these three; but the greatest of these is charity" (I Cor. 13:12–13). Yet Augustine chooses this same passage as summarizing the entire content of the Bible (*On Christian Doctrine,* I. xxvi), and if Augustine has influenced Spinoza in his choice of it as key, one might well wonder whether Spinoza's interpretation is therefore intrinsic or extrinsic. For a particularly clear discussion of these issues, see Lang, "Politics of Interpretation."

15. For the reasons given here, I cannot agree with Reedy's contention (*Bible and Reason,* p. 27) that Toland's hermeneutic monism is merely a reiteration of "Spinoza's doctrine about studying Scripture without prejudice."

16. Here the principle of "sola scriptura" means nearly the opposite of what it ordinarily does: namely, that everything necessary to know is plain. Spinoza believes this as well, as we will see; but for him the "necessary" comprehends only a small fraction of Scripture.

17. Reedy, "Socinians," p. 298. Grondin, however, pushes back universal hermeneutics to much earlier, to Augustine (*Einführung,* pp. 42–52).

18. See Locke, *Essay Concerning Human Understanding,* 4. 2. 1–2. Reventlow summarizes the other respects in which Toland borrows from Locke in *Authority of the Bible,* p. 295. Yet it cannot be said that Toland's tract is a reply to Locke's *Reasonableness of Christianity,* published a year earlier. It seems that Toland had written his piece a year earlier still and that Locke in fact saw it in manuscript. See Biddle, "Locke's Critique," and Jacob, *Newtonians,* p. 214.

19. Collins makes this equation clear when he writes, "To understand such a book [as Scripture] literally, and not make use of common sense whereby to adjust the several popular expressions wherewith it abounds to the maxims of reason and philosophy would be unreasonable in itself" (*Essay Concerning Propositions,* p. 19).

20. Jacob notes this deviation from Newton in "John Toland," p. 321.

21. Compare Culler: "To assimilate or interpret something is to bring it within the modes of order which culture makes available, and this is usually done by talking about it in a mode of discourse which a culture takes as natural. . . . 'Naturalization' emphasizes the fact that the strange or deviant is brought within a discursive order and thus made to seem natural" (*Structuralist Poetics,* p. 137).

22. In a tract that Toland may have read, Boyle makes this explicit: "Reason operates according to certain notions or ideas and certain axioms and propositions, by which, as by prototypes or models and rules and measures, it conceives things and makes estimates and judgements of them. And indeed, when we say that such a thing is 'consonant' to reason . . . we usually mean that it is either immediately or mediately deducible from, or at least consistent with . . . one or other of those standard notions or rules" ("Discourse of Things above Reason," in *Selected Philosophical Papers,* p. 220).

23. William James explains why accepting a text as true necessarily involves accommodation: "A new opinion counts as 'true' just in proportion as it gratifies the individual's desire to assimilate the novel in his experience to his beliefs in stock. . . . It makes itself true, gets itself classed as true, by the way it works, grafting itself upon the ancient body of truth. . . . The reason why we call things true is the reason why they *are* true, for 'to be true' *means* only to perform this marriage-function" ("What Pragmatism Means," pp. 135–36).

24. See Toland's first letter to Serena where (as he says in the preface) he shows "the successive growth and increase of prejudices through every step of our lives, and prov[es] that all the men in the world are joined in the same conspiracy to deprave the reason of every individual person" (*Letters to Serena,* p. xi).

25. Toland's contemporaries made this charge. See Willis: "Now I have as

little prejudice against clear ideas as I have against the infallible judge; but I am afraid that in many cases these are as hard to be found as the other" (*Reflections*, p. 13).

26. Boyle, "Discourse," p. 216, emphasis added.

27. See Gawlick's comment: "In *Christianity Not Mysterious* Toland presupposed the truth of the Christian revelation instead of questioning it or even denying it" (cited by Reventlow, *Authority of the Bible*, p. 295).

28. Toland himself raises doubts about the canon when he produces a long list of apocrypha formerly taken as authentic in "A Catalogue of Books Mentioned by the Fathers," in *Collection*, 1:360–403.

29. Of course, Toland was not alone in his suspicion of the "word" as a guide to faith. Tindal repeats again and again that "the letter killeth" and cites Athanasius, St. Cyril, St. Gregory, St. Jerome, and Gregory of Nyssa against the authority of the literal (*Christianity as Old as Creation*, p. 207). Toland is less aware than Tindal of how close he is to the allegorizing Fathers.

30. Korshin traces the Restoration reaction against interpretive excess in *Typologies in England*, pp. 39–74.

31. Johnson, "*Rasselas*," p. 623.

32. In *Spinoza's Critique of Religion*, p. 174, Strauss sides with Spinoza in arguing thus: "If the true meaning of a passage in Scripture can be brought out only by the interpretation of the passage with a view to the truth of the matter spoken of in the passage, then that objective truth must have been established beyond doubt." I would argue that, even if it is not an established fact, one must accept the truth of the passage as one must accept a regulative principle upon which the possibility of understanding depends.

33. For a modern elaboration of this thesis, see Hirsch, "Stylistics and Synonymity."

34. Compare Gadamer's conclusion: "Not only does the reader assume an immanent unity of meaning, but his understanding is likewise guided by the constant transcendent expectations of meaning that proceed from the relation to the truth of what is being said" (*Truth and Method*, p. 294). Gadamer is not replying to Spinoza here; but from the notes, one sees that Strauss's commentary on the *Tractatus* is in the back of his mind.

35. Frei, *Eclipse of Biblical Narrative*, p. 85. Frei is writing about Collins here, but the same observation can be made with respect to Toland, who was in some respects Collins's mentor.

36. Compare Davidson: "If we cannot find a way to interpret the utterances and other behaviour of a creature as revealing a set of beliefs largely consistent and true by our own standards, we have no reason to count that creature as rational, as having beliefs, or as saying anything" ("Radical Interpretation," p. 137).

37. It follows that what is concealed must be humanly concealed, and thus Toland enjoins the reader of his *Pantheisticon* not to "make the wicked

or the ignorant nor any except the brethren alone . . . partake of esoterics. . . . The pantheists shall not be more open till they are at full liberty to think as they please and speak as they think" (p. 108).

38. Toland asserts that we are "absolutely ignorant" of the "real essence" of everything (84). He does not seem to notice that his doctrine that the unknowable is nothing to us would, if pressed to its conclusion, therefore render meaningless the notion of real essence. Stillingfleet notices it, however: "I do not wonder that the gentlemen of this new way of reasoning have almost discarded substance out of the reasonable part of the world" (*Discourse in Vindication of the Doctrine of the Trinity* (1697), cited in Carabelli, *Tolandiana,* p. 27).

39. Compare Peirce: "Over against any [particular] cognition, there is an unknown but knowable reality; but over against all possible cognition, there is only the self-contradictory. In short, *cognizability* and *being* are not merely metaphysically the same, but are synonymous terms" (*Essential Writings,* pp. 82–83).

Chapter 3. Bolingbroke on History

1. In masterly fashion Skinner has explained how historians in the tradition of Namier have "failed to take seriously the possibility that there might be anything to be said about the content of [Bolingbroke's] ideas" ("Principles and Practice of Opposition").

2. For general biographical background, see Sichel, *Bolingbroke and His Times,* esp. vol. 2, chap. 2; and, more reliable, Dickinson, *Bolingbroke,* esp. chap. 9. On Bolingbroke's Deism, see Merrill, *Statesman to Philosopher.* On Bolingbroke's partisanship, see Mansfield, *Statesmanship and Party Government.* On Bolingbroke in the tradition of Whig historiography, see Butterfield, *Englishman and History;* Skinner, "Principles and Practice of Opposition"; and Kramnick, "Augustan Politics."

3. Compared to Bolingbroke, Hume was undoubtedly the superior historian, but, as Mossner writes, "he nowhere once and for all sets down together all his attitudes judiciously systematized" ("Apology for David Hume," p. 660).

4. Parenthetical references to *Letters on the Study and Use of History* refer to vol. 1 of *Works.* References to other items in the collected works are identified by volume number.

5. See Nadel, "Bolingbroke's Letters on History." Meinecke considers these the best of the *Letters* (*Historism,* p. 94).

6. The quoted phrase is from Nadel's excellent survey, "Philosophy of History," p. 293. Kramnick traces Bolingbroke's interest in French historiography to the Abbé Joseph Alary (*Bolingbroke and His Circle,* p. 16). Additional information on the intellectual background of the letters is to be found in Kramnick's fine introduction to *Lord Bolingbroke.* See also Barrell, *Bolingbroke and France,* esp. pp. 52–60.

7. Kramnick (ed.), *Lord Bolingbroke,* p. xv. The case of Bolingbroke is evidence for Shapiro's claim, though she is concerned primarily with the earlier period, that "it will be necessary to modify the traditional view that the humanities and the natural sciences belonged to different, and perhaps mutually exclusive, traditions. . . . Even if the notion of two conflicting traditions or cultures is to be maintained, history as a discipline belonged fully to neither" (*Probability and Certainty,* p. 160).

8. For the impact of the battle of the ancients and the moderns on English historiography, see Levine, *Humanism and History,* esp. chaps. 6 and 7, and, more recently, *Battle of the Books,* esp. chap. 9.

9. Stephen, *English Thought,* 2:143.

10. D. G. James, *Life of Reason,* p. 204.

11. Kramnick (ed.), *Lord Bolingbroke,* p. xxvii.

12. Ibid., p. li.

13. Various dates have been suggested for the decline of exemplary history. Shapiro suggests 1650 (*Probability and Certainty,* p. 160). For the place of example in Renaissance rhetoric, see inter alia Wallace, "'Examples are Best Precepts'"; Kahn, "Humanism and Resistance to Theory"; and Hampton, *Writing from History.*

14. Kant, *Critique of Pure Reason,* p. 177.

15. Hegel, *Philosophy of History,* p. 6.

16. Ranke, *Theory and Practice of History,* esp. part 2.

17. On philosophic history among the *philosophes,* see Becker, *Heavenly City,* chap. 3.

18. On the other hand, in comparing examples to images, Bolingbroke suggests that history is static, like a tableau.

19. Fielding, *Tom Jones,* p. 7.

20. On the function of example in ethical philosophy, see O'Neill, "Power of Example."

21. See Freedberg, *Power of Images,* and Griffin, *Pornography and Silence.*

22. I have compared Johnson's *Rambler* 4 with Bolingbroke's *Letters* in "Fiction and Force of Example."

23. Hume, *Essays,* p. 566.

24. Kramnick makes this charge in *Lord Bolingbroke,* p. xix; see also Douglas, *English Scholars,* p. 277. On a more sympathetic reading, in addressing history to actively engaged statesmen, Bolingbroke anticipates Nietzsche's suggestion that only those can understand the past who are building the future. See Nietzsche, *Use and Abuse of History,* p. 41.

25. Locke, *Conduct of Understanding,* pp. 64–65.

26. Womersley touches on this distinction, only to collapse it, in "Lord Bolingbroke," (p. 226).

27. Varey emphasizes the rhetorical side of Bolingbroke in *Henry St. John,* esp. chap. 2.

28. Lennox, *Female Quixote,* pp. 376–77. On the possibility that Samuel Johnson wrote the passages cited, see ibid., pp. 414–15.

29. For a contrasting view, see Momigliano: "The whole modern method of historical research is founded upon the distinction between original and derivative authorities" ("Ancient History," p. 2).

30. As I noted in the Introduction, decoding as a mode of interpretation had come under ridicule by reason of its connection with political conspiracy theories on the one hand and Cabbalism and other forms of religious mysticism on the other. For an example of Bolingbroke's satire of the first, see no. 319 in *Contributions to the Craftsman*, pp. 138–40; and for an example of the second, *Works*, 3:241–42.

31. See Akstens, "Pope and Bolingbroke on 'Examples'"; Hammond, *Pope and Bolingbroke;* and Erskine-Hill, *Social Milieu.*

32. The analogue of imitation in the sphere of rhetoric is metaphor—which, Bolingbroke claims, by "transferring ideas from one subject to another, makes that become graceful and reasonable, and thereby useful when the application is judicious, which would be monstrous and absurd, and thereby hurtful without it" (3:128). Bolingbroke suggests further that the association of ideas that Locke described is held together by metaphorical links—that is to say, metaphor is not a special or peculiar act of mind.

33. Dryden, *Essays*, 1:240.

34. Ibid., 1:241.

35. Braudy notes that Bolingbroke conceives of history as having a literary structure (*Narrative Form*, p. 27).

36. Contrast Gibbon: "I should shrink with terror from the modern history of English, where every character is a problem and every reader a friend or an enemy, where a writer is supposed to hoist a flag of party, and is devoted to damnation by the adverse faction" (*Autobiography*, p. 140).

37. Pocock, *Ancient Constitution*, p. 246. For a similar sentiment, see Croce, *History*, p. 31.

38. Temple, *Works*, 3:69.

39. On Bodin, see Kelley, "Development and Context of Bodin's Method."

Chapter 4. Hume on Others

1. In parenthetical citations, the titles of Hume's works are abbreviated as follows: T = *Treatise of Human Nature*; ECHU = *Enquiry Concerning the Human Understanding*; ECPM = *Enquiry Concerning the Principles of Morals; Essays = Essays: Moral, Political, and Literary.*

2. See Hume's anonymous *Letter from a Gentleman*, pp. 19–21: "As to the scepticism with which the author is charged, . . . all he means by these scruples is to abate the pride of *mere human reasoners*. . . . In reality, whence come all the various tribes of heretics, the *Arians, Socinians,* and *Deists,* but from too great a confidence in mere human reason, which they regard as the *standard* of everything."

3. "When I read a volume, I enter into the mind and intention of the

author; I become him, in a manner. . . . But so near an approach we never surely can make to the Deity. . . . And this volume of nature contains a great and inexplicable riddle, more than any intelligible discourse or reasoning" (Hume, *Dialogues Concerning Natural Religion,* p. 26).

4. Noxon, *Hume's Philosophical Development,* p. 191.

5. Hume, *Four Dissertations,* p. 80.

6. See Butler, "T and Sympathy."

7. Bernstein, *Praxis and Action,* p. 233. Once we recall that Husserl claims Hume as a founder of phenomenology, that Peirce claims him for pragmatism, and Bentham for utilitarianism, it should perhaps be admitted that such claims don't have much cash value.

8. That Hume views custom, not reason, as the basis of cognitive life does not alter this fact, insofar as what he means by custom is not tradition (collective, communal cognition), but rather habit, the automatization of private experience.

9. Hume, *Abstract,* p. 25.

10. Contrast Shaftesbury: "All things in this world are united. For as the branch is united with the tree, so is the tree as immediately with the earth, air, and water which feed it. . . . Thus too in the system of the bigger world. See there the mutual dependency of things!" (*Characteristics,* pp. 64–65).

11. Stewart, *Moral and Political Philosophy,* pp. 123–24.

12. Norton, *David Hume;* Livingston, *Hume's Philosophy.* These are perhaps the two best recent books on Hume.

13. Farr describes this model, contrasting it with Hume's, in his groundbreaking article, "Hume, Hermeneutics, and History." See also his "Humean Explanations."

14. Shaftesbury, *Characteristics,* pp. 78–81.

15. "The problem of the origin of society," Cumming concludes, "is a pseudo-problem for Hume" (*Human Nature and History,* 2:163).

16. Christensen, *Practicing Enlightenment,* p. 21.

17. See Livingston, *Hume's Philosophy,* pp. 200–09, for a full discussion of this maxim.

18. Compare Hegel: "Das Selbstbewußtsein ist an und für sich, indem, und dadurch, daß es für ein Anderes an und für sich ist; d.h. es ist nur als ein Anerkanntes" ("Self-consciousness is in and for itself in that it is for another in and for itself; that is, it is only as something recognized") (*Phänomenologie des Geistes,* p. 148). Willey (*Eighteenth Century Background,* p. 123) and others have so overemphasized the tendency of Humean "reflection" toward an ethics of respectability that they have overlooked the way in which mutual recognition leads to a Hegelian dialectic of self and other. See my article "'Give Me Something to Desire'."

19. Farr and Livingston (cited in n. 13 and 12, respectively) ally Hume's

moral science with *verstehen:* Farr with the accounts of Dilthey and Gadamer, Livingston with that of Collingwood.

20. Hutcheson, *Enquiry into the Original,* pp. 166–67. On Hume and Hutcheson, see Kivy, *Seventh Sense,* pp. 139–53, and Blakestone, *Francis Hutcheson.*

21. Shaftesbury, *Characteristics,* p. 310. See also ibid., p. 299: "Were pleasure to be computed in the same way other things commonly are, it might properly be said that out of these two branches (viz. community or participation in the pleasure of others and belief in meriting well from others) would arise more than nine-tenths of whatever is enjoyed in life."

22. In *Sympathy and Ethics,* Mercer asserts, "It would sound odd to say that one sympathized with a person who was enjoying himself and having a good time" (p. 5). But, however odd this sounds to Mercer, it conforms to Hume's usage.

23. Farr, "Hume, Hermeneutics, and History," p. 291.

24. Mercer overlooks the role that Hume assigns to our common human nature when he asserts: "It is clear that on Hume's account we can only sympathize with feelings which we ourselves have already experienced" (*Sympathy and Ethics,* p. 34).

25. Farr, "Hume, Hermeneutics, and History," p. 292.

26. See Mullan, "Sympathy and Production of Society."

27. Wright pays special attention to Hume's mechanical explanations in *Sceptical Realism.*

28. Hume mentions that contiguity also reinforces sympathy (*T* 2:112), though he returns most often to resemblance.

29. Black comes to this conclusion in *Art of History,* p. 100. For an opposing view, see Livingston, *Hume's Philosophy,* pp. 214ff. Most of Hume's comments on the theory of history and historiography are conveniently collected in *David Hume.*

30. Cited in Mossner, *Life of David Hume,* p. 293.

31. Smith, *Theory of Moral Sentiments,* p. 9.

32. See Scheler's phenomenological conclusions on this issue in "The Perception of Other Minds," in *Nature of Sympathy,* pp. 238–59. For an extended meditation on skepticism regarding other minds, see Cavell, *Claim of Reason,* part 4.

33. I concur with Noxon that Hume's "succinct reason for extending the experimental method of natural philosophy to moral subjects is that the essence of mind is as unknowable as the essence of matter, and therefore the *a priori* deductive method must be superseded in the human sciences as it had been over a century before in the physical sciences" (*Hume's Philosophical Development,* p. 7).

34. That Hume should have taken the original audience as the standard for correct understanding (or that he should have taken an orator as representative of literary art) is indicative of his own practice. As Richetti

argues, Hume's "thought is deeply embedded from its beginnings in persuasiveness. . . . Hume always conceived of his philosophy in literary terms and saw his problems as essentially rhetorical" (*Philosophical Writing*, p. 184).

35. It should be admitted, however, that on the last page of *Principles of Morals* Hume reverts to the dichotomy of reason and taste.

36. Hume, *Letters*, 1:34. Citing this passage, Siebert concludes (mistakenly, I think) that Hume did not in fact prefer Cicero, either because Hume was playing "a game in relativistic ethics" or because the *Offices* and *Whole Duty* are so similar as to leave little to choose between them (*Moral Animus*, p. 22).

37. For much useful bibliography on the issues surrounding prudence in the mid-eighteenth century, see Haakonssen's notes to Reid's *Practical Ethics*, pp. 311–13; see also Battestin's excellent survey of eighteenth-century references to prudence in "Fielding's Definition of Wisdom."

Chapter 5. Reid on Common Sense

1. Gadamer, *Truth and Method*, p. 24.
2. Ibid., p. 23.
3. Parenthetical citations refer to Reid's *Philosophical Works*.
4. Peirce, who called himself a "commonsensist" out of respect for his Scots predecessor, shows why the "acritically indubitable is invariably vague" (*Collected Papers*, 5.446, 6.495, and 8.208).
5. No satisfactory history of the phrase or concept is, to my knowledge, available. But see Appendix A in Hamilton's edition of Reid's *Philosophical Works*; Foxe, *Common Sense*; and esp. van Holtoon and Olson, eds., *Common Sense*, part 2.
6. This is the title of Bracken's introduction to the Olm reprint of Reid's *Philosophical Works*.
7. Shaftesbury, *Sensus Communis*, in *Characteristics*, 1:55–56.
8. Reprinted in Marcil-Lacoste, *Claude Buffier and Thomas Reid*, p. 189.
9. Shaftesbury, *Sensus Communis*, 1:70.
10. Cited in Butger, "Sensus Communis," p. 90.
11. Kant, *Critique of Judgment*, p. 160.
12. Shaftesbury, *Sensus Communis*, 1:94.
13. Kant, *Critique of Judgment*, p. 162. On the hermeneutic significance of Kant on common sense, see Makkreel, *Imagination and Interpretation*, chap. 8.
14. Interestingly, it has recently been argued in detail that Reid himself developed a non-Euclidean geometry. See Daniels, *Thomas Reid's "Inquiry."*
15. Beattie, *Essay*, p. 84.
16. Ibid., p. 31.

17. Grave speaks of the "unanswerable finality" that attends the pronouncements of common sense (*Scottish Philosophy of Common Sense*, p. 124).

18. To this assertion Priestley responded, "There is this difference between the ancient and these modern skeptics, that the ancients professed neither to *understand* nor *believe* anything, whereas these moderns believe everything, though they profess to understand nothing" (cited in Jones, *Empiricism and Intuitionism*, p. 74).

19. On Reid and the experimental method, see Marcil-Lacoste, *Claude Buffier and Thomas Reid*, esp. p. 120.

20. Toland had similarly identified reason and common sense (*Christianity Not Mysterious*, p. 9).

21. See Grave, *Scottish Philosophy of Common Sense*, p. 124; Seth, *Scottish Philosophy*, p. 111; Norton, "Hume and His Scottish Critics," p. 318.

22. For the notion that sense includes judgment and is in that respect interpretive, Reid is borrowing heavily from his predecessors. In his *New Theory of Vision*, Berkeley, e.g., mentions as a matter "agreed by all" that "distance of itself, and immediately, cannot be seen" and that "the estimate we make of the distance of objects considerably remote is rather an act of judgment grounded on experience than of sense" (*Works*, 1:35).

23. In his life of Reid prefacing the *Philosophical Works*, Dugald Stewart notes that commonsense principles "have been called by a very ingenious foreigner, (M. Trembley of Geneva,) but certainly with a singular infelicity of language, *Préjugés Légitimes*" (27).

24. Ferguson points out the similarities between Reid's commonsensism and Davidson's theory of interpretation in *Common Sense*, pp. 167–69.

25. Yet Reid counts the adequacy of reflection among the maxims of common sense. "It is not impossible that what is only a vulgar prejudice may be mistaken for a first principle," he admits (231).

26. I am not concerned with the adequacy of Reid's interpretations of his predecessors. But it should not go unmentioned that there is a long tradition of Reid scholarship (indeed, Hume was perhaps first in the line) which holds that Reid pretty thoroughly misunderstood post-Cartesian philosophy. Yolton, notably, speaks of "Reid's seminal misinterpretations of the way of ideas" and conceives his own book as correcting this "long misunderstanding" (*Perceptual Acquaintance*, pp. 15 and 222).

27. For a survey of seventeenth- and eighteenth-century semiotics, see Patey, *Probability and Literary Form*, esp. pp. 35–133.

28. Foucault, *Order of Things*, p. 29.

29. Reid, "Abstract of the *Inquiry*," p. 129.

30. Yolton finds this definition of the sign as early as Descartes (*Perceptual Acquaintance*, p. 24).

31. On the inadequacies of the term "suggestion," see Winch, "Notion of 'Suggestion'."

32. So Dugald Stewart seems to understand the matter. See his *Elements,* p. 92.

33. Compare Peirce's definition: "A *symbol* is a sign which would lose the character which renders it a sign if there were no interpretant. Such is any utterance of speech which signifies what it does only by virtue of its being understood to have that signification" (*Collected Papers,* 2:304).

34. Hamlyn seems not to recognize the distinction between logical inference and interpretation when he accuses Reid of incoherence on this point (*Sensation and Perception,* p. 129.

35. Interestingly, when Reid treats of prudence as an ethical matter, it becomes, as Haakonssen remarks, a "principle of cool, rational self-interest" (in Reid, *Practical Ethics,* p. 48).

36. Quoted by Marcil-Lacoste, *Claude Buffier and Thomas Reid,* p. 188.

37. Compare Vico: "Common sense arises from perceptions based on ver-isimilitude." This he allies with the "capacity to perceive the analogies existing between matters lying far apart and, apparently, most dissim-ilar" (*Study Methods,* pp. 13 and 24). On Vico and common sense, see Krois, "Vico's and Peirce's 'Sensus Communis'"; Grassi, "Priority of Common Sense"; and esp. Schaeffer, *Sensus Communis.* Schaeffer ac-tually (mis)translates Vico's *verisimile* as "similitude" (ibid., p. 69).

38. In "Reid and Wittgenstein," Jensen compares the two philosophers. Lehrer believes that Reid actually influenced Wittgenstein, at least through G. E. Moore (*Thomas Reid,* p. 6).

39. Ferreira, *Scepticism and Reasonable Doubt,* p. 122.

40. On the implicit commonsense thesis that philosophy must abide by the structures of common language, see Madden, "Metaphilosophy of Commonsense." Bracken compared Reid's thought on language to Chomsky's "Cartesian linguistics" in "Innate Ideas." For an argument that Reid explains language "in terms of its use rather than in terms of the mental substratum," see Land, *Philosophy of Language,* p. 231.

41. For more on Wilkins, see Knowlson, *Universal Language Schemes,* chap. 3.

Chapter 6. Blackstone on Equity

1. Dicey, "Blackstone's *Commentaries,*" p. 657.

2. Ibid., p. 656.

3. Ibid., p. 661.

4. Ibid.

5. There is, however, plenty of evidence that this expectation is changing and that the issues of literary and juridical interpretation are now per-ceived to overlap. Among the first to propose reassessment of the centuries-long division of the two was Gadamer, in *Truth and Method.* For a more recent discussion of the issue, see Michaels, "Against For-

malism." *Texas Law Review* 60:3 (1982) includes articles by Ronald Dworkin, "Law as Interpretation"; Stanley Fish, "Working on the Chain Gang: Interpretation in the Law and in Literary Criticism"; Sanford Levinson, "Law as Literature"; James Boyd White, "Law as Language: Reading Law and Reading Literature"; and Michael Hancher, "Dead Letters: Wills and Poems." See also two essays by Abraham: "Statutory Interpretation" and "Three Fallacies." Some of the above are reprinted along with other pertinent essays in Levinson and Mailloux, eds., *Interpreting Law and Literature*.

Not just a commentator on legal matters, Blackstone wrote critical notes on Shakespeare's plays, which appeared in Malone's supplement to Johnson's edition. See Lockmiller, *Sir William Blackstone*, p. 80.

6. William Carey Jones, Preface, to Blackstone, *Commentaries*, 1:ix. All citations from the *Commentaries* are from this edition, which follows the standard page and volume numbering. Since it incorporates all Hammond's notes and adds Carey's own, it amounts to the most recent "variorum" edition of the *Commentaries*. The Jones edition was among the last to be used as a textbook in American (or any other) law schools. As Orth observes, "the Commentator exercised his profoundest influence in the New World" ("Sir William Blackstone," p. 158).

7. Dicey, "Blackstone's *Commentaries*," p. 663.

8. Johnson, "*Rasselas*," p. 528. See Lucas: "Dr. Blackstone's desire that the gentlemen of England should dominate the legal profession was not original. The novelty of his proposal lay in its method: he would have had a university education be a prerequisite for the bar" ("Blackstone and Reform," p. 467). To Lucas's first proposition, Willman replies, "I think I would emphasize rather more strongly than Lucas does that what Blackstone wanted was not simply the preservation of the aristocracy as such, but the preservation of its constitutional function" ("Blackstone and English Law," p. 68).

9. Dicey, "Blackstone's *Commentaries*," p. 663.

10. Concerning Blackstone's own experience in the courts, Lockmiller writes that "most of his courtroom activities had to do with appellate practice as distinguished from trial practice, and as a member of the common law bar he specialized in actions at law rather than in equity proceedings" (*Sir William Blackstone*, p. 66).

11. Wende emphasizes this complementarity in "Vernuft und Tradition."

12. Bentham, "*Comment on the Commentaries*," p. 13.

13. This premise underlies the "legal positivism" of H. L. A. Hart, which Dworkin summarizes in three propositions: "The law of a community is a set of special rules"; "the set of these valid legal rules is exhaustive of the 'law'"; "to say that someone has a 'legal obligation' is to say that his case falls under a valid legal rule" (*Taking Rights Seriously*, p. 17).

14. As the sole exception of which I am aware, Dworkin (see previous note) argues against Hart that laws cannot be understood as rules. My

argument will be that Blackstone anticipates and offers explicit evidence for this thesis.

15. Johnson, "*Rasselas*," pp. 239–40.

16. For the enormous significance of this notion in the history of British historiography, see Pocock, *Ancient Constitution*.

17. "Few decisions were embodied in authoritative texts or records," Baker writes, "and so the means by which the common law of England was brought into being are largely lost to historians" (*Introduction*, p. 13).

18. Boorstin's otherwise excellent *Mysterious Science of Law* is flawed in its insistence on reading Blackstone's nondifferentiations (e.g., of history and reason) as unconscious duplicity.

19. On Blackstone's combining a study of law in the abstract with an examination of how laws actually "operated in society," see Richard Posner, "Blackstone and Bentham," *Journal of Law and Economics* 19 (1976):572; cited by Willman, "Blackstone and English Law," p. 44n.

20. Sterne, *Tristram Shandy*, p. 329.

21. "There is no foundation in nature or in natural law why a set of words upon parchment should convey the dominion of land, why the son should have a right to exclude his fellow-creatures from a determinate spot of ground because his father had done so before him" (2:2).

22. Pound, *Spirit of Common Law*, pp. 60–61.

23. Sterne, *Tristram Shandy*, p. 331.

24. To my knowledge, the most thorough and thoughtful exposition of the relation of law and equity in theory and fact is that of Newman, *Equity and Law*.

25. West, *Second Part of Symboleography*, p. 176.

26. Sterne, *Tristram Shandy*, p. 140.

27. "It is the height of irony that the court which originated to provide an escape from the defects of common law procedure should in its later history have developed procedural defects worse by far than those of the law. For two centuries before Dickens wrote *Bleak House*, the word 'Chancery' had been synonymous with expense, delay and despair" (Baker, *Introduction*, p. 95).

28. Holdsworth concedes (what is most relevant here) that Blackstone and Mansfield, whose views he shared, anticipated the Judicature Acts (1873), which fused equity and law in matters of jurisdiction, procedure, and pleading. Yet Holdsworth argues that Blackstone was mistaken in believing that any substantive fusion of the rules of law and equity had already been completed or even begun ("Blackstone's Treatment of Equity").

29. Absence of legislative intention about a particular case is one factor that can make it a "hard case." See Pound's statement that "interpretation is difficult, when it is difficult, just because the legislature had no actual intent to ascertain" (*Introduction to Philosophy of Law*, p. 52). This implies

that, insofar as interpretation means determining intention, in hard cases interpretation is not difficult but impossible.

30. Although Blackstone cites Grotius, *De Jure Belli ac Pacis,* it should be emphasized that Grotius draws his theory of equity in large part from a classical source, Aristotle's *Nichomachean Ethics,* book 5. The main Renaissance treatises on this subject are St. German, *Doctor and Student,* and Hake, *Epieikeia.*

31. By contrast, compare what Cross calls Bentham's "naive belief . . . that it is possible for the laws of a sophisticated society to be formulated in terms of indisputable comprehensibility" ("Blackstone vs. Bentham," p. 520).

32. Johnson, *Rambler* 148, in "*Rasselas,*" pp. 116–17.

33. Maitland, *Equity,* pp. 1 and 13.

34. On this reconciliation, see Lieberman's important discussion in *Province,* p. 85.

35. Specifically, Blackstone's target is *Principles of Equity,* by Henry Home, Lord Kames.

Chapter 7. Burke on Taste

1. It must be admitted, as O'Gorman notes, that in some respects Burke's "thinking was just as abstract and as speculative as that of the writers whom he attacked" (*Edmund Burke,* p. 107). Perhaps Burke's own abstractness offers some excuse for the fact that in O'Gorman's, my own, and many other expositions of his thought, Burke is typically made much more of a political philosopher than a politician.

2. I have employed the following abbreviations in parenthetical references: *A = Appeal from the New to the Old Whigs; C = Speech on the Reform of Representation in the Commons; D = Hints for an Essay on the Drama; E = A Philosophical Enquiry into the Origin of Our Ideas of the Sublime and Beautiful; L = Letters on a Regicide Peace; M = Speech Relative to the Middlesex Election; N = Letter to a Noble Lord; R = Reflections on the Revolution in France; S = Letter to the Sheriffs of Bristol; T = Thoughts on the Present Discontents; U = Speech on the Petition of the Unitarians; V = A Vindication of Natural Society.*

   E is cited from the edition of J. T. Boulton; *R* and *T* from *Writings and Speeches,* vols. 2 and 8; and all the others from *Works.*

3. I concur with Strauss that "Burke's remarks on the problem of theory and practice are the most important of his work" (*Natural Right,* p. 303).

4. Chapman, *Edmund Burke,* p. 2. Chapman leaves the aesthetic side of political "imagination" undeveloped.

5. Although he does not mention the role of judgment in Burke's politics, Beiner offers a very stimulating discussion of Aristotle and Kant in *Political Judgment.*

6. Pocock, *Virtue*, p. 196. Pocock also rightly ascribes Burke's emphasis on taste to his belonging to the common law tradition in "Burke and the Ancient Constitution." For the relation of taste to the clothing imagery of the *Reflections*, discussed below, see Fussell's masterly treatment in *Rhetorical World*, chap. 9.

7. Stephen (*History of English Thought*, 2:207) sees Burke's denunciation of the monstrous only as "foaming at the mouth"—rhetoric gone mad. The Horatian background, I hope, will somewhat allay that impression.

8. All citations from Horace refer to *Art of Poetry*, translated by Burton Raffel with a literal version by James Hynd. Hynd translates the opening as follows: "Suppose: a painter starts from a human head, he joins it to a horse's neck, he inserts a variety of feathers on limbs assembled from any and everywhere."

9. An unsympathetic listener might wonder how Athenian spectators reacted to Euripides' *Bacchae*, which appears to combine the demonic and carnivalesque in a manner similar to the "triumph" in Paris.

10. See Benjamin: "The logical result of fascism is the introduction of aesthetics into politics. . . . All efforts to render politics aesthetic culminate in one thing: war" (*Illuminations*, p. 241); and Lyotard: "It is not true that one can do an aesthetic politics. It is not true that the search for intensities or things of that type can ground politics, because there is the problem of injustice" (in Lyotard and Thébaud, *Just Gaming*, p. 90).

11. In "Edmund Burke," MacPherson charges that Burke's notion of natural law is "emptied of specific moral content" (p. 236). Cobban says similarly that it is "only with very considerable qualifications" that Burke "can be said to belong to the natural rights school of thought" because, however he professed his veneration for natural rights, Burke "puts little value on attempts to codify them" (*Edmund Burke*, p. 45). This is quite true; yet it may be that at least the Aristotelian wing of the natural right school, where Strauss situates Burke (*Natural Right*, p. 303), saw natural law as precisely that which resists codification.

12. Mansfield, *Statesmanship and Party Government*, p. 243.

13. Sterne, *Tristram Shandy*, p. 26.

14. Warton, *History of English Poetry*, 2:462–63.

15. When Pocock observes that Burke's account of political society is "in a fairly obvious sense anti-rationalist" ("Burke and the Ancient Constitution," p. 203), he is talking about Burke's opposition to rationalism, not reason. The fact that Burke is contesting a narrow notion of reason, not advocating the rejection of reason per se, seems to go unnoticed by Kramnick when he speaks of Burke as expressing "the eternal longing of the conservative for the elimination of rational thought from politics" (*Rage of Edmund Burke*, p. 23).

16. Reynolds, *Discourses*, p. 44.

17. Ibid., p. 122.

18. Ibid.
19. Ibid.
20. Ibid., p. 140.
21. Hume, *Essays,* p. 32. See also Ernst Vollrath, "'That All Governments Rest on Opinion,'" *Social Research* 43 (1976): 46–61. "It is futile to seek in Hume a developed theory about the connection between taste and action, mediated by opinion," writes Vollrath (ibid., p. 57). "It is equally futile to seek such a connection in Edmund Burke. . . . The political implications of a doctrine of taste have been lost in the eighteenth century." Clearly, I consider this view mistaken.
22. This, in my view, is what distinguishes Burke from the skeptical tradition. See Kramnick, "Skepticism." Burke belonged to the ranks not only of political thinkers but of politicians, and the latter cannot afford the luxury of skepticism but must act. As Hume says, "The great subverter of pyrrhonism or the excessive principles of scepticism is action" (*ECHU* 158–59).
23. See Stanlis, *Edmund Burke,* pp. 125–27.
24. See Kramnick, *Rage of Edmund Burke,* chap. 1.
25. Contrast Price: "Obedience, therefore, to the laws and to magistrates are necessary expressions of our regard to the community" ("Discourse," p. 27). Price and Burke agree that obedience must be founded on "regard" for country or community; the question is whether these can be embodied in its rulers.

Epilogue

1. Reynolds, *Discourses,* p. 44.
2. Ibid., pp. 230–31.
3. Shaftesbury, *Characteristics,* p. 94.

Works Cited

Aarsleff, Hans. *From Locke to Saussure: Essays on the Study of Language and Intellectual History.* Minneapolis: Univ. of Minnesota Press, 1982.
———. *The Study of Language in England, 1780–1860.* 2d ed. Minneapolis: Univ. of Minnesota Press, 1983.
Abraham, Kenneth S. "Statutory Interpretation and Literary Theory: Some Common Concerns of an Unlikely Pair." *Rutgers Law Review* 32 (1979):676–94.
———. "Three Fallacies of Interpretation: A Comment on Precedent and Judicial Decision." *Arizona Law Review* 23 (1981):771–83.
Akstens, Thomas. "Pope and Bolingbroke on 'Examples': An Echo of the *Letters on History* in Pope's Correspondence." *Philological Quarterly* 52 (1973):232–38.
Andreasen, N. J. C. "Swift's Satire on the Occult in *A Tale of a Tub.*" *Texas Studies in Literature and Language* 5 (1963):410–21.
Baker, J. H. *An Introduction to English Legal History.* 2d ed. London: Butterworths, 1979.
Barrell, Rex A. *Bolingbroke and France.* Lanham, Md.: Univ. Press of America, 1988.
Battestin, Martin C. "Fielding's Definition of Wisdom: Some Functions of Ambiguity and Emblem in *Tom Jones.*" *ELH* 35 (1968):188–217.
Beattie, James. *An Essay on the Nature and Immutability of Truth in Opposition to Scepticism.* 1776. Reprint. New York: Garland, 1971.
Becker, Carl. *The Heavenly City of Eighteenth-Century Philosophers.* New Haven: Yale Univ. Press, 1932.
Beiner, Ronald. *Political Judgment.* Chicago: Univ. of Chicago Press, 1983.

Benjamin, Walter. *Illuminations.* Edited by Hannah Arendt. Translated by Harry Zohn. New York: Schocken Books, 1969.

Bentham, Jeremy. *"A Comment on the Commentaries" and "A Fragment of Government",* Edited by J. H. Burns and H. L. A. Hart. In *The Collected Works of Jeremy Bentham,* vol. 1, Edited by J. H. Burns. London: Athlone Press, 1977.

Berkeley, George. *The Works,* 4 vols. Edited by A. C. Fraser. Oxford: Clarendon Press, 1871.

Bernstein, Richard. *Praxis and Action.* Philadelphia: Univ. of Pennsylvania Press, 1971.

Biddle, John. "John Locke's Essay on Infallibility: Introduction, Text, and Translation." *Journal of Church and State* 19 (1977):301–27.

———. "Locke's Critique of Innate Principles and Toland's Deism." *Journal of the History of Ideas* 37 (1976):411–22.

Black, J. B. *The Art of History.* New York: Crofts, 1926.

Blackstone, Sir William. *Commentaries on the Laws of England,* 4 vols. in 2. Edited by William Carey Jones. San Francisco: Bancroft-Whitney Co., 1915.

Blakestone, William T. *Francis Hutcheson and Contemporary Ethical Theory.* Athens: Univ. of Georgia Press, 1965.

Bloom, Harold. *Kabbalah and Criticism.* New York: Seabury Press, 1975.

Bolingbroke. *Lord Bolingbroke: Contributions to the Craftsman.* Edited by Simon Varey. Oxford: Clarendon Press, 1982.

———. *The Works of Lord Bolingbroke,* 4 vols. 1844. Reprint. London: Cass, 1967.

Boorstin, Daniel. *The Mysterious Science of the Law.* Cambridge, Mass.: Harvard Univ. Press, 1941.

Boyle, Robert. *Selected Philosophical Papers of Robert Boyle.* Edited by M. A. Stewart. Manchester: Manchester Univ. Press, 1979.

Bracken, Harry A. "Innate Ideas—Then and Now." *Dialogue: Canadian Philosophical Review* 6 (1967):334–46.

Braudy, Leo. *Narrative Form in History and Fiction.* Princeton: Princeton Univ. Press, 1970.

Burke, Edmund. *A Philosophical Enquiry into the Origin of Our Ideas of the Sublime and Beautiful.* Edited by J. T. Boulton. Notre Dame, Ind.: Univ. of Notre Dame Press, 1968.

———. *The Works of the Right Honorable Edmund Burke,* 8 vols. 7th ed. Boston: Little, Brown, 1881.

———. *The Writings and Speeches of Edmund Burke.* Edited by Paul Langford. Oxford: Clarendon, 1989– .

Burrow, Richard. "Credulity and Curiosity in *A Tale of a Tub.*" *Interpretation: A Journal of Political Philosophy* 15 (1987):309–22.

Butger, S. E. W. "Sensus Communis in the Works of M. Tullius Cicero." In *Common Sense: The Foundations for Social Science,* edited by F. van

Holtoon and D. R. Olson, pp. 83–97. Lanham, Md.: Univ. Press of America, 1987.

Butler, R. J. "T and Sympathy." In *Proceedings of the Aristotelian Society,* pp. 1–20. London: Methuen, 1975.

Butterfield, Herbert. *The Englishman and His History.* Cambridge: Cambridge Univ. Press, 1944.

Carabelli, Giancarlo. *Tolandiana.* Florence: La Nuova Italia, 1975.

Cavell, Stanley. *The Claim of Reason: Wittgenstein, Skepticism, Morality, and Tragedy.* New York: Oxford Univ. Press, 1979.

Chapman, Gerald. *Edmund Burke: The Practical Imagination.* Cambridge, Mass.: Harvard Univ. Press, 1967.

Chiasson, Elias J. "Swift's Clothes Philosophy in the *Tale* and Hooker's Concept of Law." *Studies in Philology* 59 (1962):64–82.

Christensen, Jerome. *Practicing Enlightenment: Hume and the Formation of a Literary Career.* Madison: Univ. of Wisconsin Press, 1987.

Clarke, John. *Form and Frenzy in Swift's Tale of a Tub.* Ithaca: Cornell Univ. Press, 1970.

Cobban, Alfred. *Edmund Burke and the Revolt against the Eighteenth Century.* London: Allen and Unwin, 1929.

Coleridge, S. T. *Biographia Literaria.* Edited by J. Shawcross. London: Oxford Univ. Press, 1907.

Colie, Rosalie. "Spinoza and the Early English Deists." *Journal of the History of Ideas* 20 (1959):23–46.

Collins, Anthony. *An Essay Concerning the Use of Reason in Propositions.* 1707. Reprint. New York: Garland, 1984.

Cope, Kevin. *Criteria of Certainty: Truth and Judgment in the English Enlightenment.* Lexington: Univ. of Kentucky Press, 1990.

Cranston, Maurice. *John Locke: A Biography.* London: Longmans, 1957.

Croce, Benedetto. *History as the Story of Liberty.* Translated by Sylvia Sprigge. London: Allen and Unwin, 1941.

Cross, Rupert. "Blackstone vs. Bentham." *Law Quarterly Review* 92 (1976): 516–27.

Culler, Jonathan. *Structuralist Poetics.* Ithaca: Cornell Univ. Press, 1975.

Cumming, R. D. *Human Nature and History: A Study of the Development of Liberal Political Thought,* 2 vols. Chicago: Univ. of Chicago Press, 1969.

Daniel, Stephen H. *John Toland: His Methods, Manners, and Mind.* Kingston: McGill–Queen's Univ. Press, 1984.

Daniels, Norman. *Thomas Reid's "Inquiry": The Geometry of Visibles and the Case for Realism.* Stanford: Stanford Univ. Press, 1979.

Davidson, Donald. "Radical Interpretation." In *Inquiries into Truth and Interpretation.* Oxford: Clarendon Press, 1984.

Dicey, A. F. "Blackstone's *Commentaries.*" *National Review* 54 (1909):653–75.

Dickinson, H. T. *Bolingbroke*. London: Constable, 1970.

Douglas, David. *English Scholars, 1660–1730*. 2d ed. London: Eyre and Spottiswoode, 1951.

Dryden, John. *Essays of John Dryden,* 2 vols. Edited by W. P. Ker. 1899. Reprint. New York: Russell and Russell, 1961.

———. *The Poems of John Dryden*. Edited by James Kinsley. Oxford: Clarendon Press, 1958.

Dunn, John. *The Political Thought of John Locke: An Historical Account of the Argument of the 'Two Treatises of Government'*. London: Cambridge Univ. Press, 1969.

Dworkin, Ronald. *Taking Rights Seriously*. Cambridge, Mass.: Harvard Univ. Press, 1977.

Edwards, Thomas. *The Canons of Criticism and Glossary, Being a Supplement to Mr. Warburton's Edition of Shakespear*. 6th ed. 1765. Reprint. Plymouth and London: Cass, 1970.

Erskine-Hill, Howard. *The Social Milieu of Alexander Pope: Lives, Examples, and the Poetic Response*. New Haven: Yale Univ. Press, 1975.

Evans, G. R. *The Language and Logic of the Bible: The Road to Reformation*. Cambridge: Cambridge University Press, 1985.

Farr, James. "Hume, Hermeneutics, and History: A 'Sympathetic' Account." *History and Theory* 17 (1978):285–310.

———. "Humean Explanations in the Moral Sciences." *Inquiry* 25 (1982):57–80.

Ferreira, M. Jamie. *Scepticism and Reasonable Doubt: The British Naturalist Tradition in Wilkins, Hume, Reid and Newman*. Oxford: Clarendon Press, 1986.

Fielding, Henry. *Tom Jones*. Edited by Sheridan Baker. New York: Norton, 1973.

Forguson, Lynd. *Common Sense*. London: Routledge, 1989.

Foucault, Michel. *The Order of Things: An Archaeology of the Human Sciences*. New York: Vintage, 1973.

Foxe, Arthur N. *The Common Sense from Heraclitus to Peirce: The Sources, Substance, and Possibilities of the Common Sense*. New York: Tunbridge Press, 1962.

Fraser, A. C. *Locke*. 1890. Reprint. Port Washington: Kennikat, 1970.

Freedberg, David. *The Power of Images*. Chicago: Univ. of Chicago Press, 1989.

Frei, Hans. *The Eclipse of Biblical Narrative: A Study in Eighteenth and Nineteenth Century Hermeneutics*. New Haven: Yale Univ. Press, 1974.

Fussell, Paul. *The Rhetorical World of Augustan Humanism: Ethics and Imagery from Swift to Burke*. Oxford: Clarendon Press, 1965.

Gadamer, Hans-Georg. *Truth and Method*. Revised translation by Joel Weinsheimer and Donald G. Marshall. New York: Crossroad, 1989.

Gibbon, Edward. *Autobiography*. Edited by Dero Saunders. New York: Meridian, 1961.

Gibson, James. *Locke's Theory of Knowledge and Its Historical Relations*. 1917. Reprint. London: Cambridge Univ. Press, 1960.

Grassi, Ernesto. "The Priority of Common Sense and Imagination: Vico's Philosophical Relevance Today." In *Vico and Contemporary Thought*, edited by Giorgio Tagliacozzo, Michael Mooney, and Donald Phillip Verene, pp. 163–85. Atlantic Highlands, N.J.: Humanities Press, 1976.

Grave, S. A. *The Scottish Philosophy of Common Sense*. Oxford: Clarendon Press, 1960.

Griffin, Susan. *Pornography and Silence: Culture's Revenge against Nature*. New York: Harper and Row, 1981.

Grondin, Jean. *Einführung in die philosophische Hermeneutik*. Darmstadt: Wissenschaftliche Buchgesellschaft, 1991.

Hake, Edward. *Epieikeia: A Dialogue on Equity in Three Parts*. Edited by D. E. C. Yale. 1603. Reprint. New Haven: Yale Univ. Press, 1953.

Hamlyn, D. W. *Sensation and Perception: A History of the Philosophy of Perception*. New York: Humanities Press, 1961.

Hammond, Brean. *Pope and Bolingbroke: A Study of Friendship and Influence*. Columbia: Univ. of Missouri Press, 1984.

Hampton, Timothy. *Writing from History: The Rhetoric of Exemplarity in Renaissance Literature*. Ithaca: Cornell Univ. Press, 1990.

Harth, Phillip. *Swift and Anglican Rationalism: The Religious Background of* A Tale of a Tub. Chicago: Univ. of Chicago Press, 1961.

Hegel, G. W. F. *Phänomenologie des Geistes*. Stuttgart-Bad: Frommann Verlag, 1964.

———. *The Philosophy of History*. Translated by J. Sibree. Buffalo: Prometheus Books, 1991.

Hirsch, E. D., Jr. "Stylistics and Synonymity." In *The Aims of Interpretation*, pp. 50–73. Chicago: Univ. of Chicago Press, 1976.

Holdsworth, W. S. "Blackstone's Treatment of Equity." *Harvard Law Review* 43 (1929):1–32.

Horace, *The Art of Poetry*. Translated by Burton Raffel, with a literal version by James Hynd. Albany: State Univ. of New York Press, 1974.

Hume, David. *An Abstract of a Treatise of Human Nature*. Edited by J. M. Keynes and P. Straffa. Cambridge: Cambridge Univ. Press, 1938.

———. *David Hume: Philosophical Historian*. Edited by David Fate Norton and Richard H. Popkin. Indianapolis: Bobbs-Merrill, 1965.

———. *Dialogues Concerning Natural Religion*. Indianapolis: Hackett, 1980.

———. *Enquiry Concerning the Human Understanding* and *Concerning the Principles of Morals*, 2 vols. in 1. Edited by L. A. Selby-Bigge. 2d ed. Oxford: Clarendon Press, 1962.

———. *Essays: Moral, Political, and Literary*. Edited by Eugene F. Miller. Indianapolis: Liberty Press, 1985.

————. *Four Dissertations.* 1757. Reprint. New York: Garland, 1970.

————. *A Letter from a Gentleman to His Friend in Edinburgh.* 1745. Reprint. Edinburgh: Edinburgh Univ. Press, 1967.

————. *The Letters of David Hume,* 2 vols. Edited by J. Y. T. Grieg. Oxford: Clarendon Press, 1932.

————. *Treatise of Human Nature.* Edited by L. A. Selby-Bigge. 2d ed. Oxford: Clarendon Press, 1888.

Hurley, Michael, S.J. "'Scriptura Sola': Wyclif and His Critics." *Traditio* 16 (1960):275–352.

Hutcheson, Francis. *An Enquiry into the Original of Our Ideas of Beauty and Virtue.* 1738. Reprint. Westmead: Gregg Publishers, 1969.

Idel, Moshe. *Kabbalah: New Perspectives.* New Haven: Yale Univ. Press, 1988.

Jacob, Margaret. "John Toland and the Newtonian Ideology." *Journal of the Warburg and Courtauld Institutes* 32 (1969):307–31.

————. *The Newtonians and the English Revolution, 1689–1720.* Ithaca: Cornell Univ. Press, 1976.

James, D. G. *The Life of Reason: Hobbes, Locke, Bolingbroke.* London: Longmans, Green, and Co., 1949.

James, William. "What Pragmatism Means." In *Classic American Philosophers,* edited by Max H. Fisch, pp. 128–36. New York: Appleton-Century-Crofts, 1951.

Jensen, Henning. "Reid and Wittgenstein on Philosophy and Language." *Philosophical Studies* 36 (1979):359–76.

Johnson, Samuel. *"Rasselas," Poems, and Selected Prose.* Edited by Bertrand Bronson. 3d ed. San Francisco: Rinehart, 1958.

Jones, Olin McKendree. *Empiricism and Intuitionism in Reid's Common Sense Philosophy.* Princeton: Princeton Univ. Press, 1927.

Kahn, Victoria. "Humanism and the Resistance to Theory." In *Literary Theory/Renaissance Texts,* edited by Patricia Parker and David Quint, pp. 373–96. Baltimore: Johns Hopkins Univ. Press, 1986.

Kant, Immanuel. *Critique of Judgment.* Translated by Werner S. Pluhar. Indianapolis: Hackett, 1987.

————. *Critique of Pure Reason.* Translated by Norman Kemp Smith. London: Macmillan, 1961.

Kelley, D. R. "The Development and Context of Bodin's Method." In *History, Law, and the Human Sciences: Medieval and Renaissance Perspectives,* part 8 (pages not numbered consecutively). London: Variorum Reprints, 1984.

Kivy, Peter. *The Seventh Sense: A Study of Francis Hutcheson's Aesthetics and Its Influence in Eighteenth Century Britain.* New York: Burt Franklin, 1976.

Knowlson, James. *Universal Language Schemes in England and France, 1600–1800.* Toronto: Univ. of Toronto Press, 1975.

Korshin, Paul. *Typologies in England, 1650–1820*. Princeton: Princeton Univ. Press, 1982.

Kramnick, Isaac. "Augustan Politics and English Historiography: The Debate on the English Past, 1730–35." *History and Theory* 6 (1967):33–56.

———. *Bolingbroke and His Circle: The Politics of Nostalgia in the Age of Walpole*. Cambridge, Mass.: Harvard Univ. Press, 1968.

———. *The Rage of Edmund Burke: Portrait of an Ambivalent Conservative*. New York: Basic Books, 1977.

———. "Skepticism in English Political Thought: From Temple to Burke." *Studies in Burke and His Time* 12 (1970):1627–60.

———, ed. *Lord Bolingbroke: Historical Writings*. Chicago: Univ. of Chicago Press, 1972.

Krois, John Michael. "Vico's and Peirce's 'Sensus Communis.'" In *Vico: Past and Present*, edited by Giorgia Tagliacozzo, pp. 58–71. Atlantic Highlands, N.J.: Humanities Press, 1981.

Land, Stephen K. *The Philosophy of Language in Britain: Major Theories from Hobbes to Thomas Reid*. New York: AMS Press, 1986.

Lang, Berel. "The Politics of Interpretation: Spinoza's Modernist Turn." *Review of Metaphysics* 43 (1989):327–56.

Lee, Henry. *Anti-Scepticism*. 1702. Reprint. New York: Garland, 1978.

Lehrer, Keith. *Thomas Reid*. London: Routledge, 1989.

Lennox, Charlotte. *The Female Quixote*. Edited by Margaret Dalziel. 1752. Reprint. London: Oxford Univ. Press, 1970.

Levine, Joseph M. *The Battle of the Books: History and Literature in the Augustan Age*. Ithaca: Cornell Univ. Press, 1991.

———. *Humanism and History: Origins of Modern English Historiography*. Ithaca: Cornell Univ. Press, 1987.

Levinson, Sanford, and Mailloux, Steven, eds. *Interpreting Law and Literature: A Hermeneutic Reader*. Evanston, Ill.: Northwestern Univ. Press, 1988.

Lieberman, David. *The Province of Legislation Examined: Legal Theory in Eighteenth-Century Britain*. Cambridge: Cambridge Univ. Press, 1989.

Livingston, David. *Hume's Philosophy of Common Life*. Chicago: Univ. of Chicago Press, 1984.

Locke, John. *The Correspondence of John Locke*, 8 vols. Edited by E. S. DeBeer. Oxford: Clarendon Press, 1976.

———. *An Essay Concerning Human Understanding*. Edited by Peter N. Nidditch. Oxford: Clarendon Press, 1975.

———. *Essays on the Law of Nature*. Edited by W. von Leyden. Oxford: Clarendon Press, 1954.

———. *Of the Conduct of the Understanding*. Edited by Francis W. Garforth. Classics of Education, no. 31. New York: Teachers' College Press, 1954.

———. *Paraphrases and Notes on the Epistles of St. Paul,* edited by Arthur Wainwright. Oxford: Clarendon Press, 1987.

———. *The Reasonableness of Christianity as Delivered in the Scriptures.* Edited by George W. Ewing. Chicago: Henry Regnery, 1965.

———. *Two Tracts on Government.* Edited by Philip Abrams. Cambrdige: Cambridge Univ. Press, 1967.

———. *Two Treatises of Government.* Edited by Peter Laslett. Cambridge: Cambridge Univ. Press, 1988.

———. *The Works of John Locke,* 12 vols. London: Thomas Tegg, W. Sharpe and Son, G. Offor, G. and J. Robinson, J. Evans and Co., 1823.

Lockmiller, David. *Sir William Blackstone.* Chapel Hill: Univ. of North Carolina Press, 1938.

Louis, Frances. *Swift's Anatomy of Misunderstanding.* Totowa, N.J.: Barnes and Noble, 1981.

Lucas, Paul. "Blackstone and the Reform of the Legal Profession." *English Historical Review* 77 (1962):456–89.

Lyotard, Jean-François, and Thébaud, Jean-Loup. *Just Gaming.* Translated by Wlad Godzich. Minneapolis: Univ. of Minnesota Press, 1985.

MacPherson, C. B. "Edmund Burke and the New Conservatism." *Science & Society* 22 (1958):231–39.

———. *The Political Theory of Possessive Individualism.* Oxford: Clarendon Press, 1962.

Madden, Edward H. "The Metaphilosophy of Commonsense." *American Philosophical Quarterly* 20 (1983):23–36.

Maitland, F. W. *Equity: A Course of Lectures.* Edited by A. H. Chaytor and W. J. Whittaker. Revised by John Brunyate. 2d ed. Cambridge: Cambridge Univ. press, 1936.

Makkreel, Rudolf A. *Imagination and Interpretation in Kant: The Hermeneutical Import of the "Critique of Judgment."* Chicago: Univ. of Chicago Press, 1990.

Mansfield, Harvey C., Jr. *Statesmanship and Party Government: A Study of Burke and Bolingbroke.* Chicago: Univ. of Chicago Press, 1965.

Marcil-Lacoste, Louise. *Claude Buffier and Thomas Reid: Two Common-Sense Philosophers.* Kingston: McGill–Queen's Univ. Press, 1982.

Meinecke, Friedrich. *Historism.* Translated by J. E. Anderson. London: Routledge and Kegan Paul, 1972.

Mercer, Philip. *Sympathy and Ethics: A Study of the Relationship between Sympathy and Morality with Special Reference to Hume's "Treatise".* Oxford: Clarendon Press, 1972.

Merrill, Walter. *From Statesman to Philosopher.* New York: Philosophical Library, 1949.

Michaels, W. B. "Against Formalism: The Autonomous Text in Legal and Literary Interpretation." *Poetics Today* 1 (1979):23–34.

Momigliano, Arnaldo. "Ancient History and the Antiquarian." In *Studies in Historiography,* pp. 1–39. London: Weidenfeld and Nicolson, 1966.

Mossner, Ernest. "An Apology for David Hume, Historian." *PMLA* 55 (1941):657–90.

———. *The Life of David Hume.* Oxford: Clarendon Press, 1954.

Mullan, John. "Sympathy and the Production of Society." In *Sentiment and Sociability: The Language of Feeling in the Eighteenth Century,* pp. 18–56. Oxford: Clarendon Press, 1988.

Nadel, G. H. "Bolingbroke's Letters on History." *Journal of the History of Ideas* 23 (1962):550–57.

———. "Philosophy of History before Historicism." *History and Theory* 3 (1964):291–315.

Nash, Richard. "Entrapment and Ironic Modes in *Tale of a Tub.*" *Eighteenth-Century Studies* 24 (1991):415–31.

Newman, Ralph A. *Equity and Law: A Comparative Study.* New York: Oceana, 1961.

Newton, Sir Isaac. *Theological Manuscripts.* Edited by H. McLachlan. Liverpool: Liverpool Univ. Press, 1950.

Nietzsche, F. *The Use and Abuse of History.* Translated by Adrian Collins. Indianapolis: Bobbs-Merrill, 1949.

Norton, David Fate. *David Hume: Common-Sense Moralist, Sceptical Metaphysician.* Princeton: Princeton Univ. Press, 1982.

———. "Hume and His Scottish Critics." In *McGill Hume Studies,* edited by David Fate Norton, Nicholas Capaldi, and Wade L. Robison, pp. 309–24. San Diego: Austin Hill Press, 1979.

Noxon, James. *Hume's Philosophical Development: A Study of His Methods.* Oxford: Clarendon Press, 1973.

O'Gorman, Frank. *Edmund Burke: His Political Philosophy.* Bloomington: Indiana Univ. Press, 1973.

O'Neill, Onora. "The Power of Example." *Philosophy* 61 (1986):5–29.

Orth, John V. "Sir William Blackstone: Hero of the Common Law." *American Bar Association Journal* 66 (1980):155–59.

Pahl, Gretchen Graf. "John Locke as Literary Critic and Biblical Interpreter." In *Essays Historical and Critical Dedicated to Lily B. Campbell,* pp. 139–59. Berkeley: Univ. of California Press, 1950.

Patey, Douglas L. *Probability and Literary Form: Philosophic Theory and Literary Practice in the Augustan Age.* Cambridge: Cambridge Univ. Press, 1984.

Paulson, Ronald. *Theme and Structure in Swift's Tale of a Tub.* 1960. Reprint. Hamden, Conn.: Archon, 1972.

Peirce, Charles S. *Charles S. Peirce: The Essential Writings.* Edited by Edward C. Moore. New York: Harper and Row, 1972.

———. *Collected Papers,* 8 vols. Edited by Charles Hartshorne and Paul Weiss. Cambridge, Mass.: Harvard Univ. Press, 1934–58.

Pinkus, Philip. "*A Tale of a Tub* and the Rosy Cross." *Journal of English and Germanic Philology* 59 (1960):669–79.

Pocock, J. G. A. *The Ancient Constitution and the Feudal Law: A Study of*

English Historical Thought in the Seventeenth Century. 2d ed. Cambridge: Cambridge Univ. Press, 1987.

——. "Burke and the Ancient Constitution: A Problem in the History of Ideas." In *Politics, Language and Time: Essays on Political Thought and History,* pp. 202–32. New York: Atheneum, 1971.

——. *Virtue, Commerce, and History: Essays on Political Thought and History, Chiefly in the Eighteenth Century.* Cambridge: Cambridge Univ. Press, 1985.

Pope, Alexander. "Preface to Shakespeare." In *Literary Criticism of Alexander Pope,* edited by Bertrand Goldgar, pp. 161–75. Lincoln: University of Nebraska Press, 1965.

Pound, Roscoe. *An Introduction to the Philosophy of Law.* New Haven: Yale Univ. Press, 1922.

——. *The Spirit of the Common Law.* Boston: Marshall Jones, 1921.

Price, Richard. "A Discourse on the Love of Our Country." In *Burke, Paine, Godwin and the Revolution Controversy,* edited by Marilyn Butler, pp. 23–32. Cambridge: Cambridge Univ. Press, 1984.

Ranke, Leopold. *The Theory and Practice of History.* Translated and edited by G. Iggers and K. von Moltke. Indianapolis: Bobbs-Merrill, 1973.

Rawson, Claude. *Gulliver and the Gentle Reader.* London: Routledge and Kegan Paul, 1973.

——. *Order from Confusion Sprung.* London: Allen and Unwin, 1985.

Reedy, Gerard, S.J. *The Bible and Reason: Anglicans and Scripture in Late Seventeenth-Century England.* Philadelphia: Univ. of Pennsylvania Press, 1985.

——. "Socinians, John Toland, and the Anglican Rationalists." *Harvard Theological Review* 70 (1977):285–304.

Reid, Thomas. "Abstract of the *Inquiry,*" edited by David Fate Norton. In *Thomas Reid: Critical Interpretations,* edited by Stephen F. Barker and Tom L. Beauchamp, pp. 128–30. Philadelphia: Philosophical Monographs, 1976.

——. *Philosophical Works.* Edited by William Hamilton. 1895. Reprint. Hildesheim: Georg Olms, 1967.

——. *Practical Ethics: Being Lectures and Papers on Natural Religion, Self-Government, Natural Jurisprudence, and the Law of Nations.* Edited by Knud Haakonssen. Princeton: Princeton Univ. Press, 1990.

Rembert, James. *Swift and the Dialectical Tradition.* New York: St. Martin's Press, 1988.

Reventlow, Graf Henning. *The Authority of the Bible and the Rise of the Modern World.* Translated by John Bowden. Philadelphia: Fortress Press, 1985.

Reynolds, Sir Joshua. *Discourses on Art.* Edited by Robert R. Wark. San Marino, Calif.: Huntingdon Library, 1959.

Richetti, John. *Philosophical Writing: Locke, Berkeley, Hume.* Cambridge, Mass.: Harvard Univ. Press, 1983.

St. German, Christopher. *Doctor and Student.* Edited by T. F. T. Plucknett and J. L. Barton. 1523. Reprint. London: Selden Society, 1974.

Schaeffer, John D. *Sensus Communis: Vico, Rhetoric, and the Limits of Relativism.* Durham, N.C.: Duke Univ. Press, 1990.

Scheler, Max. *The Nature of Sympathy.* Translated by Peter Heath. London: Routledge and Kegan Paul, 1954.

Schouls, Peter A. *The Imposition of Method: A Study of Descartes and Locke.* Oxford: Clarendon Press, 1980.

Seth, Andrew. *Scottish Philosophy: A Comparison of the Scottish and German Answers to Hume.* 1889. Reprint. New York: Burt Franklin, 1971.

Shaftesbury, Lord Anthony Ashley Cooper. *Characteristics of Men, Manners, Opinions, Times.* Edited by J. M. Robertson. Indianapolis: Bobbs-Merrill, 1964.

Shapiro, Barbara. *Probability and Certainty in Seventeenth-Century England: A Study of the Relationships between Natural Science, Religion, History, Law, and Literature.* Princeton: Princeton Univ. Press, 1983.

Sichel, Walter. *Bolingbroke and His Times.* 1901. Reprint. New York: Greenwood Press, 1968.

Siebert, Donald. *The Moral Animus of David Hume.* Newark: Univ. of Delaware Press, 1990.

Skinner, Quentin. "The Principles and Practice of Opposition." In *Historical Perspectives: Studies in English Thought and Society in Honour of J. H. Plumb,* edited by Neil McKendrick, pp. 93–128. London: Europa, 1974.

Smith, Adam. *The Theory of Moral Sentiments.* Edited by D. D. Raphael and A. L. Macfie. Oxford: Clarendon Press, 1976.

Spinoza, Benedict. *Theologico-Political Treatise.* In *The Chief Works of Benedict de Spinoza,* translated by R. H. M. Elwes. London: Bell, 1883.

Stanlis, Peter. *Edmund Burke and the Natural Law.* Ann Arbor: Univ. of Michigan Press, 1958.

Starkman, Miriam. *Swift's Satire on Learning in* A Tale of a Tub. Princeton: Princeton Univ. Press, 1950.

Stephen, Sir Leslie. *History of English Thought in the Eighteenth Century,* 2 vols. 1876. Reprint. New York: Harcourt, Brace and World, 1962.

Sterne, Lawrence. *Tristram Shandy.* Edited by James A. Work. New York: Odyssey, 1940.

Stewart, Dugald. *Elements of the Philosophy of the Human Mind.* 1792. Reprint. New York: Garland, 1971.

Stewart, John. *The Moral and Political Philosophy of David Hume.* New York: Columbia Univ. Press, 1963.

Stewart, M. A. "Locke, Steiner and Understanding." In *Communication and Understanding,* edited by Godfrey Vesey, pp. 20–45. Sussex: Harvester Press, 1977.

Stillingfleet, Edward. *Sermons Preached upon Several Occasions.* London: H. Lintot, 1737.

Strauss, Leo. "How to Study Spinoza's *Theologico-Political Treatise.*" In *Persecution and the Art of Writing,* pp. 142–201. Glencoe, Ill.: Free Press, 1952.

———. *Natural Right and History.* Chicago: Univ. of Chicago Press, 1953.

———. *Spinoza's Critique of Religion.* Translated by E. M. Sinclair. New York: Schocken, 1965.

Sullivan, Robert E. *John Toland and the Deist Controversy: A Study in Adaptations.* Cambridge, Mass.: Harvard Univ. Press, 1982.

Swift, Jonathan. *The Correspondence of Jonathan Swift.* Edited by Harold Williams. Oxford: Clarendon Press, 1963.

———. *Poetical Works.* Edited by Herbert Davis. London: Oxford Univ. Press, 1967.

———. *The Prose Works of Jonathan Swift.* Edited by Herbert Davis. Oxford: Blackwell, 1957.

———. *A Tale of a Tub.* Edited by A. C. Guthkelch and D. Nicol Smith. 2d ed. Oxford: Clarendon Press, 1958.

Taylor, Jeremy. *The Whole Works of Jeremy Taylor.* London: Ogle, Duncan, 1822.

Temple, Sir William. *The Works of Sir William Temple,* 4 vols. 1814. Reprint. New York: Greenwood Press, 1968.

Texas Law Review 60, no. 3 (1982), special issue devoted to issues of law and literature.

Theobald, Lewis. *Shakespeare Restored: or, a Specimen of the Many Errors as Well Committed, as Unamended, by Mr. Pope in His Late Edition of This Poet.* 1726. Reprint. New York: AMS, 1970.

Tindal, Matthew. *Christianity as Old as Creation.* Edited by Gunter Gawlick. 1730. Reprint. Stuttgart: Frommann Verlag, 1967.

Todorov, Tzvetan. *Symbolism and Interpretation.* Translated by Catherine Porter. Ithaca: Cornell Univ. Press, 1982.

Toland, John. *Christianity Not Mysterious.* 1696. Reprint. New York: Garland, 1984.

———. *A Collection of Several Pieces of Mr. John Toland.* Edited by Pierre Desmaizeaux. London: Peele, 1726.

———. *Letters to Serena.* Edited by Gunter Gawlick. Stuttgart: Frommann Verlag, 1964.

———. *Pantheisticon.* 1751. Reprint. New York: Garland, 1976.

Tooke, Horne. *The Diversions of Purley,* 2 vols. 1798. Reprint. Menston: Scolar Press, 1968.

Traugott, John. "A Tale of a Tub." In *The Character of Swift's Satire,* edited by Claude Rawson, pp. 83–126. Newark: Univ. of Delaware Press, 1983.

Tuveson, Ernest. *The Imagination as a Means of Grace: Locke and the Aesthetics of Romanticism.* Berkeley: Univ. of California Press, 1960.

Van Holtoon, Fritz, and Olson, David R., eds. *Common Sense: The Foundations for Social Science*. Lanham, Md.: Univ. Press of America, 1987.

Varey, Simon. *Henry St. John, Viscount Bolingbroke*. Boston: Twayne, 1984.

Vico, Giambattista. *On the Study Methods of Our Time*. Translated by Elio Gianturco. Itahca: Cornell Univ. Press, 1990.

Voigt, Milton. *Swift and the Twentieth Century*. Detroit: Wayne Sate Univ. Press, 1964.

Vollrath, Ernst, "'That All Governments Rest on Opinion,'" *Social Research* 43 (1976):46–61.

Wallace, John M. "'Examples Are Best Precepts': Readers and Meanings in Seventeenth-Century Poetry." *Critical Inquiry* 1 (1974):273–90.

Warton, Thomas. *The History of English Poetry*, 4 vols. New York: Johnson Reprint, 1968.

Weathers, Winston. "A Technique of Irony in *Tale of a Tub*." In *Jonathan Swift: Tercentenary Essays*, pp. 53–60. Tulsa, Okla.: Univ. of Tulsa Press, 1967.

Weinsheimer, Joel. "Fiction and the Force of Example." In *The Idea of the Novel in the Eighteenth Century*, edited by Robert W. Uphaus, pp. 1–19. East Lansing, Mich.: Colleagues Press, 1988.

———. "'Give Me Something to Desire': A Johnsonian Anthropology of Imitation." *Philological Quarterly* 64 (1985):211–23.

———. "Hermeneutic Semiotics and Peirce's 'Ethics of Terminology.'" *Semiotica* 86 (1991):43–56.

———. *Imitation*. London: Routledge and Kegan Paul, 1984.

———. "A Word is Not a Sign." In *Philosophical Hermeneutics and Literary Theory*, pp. 87–123. New Haven: Yale Univ. Press, 1991.

Wende, Peter. "Vernuft und Tradition in der englischen Staatslehre der frühen Neuzeit." *Historische Zeitschrift* 226 (1978):317–48.

West, William. *The Second Part of Symboleography . . . Whereunto is Annexed Another Treatise of Equitie: the Juristiction, and Proceedings of the High Court of Chancerie. . . . 1641*. Reprint. New York: Garland, 1979.

Willey, Basil. *The Eighteenth Century Background*. Boston: Beacon Press, 1961.

Williams, Kathleen. *Johathan Swift and the Age of Compromise*. Lawrence: Univ. of Kansas Press, 1958.

Willis, Richard. *Reflections upon Mr. Toland's Book Called "Christianity Not Mysterious"*. London: Wotton, 1697.

Willman, Robert. "Blackstone and the 'Theoretical Perfection' of English Law in the Reign of Charles II." *Historical Journal* 26 (1983):39–70.

Winch, Peter. "The Notion of 'Suggestion' in Thomas Reid's Theory of Perception." *Philosophical Quarterly* 3 (1953):327–41.

Wittgenstein, Ludwig. *Lectures and Conversations on Aesthetics, Psychology, and Religious Belief*. Edited by Cyril Barrett. Berkeley: Univ. of California Press, n.d.

Womersley, D. J. "Lord Bolingbroke and Eighteenth-Century Historiography." *Eighteenth Century: Theory and Interpretation* 28 (1987):217–34.

Wright, John P. *The Sceptical Realism of David Hume.* Manchester: Manchester Univ. Press, 1983.

Yolton, John. *Perceptual Acquaintance from Descartes to Reid.* Minneapolis: Univ. of Minnesota Press, 1984.

Zimmerman, Everett. *Swift's Narrative Satires: Author and Authority.* Ithaca: Cornell Univ. Press, 1983.

Zuckert, Michael P. "Fools and Knaves: Reflections on Locke's Theory of Philosophical Discourse." *Review of Politics* 36 (1974):544–64.

Index

allegory, 1, 51
antiquarianism, 84, 100, 168, 226
appearance, 5; and truth, 216–19, 221,
    232. *See also* self-evidence
application, 19, 22, 58, 183; and his-
    tory, 83, 86, 92
Aristotle, 33, 50, 137, 172, 227, 230

Beattie, J., 141
beauty, 5; and truth, 3, 229, 232
Bentham, J., 166, 169
Bentley, R., 18
Berkeley, G., 4, 91, 136
Blackstone, W., 20, 33, 130, 166–94,
    228
Boileau, N., 94
Bolingbroke, Lord, 10–11, 15, 115,
    121, 185, 231; on history, 72–102
Burke, E., 7, 195–225, 229

Cabbalism, 8
Chancery. *See* equity
Chapman, G., 197
chivalry, 212
Christensen, J., 112
Cicero, M., 77, 81, 132, 138, 227
Clarendon, Earl of, 227
Coke, E., 176–77, 181

Coleridge, S., 4
common sense, 135–65; undefinable,
    136, 164, 187; charges against,
    141–42; as judgment, 148–50
custom, 138, 170, 224

decoration, 210–12
decorum, 197, 201–02; as duality,
    209–17, 225; as unity, 218–21, 225
Derrida, J., 1
Descartes, R., 58, 114, 136, 139, 151
Dicey, A., 166–67, 194
Dionysus of Halicarnassus, 75
discretion. *See* prudence
dogmatism, 50
Dryden, J., 8–10, 15, 94

embodiment, 222–23, 231
epistemology, 26, 38, 105, 116, 136–
    39; dissolution into hermeneutics,
    42; exceeded by sympathy, 121; re-
    placed by linguistics, 160; and pol-
    itics, 196, 199
equity, 20, 166–94, 228; Chancery
    court of, 169, 178–81; as opposed
    to law, 182, 184–85; and common
    sense, 187; as arbitrariness, 187–89;
    not opposed to law, 191